120550

D1391136

TO HOLD FOR NLS
DO NOT WITHDRAW

his bo

Great Sailing Ships

OTMAR SCHÄUFFELEN

Great Sailing Ships

An illustrated encyclopaedia of 150 existing barks,
barkentines, brigs, brigantines, frigates, schooners and
other large sailing vessels built since 1628.

Translated by Inge Moore with the co-operation
of Barbara Webb

ADLARD COLES Ltd. LONDON

120550   387. 203

© Delius, Klasing & Co   Bielefeld   Berlin
This translation © Adlard Coles Ltd
First published in this edition 1969
Adlard Coles Ltd
3 Upper James St
Golden Square
London W 1
SBN 229 97372 8
Printed in West Germany by
Kunst- und Werbedruck
Bad Oeynhausen-Eidinghausen

Contents

List of ships described

How this book came about

'The two four-masted barks *Pamir* and *Passat* have left on their first post-war voyage to South America.' It was this short notice which appeared in a daily paper in 1952 that first aroused my interest in sailing ships. Short reports on the ships' voyages were published after that from time to time. The *Pamir's* tragic loss on September 21, 1957 gave rise to a spate of illustrated reports in newspapers and magazines. Much of what was written revealed a most fearful ignorance on the part of the writers of what sailing ships are all about. Instead of being informative, many of these reports merely pointed out, with great pathos, how dangerous and senseless the ships were.

I wondered what the real truth behind this tragedy was. What were, and still are, the prerequisites for an up-to-date training on a sail training vessel? How many 'tall ships' were there left, and to whom did they belong? During my quest for the answers I was converted from being merely insterested into being a ship-lover.

It all started with a short list of a handful of sailing ships, containing little more than basic data.

At first I had only a few reference books. As the number of books grew so did the amount of contradictory and discrepant information, mainly concerning dimensions and the question of whether a ship still existed and under whose ownership. The only way to find out for sure was to write to the owners. The first letter with a questionnaire went out to the famous frigate *Constitution* in Boston. It took scarely ten days for the reply to arrive and with it more pictures and information that I had ever asked for. The same happened in almost every case, which was very encouraging. As time went by, contacts were established all over the world. Frequently, the only information I had to go on was the ship's name and her home port or laying-up berth. Contacts passed on details of ship of which nothing was known but their names.

One day someone replying from South America asked when and where the finished 'book' could be bought. It was then that the idea of a book was born. The accumulated material was eminently suitable. On a few ships some small details were still missing, but this presented no problems. As the work progressed even countries who had never before provided detailed technical data for such purposes co-operated. This is how, in the course of several years, an encyclopaedia of the last of the big sailing ships came about, planned in such a way as to enable ships to be directly compared with one another. Originally it was intended for private use. Now the publishers have been kind enough to take over this basic concept and produce a book which is certain to provide the answer to many questions.

Otmar Schäuffelen

Vasa

Type:
17th century warship. 64 guns, two gundecks. Wood

Country: Sweden

Owners:
Statens Sjöhistoriska Museum, Stockholm

Location:
Vasa Dockyard on the island of Djurgården, Stockholm

Year of Construction:
1628. Ordered by the King of Sweden, Gustav II Adolph in 1625 and probably launched in 1627

Builders:
Royal Naval Shipyard, Stockholm (situated on the present Blasieholm)

Tonnage: about 1300 tons displacement

Dimensions:

LOA	(approx)	230 ft
Length hull	(approx)	200 ft
Length between perpendiculars	(approx)	151 ft
Breadth extreme	(approx)	38 ft
Moulded depth		28 ft
Draft, forward		14 ft
aft		16 ft

Rig:
probable sailplan: 10 sails, spritsail, spritsail topsail; fore- and mainmasts: single topsails, single topgallants, mizzen: lateen sail with single topsail

Masts and spars:
height of mainmast above keel approx 160 ft; bowsprit with spritsail yard; spritsail topmast with yard

Complement: 133 crew and 300 marines

Armament:
64 guns; 48 24-pounders, 8 3-pounders, 3 35-pounders, 2 62-pounders, 2 1-pounders and 1 16-pounder.
All barrels cast in bronze.
Total weight about 80 tons

Use: museum ship

During the Thirty Years War the Kaiser's troops reached the Baltic in the summer of 1628. Kaiser Ferdinand II had already appointed his Commander-in-Chief Wallenstein Admiral of the Baltic Fleet. Then his advance to the north was seriously hampered by the fruitless siege of Stralsund, which city had negotiated an alliance with Sweden whose Gustav II Adolph was interested in their request for help because he hoped in this way to establish a sure foothold on German soil. He needed a strong fleet to back his further plans. The opposition, under Wallenstein, was also trying to equip a fleet which would be supported by the Spanish squadron. The building of a number of large fighting ships was ordered by the Swedish king, among them the *Vasa* which was already under construction, and which was originally to have been named the *Ny Wassan*. The Dutch shipbuilder Henrik Hybertsson de Groot had been given the job of building her, but he died in 1627 and she was completed by Hein Jacobsson. The total cost was about 100,000 Reichstaler. By July 31, 1628 all the guns had been shipped, and on August 10, 1628, between 3 and 4 o'clock in the afternoon, the *Vasa* was ready to sail on her maiden voyage under the command of Captain Söfring Hansson. First the ship was warped out, and as soon as she was free of the land her sails filled, for fore and main topsails, foresail and lateen having already been set.

Immediately the *Vasa* started to heel considerably. A few minutes later she was struck abeam by a sudden gust. Rapid attempts to trim her were unsuccessful. A great rush of water flooded in through the open gunports, the lowest of which were only four or five feet above the waterline.

Close by the island of Beckholm the *Vasa* sank to the bottom in 105 feet of water. The full complement not being aboard, only 30 members of the crew were drowned, and when she was raised 15 skeletons were found in the hull. The naval court of enquiry started on September 5, 1628 but did not succeed in placing the blame for the loss of the ship. The main cause was judged to be that at the keel her lines were too fine to take ballast, while the lower gun ports were too near the waterline. The ship was top-heavy. First salvage attempts began on August 13, 1628 and succeeded in bringing the *Vasa* to an even keel. With the help of diving-bells 54 guns were probably salvaged in 1664 and 1683.

After a two-year search Anders Franzén found the wreck again in August 1956. Twenty-nine large anchors had become fouled in her during the centuries. Divers of the 60-strong salvage team drove six 80 foot long tunnels under the hull through which were passed the wires used for raising her. The first lift took place on August 20, 1959 with the help of two pontoons, and during the next 28 days a tug towed the *Vasa* 600 yards in shoal water, grounding her 18 times so as subsequently to lift her higher in the water. Countless small pieces of the ship, including splendid carvings from the stern decorations, were found near the wreck and salvaged. Her fore lowermast was still standing when she was raised. By April 24 all preparations had been made to take her out of the water, and on May 4, 1961 she floated on her own keel in dry dock. In the meanwhile a giant pontoon had been built, and here, shortly afterwards, she found her permanent resting place.

Great difficulty was experienced with

regard to the conservation of the timber. By a long and tedious process the water was replaced by a high molecular-content alcohol, the whole ship being sprayed to prevent overrapid drying out. Smaller pieces of wood could be dealt with in baths. It is intended that only original material be used, and it still cannot be forecast when restoration will be complete. 16,000 parts were found by the archaeologists in the 13,300 cubic yards of mud removed from the hull. The *Vasa* only survives today thanks to the fact that the waters of the Baltic are too cold for teredo to exist. She lies now at the Wasa Wharf on her pontoon over which an aluminium shed has been erected—the oldest preserved and fully identified ship known at present.

Below: a cannon from the Vasa

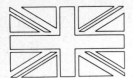

Victory

Type: First-Rate, ship-of-the-line, 3-decker. Wood
Country: Great Britain
Owners: Royal Navy (Flagship of the Portsmouth Command)
Location: Portsmouth Naval Dockyard (dry dock)
Year of construction: 1759. Keel laid on July 23, 1759, launched May 7, 1765, commissioned 1778
Builders: Single Dock, Chatham on the Medway. Built to drawings by Sir Thomas Slade, Senior Surveyor of the Royal Navy
Tonnage: approx 3500 tons displacement, approx 4000 tons displacement fully equipped, 2162 tons burden
Dimensions:

LOA	328 ft
Length hull	226 ft 4 in
Length of gun deck	186 ft
Length on main deck	152 ft
Breadth on main deck	40 ft
Breadth extreme	52 ft
Breadth overall (with studding sails)	197 ft
Depth moulded	32 ft 9 in
Draft	19 ft 8 in

Rig: full-rigged ship. Lower courses, single topsails, single topgallants, studding-sails on the fore and mainmasts
Masts and spars: all masts have topmast and topgallant masts.
Height of masts over waterline:

Foremast	180 ft
Mainmast	203 ft
Mizzen	38 ft
Bowsprit with jib boom	approx 115 ft
Bowsprit yard	64 ft
Mainyard	102 ft
Main topgallant yard	48 ft

Complement: at Trafalgar, 850 officers, men and marines
Armament: 104 guns (in 1805).
Lower gundeck 30 32-pounders; middle gundeck 28 24-pounders; upper gundeck 30 12-pounders; quarterdeck 12 12-pounders; poop 2 12-pounders and 2 68-pounder carronades.
(Maximum range of a 32-pounder was about 1½ miles)
Use: museum ship.
Still in service as flagship, permanently moored.

H.M.S. *Victory* is the fifth ship of the Royal Navy to bear this name. The first *Victory* was built in 1559 and was Sir John Hawkins' flagship in the battles against the Spanish Armada. In 1758 King George II was advised by his ministers to built 12 large ships of the line, to be led by a 100-gun ship. The English successes in the Seven Years War, particularly those in North America, were the reason for naming this ship the *Victory*.

As the war continued to go well for England both on land and at sea, it was unnecessary to built the ships too precipitately. In those days the normal time needed to built a ship of the line was five years. The *Victory's* keel was laid in 1759, and she was launched in 1765. She cost £ 57,748. Thirteen years were spent in the Medway without a commission, but when France entered the American War of Independence the *Victory* was ordered to Portsmouth in 1778. Her first commission was as flagship of the Channel Fleet under Admiral Keppel, and at Ushant she took part in an indecisive battle with a French squadron.

The *Victory* was successively the flagship of Admirals Hardy, Geary, Hyde, Parker and Kempenfelt. Then in 1782, under Lord Howe, she took part in the battles of Gibraltar and Cape Spartel. After the Treaty of Versailles in 1783 (recognizing American Independence) she was paid off. In 1793 England joined the first coalition against France, and Lord Hood aboard the *Victory* led an expedition of 22 ships to the Mediterranean. Toulon was taken but lost again due to a fierce counterattack led by the young artillery officer Napoleon Bonaparte. Later, when Calvi on the island of Corsica was under siege, the *Victory's* guns were landed and the

artillery attack was led by Captain Horatio Nelson. After this the ship returned to Portsmouth for a refit. In 1795 Admiral Hotham returned to the Mediterranean with the *Victory* and she took part in the Battle of Cape Hyeres, and two years later under Admiral Sir John Jervis in the Battle of Cape St. Vincent. The ship returned to Chatham in 1797 and was paid off. From 1798 to 1880 the *Victory* was used as a hospital ship for prisoners. In 1801 she spent two years in dock undergoing an extensive refit which had become urgent. Among other alterations the open galleries were removed, the channels moved to above the upper gun deck ports and the figurehead was changed. The ship at that time took on the appearance that she has to-day. On Nelson's instructions all his ships had an ochre band painted along the line of the gundecks, while the topsides between them and the outer side of the port lids was painted black. When the ports were shut the famous chequered pattern could be seen. The inside of the port lids was painted red. In April 1803 the ship was commissioned again. Under the overall command of Lord Nelson, the flagship *Victory* sailed with the British squadron to the Mediterranean in July. After an 18-month blockade of Toulon Admiral Villeneuve finally succeeded in breaking out with the French ships. Nelson chased him to the West Indies, but had to return to England without sighting the French vessels. On September 15, 1805 Nelson and his men sailed to lead the blockade of Cadiz, and on October 21, 1805 the decisive Battle of Trafalgar took place. The *Victory* was severely damaged and towed into Gibraltar where she was patched up with all possible haste, returning to England

with Nelson's body on board on November 3, 1805.

After extensive repairs at the Naval Dockyard at Chatham the *Victory* saw active service again from March 1808 until 1813 when she was docked for a refit. The result of the Battle of Waterloo made a new commission unnecessary and the *Victory* stayed in the reserve until 1824. From then on, with the exception of the years 1869—1889, she has been the flagship of Portsmouth Command. She lay anchor in Portsmouth Harbour until 1922, when she was moved to the world's oldest graving dock in Portsmouth and restored to her Trafalgar appearance at great cost. The job was finished on July 17, 1928. So as to spare the hull, almost all the guns and the heavy anchors have been replaced by wooden copies. The original guns stand round the dock and one of the enormous anchors lies on the shore at Southsea at the spot where Nelson left England for the last time. Every year, on the anniversary of the Battle of Trafalgar, a memorial service is held aboard the ship.

Constellation

Type: frigate, full-rigged ship. Wood
Country: U.S.A.
Owner:
 U.S. Navy (on long-term loan to the Star Spangled Banner Flag House Association of Baltimore)
Location: Baltimore, Pier 4
Year of construction:
 1797. Launched September 7, 1797
Builders:
 David Stodders Shipyard, Baltimore, Maryland
Tonnage: 1960 long tons displacement
Dimensions:

LOA	approx 259 ft 9 in
Length hull	203 ft
Length between perpendiculars	175 ft 6 in
Breadth extreme	41 ft 8 in
Moulded depth (to side decks)	30 ft 10 in
Depth in hold (to gundeck)	21 ft 4 in
Draft (loaded)	19 ft 11 in

Sail area:
 20,130 sq ft (without main and mizzen staysails and without studding sails), mainsail 3175 sq ft
Rig:
 15 sails (excluding main and mizzen staysails and studding sails). 2 head-sails, single topsails, single topgallants, royals
Masts and spars:
 Height of mainmast above deck 156 ft
 All masts have topmasts and topgallant masts.
 Length of mainyard 92 ft 3 in
 Length of main royal yard 27 ft 7 in
 Bowsprit with jib-boom and outer jib-boom approx 88 ft 7 in
 Spritsail yard
Complement:
 313 (1797) including marines
Armament:
 38 guns (1797)
 Gundeck 24 18-pounders, spardeck 12 24-pounders (carronades), foredeck 2 18-pounders. Weight of broadside 378 pounds
Use: museum-ship

After the American War of Independence, in 1783, the newly formed United States of America succeeded in opening routes for their own merchant fleet. However, in the Mediterranean the ships were constantly being attacked by pirates and corsairs from the Barbary States and their crews taken prisoner. To protect the ships and for the defence of the new nation Congress decided in 1794 to have six frigates built. Three of them were immediately contracted. Of these ships two still exist today, the *Constitution* in Boston and the *Constellation* in Baltimore.

Constellation was first equipped for sea and made sail for the first time on June 26, 1798. She was the first ship of the United States Navy and so is the oldest surviving ship of the fleet. She was the first American ship to defeat an opponent in a sea battle and the first American ship to enter Chinese waters. Her captain, Thomas Truxtun, used the first U.S. Navy signal code book, which he devised himself.

No American warship has had such a long active service life as *Constellation*. She is the only existing large ship to have taken part in the Civil War. Finally it must be mentioned that she is the oldest ship to have been afloat continuously—170 years up till now. *Constellation* was named after the group of stars in the American flag.

After a peace treaty with the Barbary States, French ships attacked the American ships. On February 9, 1799, Truxtun in the *Constellation* defeated the French frigate *L'Insurgente* in the Caribean. This feat strengthened the self-confidence of the Americans enormously. The female figurehead, which allegorically represented the spirit of the revolution, was lost in this battle. It was never replaced.

In February 1800 *Constellation* beat the French ship *La Vengeance* after a five-hour duel. Captain Truxtun played a large personal role in this success, since he attached great importance to the training of his officers and crew. *Constellation* from her inception showed a fine turn of speed so that the ship was known as 'The Yankee Race Horse'. Her fine underwater lines were subsequently taken for the design of the famous Baltimore clippers.

In the spring of 1802 the frigate joined the American Mediterranean fleet and took part in the blockade of Tripoli as part of the new war which had flared up against the Barbary States. From 1805 to the outbreak of the war of 1812 she was permanently moored in Washington. During the war with England the ship successfully foiled invasion attempts on the coast of Virginia. The Barbary pirates profited from this struggle. *Constellation* was ordered to the Mediterranean again where she remained till 1817. In June 1815 she played a part in the capture of the Algerian 48-gun frigate *Mashuda*.

From 1819 to 1821 the frigate guarded the trade routes to South America and, later, American merchant ships on the coast of Peru. After she had fought an uprising in the Caribbean from 1825 to 1826 she went on a political mission to England and France in 1831. Following that *Constellation* was with the Mediterranean fleet for another four years. In 1835 she returned to the Gulf of Mexico and took part in the defeat of the Seminol uprising in Florida.

On December 9, 1840 she began a circumnavigation during which the ship was engaged in searching American ships in the Pacific as part of the Opium War. As flag ship of the Far East fleet *Constellation* was the first American ship to penetrate Chinese inland waters. Commodore of the Fleet, Lawrence Kearny, made the first Sino-American trade agreement on this voyage. On the way home Kearny prevented the British from annexing the Sandwich Islands (Hawaii). The circumnavigation lasted until April 30, 1844. From 1845 to 1852 the ship was permanently moored at Norfolk. In 1853 *Constellation* was rebuilt and lengthened by 11½ ft. The armament at this time was 22 guns. After she had spent another three years in the Mediterranean she was taken out of service in August 1858.

During the American Civil War *Constellation* was flagship of the African fleet. She captured three slave traders and almost 1000 slaves were freed and taken back to Africa. In 1871 the Naval Academy at Annapolis took the frigate over as a training ship. There she remained for twenty years. In 1880, when Ireland had a great famine, the ship was used to transport foodstuffs there. In 1894 she came to Newport (Rhode Island) as a training ship and returned to Baltimore in 1914.

Constellation *in 1914 (left) and today (above)*

By the outbreak of the Second World War the ship had almost been forgotten and was in Newport in a very bad condition. President Roosevelt appointed the ship Flagship of the Atlantic Fleet in 1940. This was her last command.

The navy, who considered her of great historic importance, declared the vessel a National Historic Shrine. In 1955 *Constellation* was officially taken out of service and brought from Boston to Baltimore in a floating dock. She still belongs to the U.S. Fleet. The restoration is being undertaken by a patriotic organisation, the Star Spangled Banner Flag House Association of Baltimore. The cost will amount to $ 250,000. Part of this sum is covered by the sale of medals cast from copper from the replaced nails and fastenings of the ship. *Constellation* is to be restored to her

original condition at the time of building. Of course it will not be possible to alter the length of the hull, nor will the present round stern revert to the original transom, which was removed in 1829. The restoration is being done in stages. From March to September 1964 the vessel lay in drydock. While working on the hull, the restorers were able to establish beyond doubt that the ship is indeed a 1797 frigate and not, as often claimed, a corvette built in 1853. Several nails bear the date stamps 1797, 1808 and 1812.

After completion *Constellation* will be exhibited in several U.S. ports and finally remain in Baltimore.

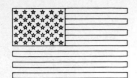

Constitution

Type: frigate, full-rigged ship. Wood
Country: U.S.A.
Owner: U.S. Navy
Location: Boston, Massachusetts
Year of construction:
1797; launched October 21, 1797
Builders:
Hartt's Shipyard, Boston, Massachusetts
Designed by Joshua Humphreys
Tonnage: 2200 tons displacement
Dimensions:

LOA	305 ft	
Hull length	204 ft	
Length between		
perpendiculars	175 ft	
Breadth extreme	43 ft	6 in
Breadth at maindeck	38 ft	5 in
Depth moulded	36 ft	
Draft	19 ft	8 in

Sails area:
42,720 sq ft (with studding sails),
main topsail 3390 sq ft
Rig:
36 sails (including studding sails,
original rig). Single topsails, single
topgallants, royals, skysails and
studding sails
Masts and spars:

Height of mainmast		
above deck	170 ft	6 in
Length mainyard	91 ft	10 in
Length of main royal yard	29 ft	6 in
Bowsprit with jib-boom	95 ft	2 in

Complement:
approx 475 (including marines)
Armament:
at the time of building 44 guns.
In the war of 1812: gundeck 30
24-pounders, spardeck 16 32-pounders, fore-spardeck 2 24-pounders,
1 16-pounder, 6 32-pounders;
a total of 55 guns.
Use: Permanently moored flagship.
Museum ship

The reasons for the construction of the *Constitution* and the *Constellation* have already been given in the notes on the *Constellation*. During the war against England from 1812—1815 the *Constitution* fought a successful battle against the 38-gun frigate *Guerriere* as well as one against the frigate *Java*. Because her gun deck lay high above the water line (over 8 feet) the *Constitution* could be sailed hard in rough seas which often gave her the advantage over her enemy. She logged up to $13\frac{1}{2}$ knots.

On February 20, 1815, during her last voyage on active service, she won a battle against the British frigate *Cyane* and the gun-sloop *Levant*, after which she underwent an extensive refit in Boston until 1821. On May 13, 1821 the *Constitution* became the flagship of the Mediterranean Fleet. In July 1828 a commission deemed her unfit for sea and it was thereupon decided to break her up. A poem by Oliver Wendell Holmes, 'Old Ironsides', which appeared in many newspapers, resulted in the saving of the frigate. Her nickname 'Ironsides', arose because the sailors had seen how the enemy bullets ricocheted off her hard topsides.

A complete overhaul at a Boston yard lasted from 1833 to 1834 and the following year the *Constitution* returned to join the Mediterranean Fleet. In 1839 she made a passage round Cape Horn to the South Pacific, followed in 1844 by a voyage to China. Then in 1848 she went to the Mediterranean and Pope Pius IX visited the frigate, the first occasion a Pope had set foot on American territory.

In 1852 the *Constitution* cruised the West coast of Africa to control and fight against the slave trade. From 1855 to 1860 she was again extensively overhauled in Portsmouth, New Hampshire, after which the Marine Academy of Annapolis took her over on July 1, 1860. In 1861, on account of the Civil War, the academy had to transfer her to Newport, Rhode Island, for safety. The frigate served as their training ship and returned to Annapolis in 1865. In 1871 she lay in dock in Philadelphia and in 1878 she carried goods to France for the Paris Exhibition. During the eighties the *Constitution* was reception ship in Portsmouth. Through the influence of John F. Fitzgerald, grandfather of President John F. Kennedy, the frigate was restored for her hundredth birthday in 1897, part of the earlier repairs having been poorly carried out. By 1905 the condition of the ship was again bad and it was decided to make her the target-ship of the fleet. Again she was saved by public outcry. Restoration costs in 1906 totalled $ 100,000.

For the next 20 years the frigate was a museum, but she continued to deteriorate steadily. In 1925 Congress decided on a complete restoration but initially voted no funds towards it. For the most part costs were covered by public subscription though later the state also contributed. Work began on June 16, 1927 in Constitution Drydock in Boston. Douglas fir for the masts was brought all the way from the west coast, and on this occasion the total cost was $ 92,100.

The frigate remained in dock until March 16, 1931, and on July 2, that year she started a three-year journey under tow which took her into 90 American ports, where she was visited by 4,614,792 people. A total of 22,000 miles was covered. Since 1932 the *Constitution* has been moored in Boston

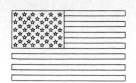

Niagara

Harbour, the flagship of the Commander of the First Naval District and the oldest active warship in the world. Annually the frigate is ceremonially warped round to present her other side to the weather.

Type: brig. Wood

Country: U.S.A.

Owners:
The Pennsylvania Historical and Museum Commission, Harrisburg Pennsylvania

Location: Niagara Park, Erie, Pennsylvania

Year of construction:
1812. Launched in June, 1813

Builders: Presque Isle Shipyard, Erie, Pennsylvania

Tonnage: 500 tons gross

Dimensions:

LOA	157 ft
Length between perpendiculars	110 ft
Breadth extreme	29 ft
Depth in hold (keel to lowest deck)	5 ft 6 in
Draft	12 ft

Rig:
9 sails. 2 headsails.
Single topsails, single topgallants

Masts and spars:
topmasts and topgallant masts.
Bowsprit with jib-boom. Height of mainmast above the deck 99 ft

Complement: about 100

Armament:
17 guns;
2 12-pounders, 15 32-pounders

Use: museum ship

During the 1812-1815 war between the U.S.A. and England, both powers strove to gain control of the Great Lakes. The Americans' main objective was the prevention of a further English advance to the south, while for their part the English wished to penetrate further into Canada. At the very beginning of the war the U.S.A. started to gather a small fleet for use on Lake Erie, the largest vessels being the *Niagara* and her sister ship the *Lawrence*. The fleet was under the command of Captain Oliver Hazard Perry.

On September 10, 1813 there was a battle in Put-In Bay, Ohio, in which the English were beaten. The Americans had two brigs, two gun-boats and four small armed vessels, while the English had two full-rigged ships, two brigs, one schooner and one sloop.
Perry found that his flagship was in major trouble so he lowered his flag with 'Don't give up the ship' embroidered on it, go into one of the ship's boats and rowed trough the harbour under fire complete with his flag to the *Niagara* where he hoisted it, attacked again and won the battle.
The Peace of Ghent, signed on December 24, 1814, brought the war to an end.
Since then the ship has been thoroughly restored twice. A 79 ft long piece of the original keel and most of the timbers have had to be replaced.
Once these swift fighting-brigs were fearsome opponents, but now the *Niagara* is the last surviving example. She has been set up as a memorial in Niagara Park, Erie, Pennsylvania.

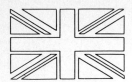

Foudroyant

ex *Trincomalee*

Type:
frigate (full-rigged ship), teak.
Fifth Rate, 46 guns

Country: Great Britain

Owner: The Foudroyant Trust

Location: Portsmouth (Gosport)

Year of construction:
1817. Keel laid May 1816. Launched
October 19, 1817

Builders: Wadia Shipyard, Bombay

Tonnage:
1447 tons displacement, 1066 tons
gross

Dimensions:

Length on deck	150 ft	4 in
Length of keel	125 ft	7 in
Breadth extreme	40 ft	3 in
Depth in hold	12 ft	9 in
Draft (at the time of building with 30 tons of ballast)		
Forward	12 ft	9 in
Aft	13 ft	6 in

Rig: low-setting single topsails

Complement:
on active service about 300

Armament:
until 1847: 46 guns. Then 26 guns and
later 24 guns

Use: stationary schoolship

This frigate, which was originally named the *Trincomalee* after the harbour on the East Coast of Ceylon, was built in Bombay and then sailed to England where she spent 25 years laid up in Portsmouth. It was not until 1847 that she had her first commission, and then with much reduced armament. She served in North American and West Indian waters until 1852. During the Crimean War the frigate patrolled in the Pacific for the four years starting in June 1852. Then she was laid up again in Chatham until 1861 when she became the training ship of the Royal Naval Reserve in Sunderland. In 1863 she was transferred to West Hartlepool, and subsequently to Southampton. On May 19, 1897 the R.N.R. sold the ship to the firm of J. Read to be broken up, but a further change of ownership followed immediately and the *Trincomalee* reverted to being a training ship when Mr. Wheatley Cobb bought her and renamed her the *Foudroyant*.
Mr. Cobb had earlier restored a 74-gun ship of that name which had once been Nelson's flagship, so as to use her as a training ship for youngsters, but she had unfortunately been lost in 1893 in a storm.
Until Cobb's death the training ship lay in Falmouth Harbour. Later she was transferred to Portsmouth and lay near H.M.S. *Implacable*. After the *Implacable* had been sunk with full honours in the English Channel the *Foudroyant* took over her training duties which she still performs to-day. From March to October courses are held for young boys and girls of 11 years and upwards, teaching sailing, boat handling, seamanship etc. All the pupils sleep in hammocks.
Between the years 1800 and 1830,

thirty-two similar frigates were built, but apart from the *Foudroyant* only the *Unicorn* in Dundee survives. There are plans afoot to re-rig her and have her as the main attraction for a Marine Centre at Bucklers Hard in the Beaulieu River near Southampon.

Foudroyant *after restoration (below) and today (right)*

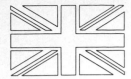

Unicorn

ex *Cressy*
ex *Unicorn II*
ex *Unicorn*

Type:
frigate (full-rigged ship). Wood.
Fifth Rate, 46 guns

Country: Great Britain

Owners:
The Unicorn Preservation Society,
Dundee

Location: Dundee, Victoria Dock

Year of construction:
1794—1824. Keel laid 1794. Launched
March 30, 1824

Builders:
Naval Dockyard, Chatham (Medway).
Designed by R. Seppings

Tonnage: 1077 tons displacement

Dimensions:

Length hull	166 ft
Length on deck	151 ft 9 in
Length between	
perpendiculars	140 ft 9 in
Breadth extreme	39 ft 11 in
Depth in hold	12 ft 9 in
Draft	approx 13 ft 1 in

Rig:
Originally low setting, single topsails,
single topgallants, royals

Masts and spars: (originally)

Height of mainmast above	
deck about	131 ft 3 in
Main yard	78 ft 9 in
Main royal yard	26 ft 3 in

Complement:
on active service provision was made
for 334 officers and men

Armament: originally 46 guns

Use: museum ship

Although the *Unicorn* is no 'famous' vessel (she never even saw active service) she is one of the oldest sailing ships to survive, due to her adaptability. She has been the training ship of the Royal Naval Reserve for many years. Up to the year 1554 when the English captured the Scottish galley *Unicorn,* all the flagships of the Scottish fleet bore this name. The English, too, have always had a ship named *Unicorn* in their fleet, and the present ship is the thirteenth. Her keel was laid in 1794, but it was not until 1822 that actual building began. Nor was she ever fully fitted out for sea; from the beginning she was in the reserves and in case of need could rapidly have been put into commission. In 1855 she was stripped and used as a powder store in Woolwich until 1862.

The *Unicorn,* who, incidentally, is a sister-ship of the *Foudroyant,* was then laid up in Sheerness for ten years. In October 1871 the Medwey Sanitary Authorities had asked to use as a cholera ship, but this was never put into effect. Instead the former frigate was converted into a training ship for the Naval Reserve and was decked over. Her official title then was H.M.S. *Unicorn,* Headquarters Tay Division, Royal Naval Reserve. In those days she had ten guns for artillery training: one 9-inch, one 6-inch, four 64-pounders and four 32-pounders. On November 9, 1873 she was towed to the Earl Grey Dock in Dundee. Naturally, over the years the ship was adapted to modern needs. Until recently, her guns were on the top deck. On the main deck were the officers' quarters, messes, offices, mine detection equipment and recreation rooms, while the lower deck housed weapons and clothing stores, a room for gunnery instruction and a practice room for the band.

In 1939 an aircraft carrier was given the traditional name *Unicorn* so the frigate was officially called the *Unicorn II* until on November 20, 1941 she was renamed the *Cressy.* In 1959 when the aircraft carrier was broken up she reverted to her old name. During the Second World War the ship served as Administration Centre for the Marine base at Dundee. From April 1946 she again came under the R.N.R. In 1962 she was transferred from the Earl Grey Dock to the Camperdown Dock because the building of the new Tay Bridge necessitated the filling-in of her former mooring place.

In the autumn of 1968 the Royal Naval Reserve moved to premises on land and the *Unicorn* was handed over to the Unicorn Preservation Society. She is now a floating museum and it is well possible that one day she will be re-rigged. One surprising fact is that after nearly 150 years in the water the hull hardly leaks at all.

23

Charles W. Morgan

Type: full-rigged ship. Wood

Country: U.S.A.

Owner:
Marine Historical Association Inc., Mystic, Connecticut

Location: Mystic Seaport, Connecticut

Year of construction:
1841. Launched July 21, 1841. First whaling expedition September 4, 1841

Builders:
Jethro and Zachariah Hillmann Brothers, Fairhaven, near New Bedford, Massachusetts

Tonnage: 313 tons gross, 298 tons net

Dimensions:
LOA	169 ft	
Length between perpendiculars	105 ft	6 in
Breadth extreme	27 ft	7 in
Depth moulded	17 ft	6 in

Rig:
20 sails. Single topsails, single topgallants, royals

Masts: all with top and topgallant masts

Engine:
no auxiliary motor, even at a later date

Complement: an average of 28

Use: museum ship

The *Charles W. Morgan* is the only surviving wooden whaling ship. Her first owner was the Quaker merchant Charles W. Morgan. Subsequent owners were Edward Mott Robinson, I. Howland & Co, J. & W. R. Cleveland, John A. Cook and Whaling Enshrined. The ship had a painted line of gunports dating from the time of her construction which were intended to deter raiding pirates. During her 80 years of whaling *Charles W. Morgan* made 37 voyages in all seas. These often lasted several years, for it was only when she was fully laden that she returned home. Over one thousand whale fishermen sailed in the *Charles W. Morgan* and altogether more than 2,500 whales were harpooned and killed by her boats.

She carried up to seven boats, which were usually manned by six men—four men on the oars, the harpooner and the helmsman.

From 1841 to 1866 her home port was New Bedford, from 1867 to 1906 San Francisco. Then she returned to New Bedford from which port she made her last seven whaling trips which lasted until 1921. That year she once more set sail for the film 'Down to the sea in ships.' In November 1941 the *Charles W. Morgan* was towed from Round Hills, Dartmouth, Massachusetts to Mystic Seaport in Connecticut where she lies today as one of the main attractions.

The Tall Ships

A visit by one of the 'tall ships' to a foreign port is today an event of premier importance, reported on the radio and TV. Even provincial newspapers far inland publish articles describing the ship and her crew. Public interest is so strong that reports are published by the press of a country even when the ship is a foreign ship and is visiting some other continent. Many of the large sail training ships are famous and their routes across the oceans of the world are followed with intense interest.

While a 'tall ship' is in port the general public is usually invited to come on board and have a look round. An example will serve to show with what enthusiasm this gesture is met. In 1963 the newly-built Argentine training ship *Libertad* visited Europe. During her fifteen-day stay in Hamburg 30,000 visitors went on board.

Nautical literature offers a large number of specialized works on the big sailing ships: not just narratives on the glorious age of the square-riggers, but in the main technical books concerning the history of these ships, their design, sails and rigging, as well as accounts of their long voyages.

Why is there such a great interest in these ships, even amongst people who will never, or rarely, set eyes on a 'tall ship', let alone see her under sail?

The sail is one of the oldest mechanical devices known to mankind. During more than 6,000 years of history the sailing ship has developed in a more consistent and logical way than most other technical inventions. Many other means of transport, the cart for example, have an equally long history. But the forces that propelled them kept changing, and this was bound to make their development erratic.

The sailing ship has always used the same motive power: the wind. If designers and shipyards exploit technical progress and improved materials, they do this with but one aim in mind: to produce a ship which can convert the same natural power into even more speed. The ships themselves are proof that fast can mean elegant, and beautiful, at the same time. There are very few examples of man-made devices of similar dimensions, especially where profitability has been a major consideration, which have attained the aesthetic appeal and the beauty of the large sailing ships. This may be one of the reasons for the irresistable attraction of these ships and the large amount of public interest which is being focussed on them today as it has been in the past. The heyday of the 'tall ships' was in the eighteen-eighties and nineties. Even then their noblest representatives, the clippers, had already come to the end of their era. The rapid development of the steam engine and internal combustion engine spelt death to the square-riggers. A steamer may impress through the sheer power of its engines, but it lacked the beauty of a graceful ship. Increasingly powerful mechanical propulsion was more important than the shape of hull and superstructure, so designers tended to neglect these at first. Only recently have ships been built which show that the hull of a motor vessel, too, can be graceful and elegant. For even the performance of these powerful liners is effected by wind and waves. As long as the designer bears this in mind he is unlikely to produce anything but aesthetically appealing shapes.

Only a half-century ago the ports of the world were so crammed with sailing ships that people referred to 'a forest of masts.' In those days they were purely cargo-carriers and passenger ships. Not long afterwards some lines started to run cargo-carrying training ships, but pure training ships of the type we have nowadays were quite unknown then. Shipping as such and the traffic in ports has basically changed very little since those days. Cargo-ships still come and go, even if they do so in a frantic hurry, for time is money. The cargo they carry is largely the same as it used to be, even if it is discharged and loaded by modern, fast-working gear that cuts a ship's stay in port to a minimum. The men who work on board these ships are basically the same. It is the sailor's tool, his ship, which has undergone a transformation. Even though quite a few square-riggers can still be found all over the world there are no longer any of those genuine, large merchant sailers which used to put their crews through a hard and merciless school.

The disappearance of the large quare-riggers and the type of seaman who manned them made way for an entirely new profession, at least in the merchant navy. Conditions of employment are now, in many respects, not dissimilar to those on land. The main considerations are good working conditions and social security, which is no more than fair and helps to make life at sea reasonably attractive. That is not to say that life on one of the old sailing ships was wholly detrimental to health. Quite the contrary! Many colds and infectious diseases were quite unknown on board a sailing ship at sea. But the preservation of food, for example, without the help of refrigeration, used to be a big problem.

Simultaneously with the introduction of steam and internal combustion engines, technical progress has made people's private lives easier and more agreeable.

The fact alone that safe and reliable means of transport have enabled people to plan their lives round time schedules has brought about a far reaching change. A system of modern communications has enabled us to establish rapid connections with any part of the world at any time. It is hardly surprising that shipping in particular has fully exploited this technological progress, and this has reduced the occupational hazard involved in going to sea quite considerably. The sailor knows his ship's time-table, he knows when he will be home. He is entitled to leave, it makes sense to plan a life ashore. His place of work is rather like a floating machine plant or factory. No more damp bunks and the attendant miseries in the forecastle of a square-rigger.

Instead, there are light and comfortable cabins. Modern navigation instruments ensure a reasonably safe voyage. Without these and many other facilities and comforts no-one would sign on a ship nowadays. Of course, the seaman's outlook has changed fundamentally. His relationship to his ship has become rather distant because there is no longer that vital, mutual dependence between man and ship which characterised the big sailing ships. Machines and reliable instruments are there to help him. When a sailor signed on a big square-rigger he knew full well that he would have to subject himself to a discipline the like of which was not found in any occupation on land, not even in the army, at least not in peace-time. His employment finished when the ship reached her destination, which could take six months or more. The strict rules and tough training were in the ultimate aimed at ensuring the safety of the ship and crew. Discipline for its own sake had no place on these ships. Only if every-body knew his job, and everything was in its place, could the ship be manoeuvred quickly and safely in every situation, especially at night.

Even if it was a tough and spartan life compared with a shore-bound existence, good ships, and in particular, fast ships, with ambitious captains had no difficulty in finding crews.

All work on board a large sailing ship was done by hand. Manual strength had to cope with vast sail areas and shift yards weighing a ton. Even if the work was made easier by tackles and occasionally even steam winches, a single man could never do it alone. Only a team in which every man knew that success depended on him personally, in which one man could rely on another, could make a ship come to life.

For a ship is a living thing. There is nothing stiff and dead about it, everything is dynamic. The whole ship is like a body which can be anatomically dissected. Its particular attraction lies in the fact that nothing is hidden. All parts are visible. In the centre there is the skeleton of masts, topmasts and yards. This is surrounded by the filigree of countless ropes and cables, some of which serve the purpose of staying the masts, others that of transmitting the effort applied at deck level to the yards and sails. The physical animation of one of these 'tall ships' becomes most convincing when every stitch of canvas is set on the towering rig.

A structure as complicated as this cannot move forward in an intelligent manner unless it is under a central command. The man in command is backed up by the crew, who have to obey all orders without question. If either condition is neglected, the ship and all of her crew are in peril. This relationship between Man and ship, this mutual dependence, used to forge a very close community on board a ship, such as was not found elsewhere. The ship served Man, Man served the ship, and he loved his ship. The men were pround of 'their' ship as she lay alongside the quay all shipshape after a fast run, with the newspapers reporting a good voyage. Each one of them had played a part in the success. More often than not a sailing ship was identified not only by her name, but by a figurehead which was somehow related to the name and was tended with loving care. It gave a ship her personality. The seamen were very conscious that their ships were something special. It is remarkable that a man-made contrivance should have been held in such esteem and had so much attention devoted to it by its users during its actual working life. With most other things this appreciation comes from outsiders and even then it is not usually forthcoming until the object in question has attained historic significance. Further proof of how close these men were to their ships can be found in the many pictures and models made by both masters and crewmen.

To the captains of the last two cargo-carrying training ships, the German ships *Pamir* and *Passat,* boat drills were not just intended as a means of familiarising the boys with the lifeboats. They attached great importance to the cadets getting a good view of their ship in her full glory in the open sea. For most of them this must have been a memorable experience. It was designed to strengthen the feeling of belonging to the ship, and this it undoubtedly did in many boys.

Today all the great cargo-carrying sailing ships have disappeared from the oceans of the world. Steamers and motor vessels have replaced them after a keen competitive struggle. By modern standards of profitability in ships, the ancient square-riggers had to have too large a crew in relation to their cargo capacity. This necessity was imposed not by the sail area, but by the number of masts. Frequently all the sails had to be handled at the same time to prevent the ship from losing way or searoom or being otherwise endangered. This means that there had to be a certain number of hands per mast. The largest of the square-riggers with a capacity of under 6,000 gross register tons had five masts. For a motor vessel this would not be very big. But in the case of a five-master like the full-rigged *Preussen* it called for a crew of forty-eight. In order to have a larger gross tonnage, sailing ships would have had to carry six or seven masts. There were some such ships, but they were short-lived both for technical and economical reasons. Today motor ships have schedules and, on the whole, they manage to keep to them. A highly competitive market requires the goods to arrive quickly and on time. Although some sailing ships plied on certain routes with remarkable regularity, the time taken for an individual run could never be reliably predicted. Sailing ships were at the mercy of calms and storms.

Under certain conditions cargo-carrying sailing ships could still be run profitably today. But the long-term business risk is too great. Sails and ropes made from traditional materials remain strong and pliable only if they are in constant use. And if a set of sails is lost in a storm the damage in a large ship can be expected to exceed the £ 10,000 mark. Contrary to a motor vessel, a sailing vessel constantly exposes its most fragile parts to the ravages of wind and weather. On the other hand, very few shipping lines could afford to rig their ships with Terylene or Dacron sails and rope. Which is why the only sailing vessels still afloat today are training ships and pleasure yachts. Some of the few remaining merchant sailers have been turned into museums and are permanently moored in harbours. It is to be hoped that these, at least, will be preserved for posterity. They must, of course, serve some purpose to remain in existence, but this should be no problem because there is ample space below decks to accommodate a variety of activities.

The last sail training vessels which also carried cargo were the two German four-masted barques, *Pamir* and *Passat*. In their case an attempt was made to cover at least part of the considerable running costs by a profit from trading. In the end they could only be kept afloat with the help of forty German shipping firms who set up the '*Pamir und Passat*' foundation and thus became the sponsors of the whole enterprise. *Pamir's* tragic loss in September 1957 also put an end to *Passat's* sailing days. Pure sail training vessels run by the merchant navies of various countries did not come into being until the beginning of the century. In Germany, for example, the Deutsche Schulschiff-Verein (German Sail Training Association) led the way in the training of cadet officers for the merchant navy. Its first ship, the full-rigged *Grossherzogin Elisabeth*, which was launched in 1901, was built as a pure training vessel. None of the ships that succeeded her under the auspices of the association carried any cargo either.

The sail training ships of both the navy and the merchant navy have always held an entirely different position to that of merchant ships. They are financially independent, being granted an annual budget which is sufficient to cover the running costs, and, above all, keep the ship in top trim for safety at all times. Many a merchant sailer ran into considerable danger because money had been saved in the wrong place! This was especially true when it came to stability. Stability enables a ship to right herself after heeling to any angle, and it was a much greater problem in sailing ships with their high and heavy rigs than it is in motor vessels. The leverage of the high masts counteracting the righting forces of the hull is much more powerful than that of the rather lower superstructure of a motor ship. In the old ships stability was ensured by the cargo, or, if the ship was empty, by ballast, which had to be discharged before reloading the ship. But even if nothing more than stones was used for ballast, they still had to be bought. Modern sail training ships have sufficient stability at all times. They usually carry their ballast in the shape of reinforced concrete which is permanently fixed in the hull. This still leaves plenty of room in the former holds for lecture rooms and living quarters.

Thanks to the financial backing sail training ships get, vital parts can be replaced long before it is really necessary. The boys' safety comes before everything, which explains why accidents rarely happen. Apart from the financial security it is the large crew which ensures that the ship is always kept in tip-top trim.

The sail training of future naval officers is not universally approved of. Voices are always raised in disapproval at this kind of training. The main argument of these opponents, discounting those who merely claim that it is 'dangerous', is that it is antiquated and superfluous in this modern age of motorized vessels.

The point is often made that, after all, car drivers do not practise in horse-drawn carriages. 'Romanticism' and 'foolhardiness' are favourite slogans used to stress the uselessness of the exercise.

Training on a big sailing ship is anything but romantic. In being enthusiastic about it the boys show that their outlook to their profession is sober, honest and undramatic. There is no room in training at sea for dreamers and spectators. From the very beginning every one of them has to dedicate himself wholly to the job in hand in order not to endager his comrades or the ship. The fact that there is still room in our mechanised and prosaic age for a type of sea-going vessel which is not only efficient but beautiful, ought to be cause for joy rather than superficial sentimentality. Arguments against the running of sail training ships inevitably prove that their advocates have no idea of what the training is all about. The boys are by no means expected to learn to sail or command a sailing vessel, nor even to be leaders, although most of them are training to be officers. Initially, the objective is to teach the youngsters to fit into a large community living in a very restricted space. Living and working under these conditions make consideration, team-spirit and co-operation so necessary that within a very short time they become a matter of course to every boy.

It goes without saying that working high up in the rigging calls for courage, determination and presence of mind. The communal life on board and the handling of the sails alone offer countless opportunities for character training of a kind which only a big sailing ship can offer.

Most of the other work on a sail training vessel, besides the work aloft, is done in the open. This makes for a much closer relationship with the weather and the sea than would be possible in a motor vessel. Even today an intimate knowledge of the natural elements is essential for the safe handling of a ship, no matter what its size. There have been a number of serious accidents at sea in recent times, not in spite of the very latest navigation aids with which the ships were equipped, but because men had relied on them.

Besides their educational role, the sail training ships fulfil a second function, that of representing their country during visits abroad. They manage to do this in a most impressive and memorable manner. A much admired sailing ship is certainly better fitted for the part than a warship bristling with guns.

Edwin Fox

Type: one-time full-rigged ship, later bark, now hulk. Teak
Country: New Zealand
Owners: Edwin Fox Restoration Society, Blenheim, N. Z.
Location:
  Picton Sound, Marlborough, N. Z.
Year of construction: 1853
Builders: yard at Sulkeali, Bengal, India
Tonnage: 891 tons gross, 836 tons net
Dimensions:
  Length between
  perpendiculars   144 ft
  Breadth extreme   29 ft 6 in
  Depth moulded   23 ft 7 in
Engine: no auxiliary motor
Use: museum ship

During the year-long siege of the fortress of Sebastopol in the Crimean War, the western powers lost twenty transport ships in a storm in November 1854 while they were lying in the roads. The *Edwin Fox* was the only sailing ship to survive undamaged.

Many documents concerning her history were lost in fires in London and New Zealand, but her life was so colourful and so varied that track of her is never lost.

The *Edwin Fox* was ordered by the East India Company, but during construction she was sold to Sir George Hodgkinson of Cornhill, London. Only the best teak was used in her construction. She was named after the famous Southampton Quaker. Her first voyage was with a cargo of tea for London where, after the company was dissolved, she was sold for a record £ 30,000 to the shipowner Duncan Dunbar. The English Government chartered her immediately and sent her to the Black Sea as a trooper where the incident during the siege of Sebastopol occured. The *Edwin Fox* spent eighteen months under British colours in the Crimea after which she made three consecutive trips to the East Indies before being chartered by the Government again, this time to deport political prisoners to Western Australia. She set sail again under naval command when she carried troops to fight the Indian Mutiny of 1856—58. In 1861 she was returned to her civil owners. She had just loaded a full cargo in Bombay when the Indian authorities asked her to unship it again, because all available shipping was needed to fight the great famine in the Northwest provinces. After that she made 16 trips to the disaster area with rice from Bangkok.

After Dunbar's death in 1862 the shipping company Gellatly & Co of London bought the *Edwin Fox* and she spent many years carrying tea, her somewhat squat and chubby lines causing her to be nicknamed the Tea Tub. The next chapter of her life was closely connected with the European settlement of New Zealand, which is why the New Zealanders wish to preserve her for future generations.

The British company Shaw Savill chartered the ship in 1873 to carry up to 259 emigrants a trip to New Zealand. On her first voyage she ran into a severe storm in the Atlantic which caused the death of several on board. She was taken in tow by the American packet *Copernicus* and brought to Brest where she was repaired and four weeks

Jylland

later was able to resume her voyage. Her second emigrant voyage also began with storm, damage and running aground; she was only saved from total loss by her extraordinarily strong construction.

In 1878 she was converted from full-rigged ship to bark, and her last voyage from England with emigrants aboard began in 1880. By now competition from steamships was making itself felt more and more, so she was fitted with refrigeration machines and sailed to New Zealand. In one day 500 sheep could be frozen, while a total of 20,000 sheep could be stored aboard her, which were then sent to England aboard refrigerated ships. In 1897, with only her lower masts standing, she was towed to Picton where she spent three further years as a refrigeration ship. She was then converted and used as a coal hulk until 1950, an opening being made in her topsides to allow waggons to be shunted into her.

Since 1964 there have been plans to restore her, and in 1965 the Edwin Fox Preservation Society bought her from the Picton Meat Co. for one shilling. The *Edwin Fox* is the only emigrant ship to have survived to the present day.

Type: steam frigate (full-rigged ship). Wood
Country: Denmark
Owners:
 town of Ebeltoft (National Museum Ship)
Location: Ebeltoft, Denmark (Jutland)
Year of construction:
 1857. Keel laid June 11, 1857. Launched November 20, 1860
Builders:
 Nyholm Naval Shipyard, Copenhagen
Tonnage: 2450 tons displacement
Dimensions:

LOA	approx 311 ft	8 in
Length between perpendiculars	210 ft	4 in
Breadth extreme	43 ft	4 in
Draft	19 ft	8 in

Rig:
 originally 18 sails (excluding studding sails), 4 headsails, single topsails, double topgallants (royals). Gaff sails on all masts, studding sails on foresail, mainsail, topsail and lower topgallant yards. At a later date the topgallants and studding sails were not used

Masts and spars:

Height of mainmast from waterline to truck	approx 177 ft	
Mainyard with studding sail spars	approx 139 ft	5 in
Main yard	approx 91 ft	10 in
Main topsail yard	approx 78 ft	9 in
Main topgallant yard	approx 46 ft	

Engine:
 Baumgarten and Burmeister 2 cylinder horizontal steam engine; nominal 400 hp, 1300 hp rated. Speed under power about 12 knots
Complement: 437
Armament:
 44 guns (smooth bore). Battery deck 30 30-pounders, upper deck 14 30-pounders, 16.2 cm calibre. After conversion in 1863-4 the upper deck had 8 18-pounders and 4 12-pounders (rifled bores). Later there were also some breech loaders with rifled bores
Use: museum ship

Three Danish fighting ships (1704, 1739, 1760) bore the name *Jylland* before this frigate, which was built by the famous naval shipyard on Nyholm Island in Copenhagen. About sixteen hundred 120 to 200-year old oaks were felled to build her, and she was the first Danish vessel to use wire for her standing rigging. The handsome figurehead symbolises the fruitfulness of Jutland, with a shepherd's crook, nets, ears of corn and mussels, while her stern is richly ornamented to match.

Her first commission was on May 15, 1862 as a cadet ship. Before the outbreak of the Austro-Prussian war the ship was fitted out for active service during the winter of 1863—4. War was declared on February 1, 1864 and on May 9, 1864 the *Jylland*, with the Danish Squadron under Admiral Suenson, won a battle against the Austro-Prussian squadron (steam frigate *Fürst Felix Schwarzenberg* under Tegetthoff) off Heligoland. After the war the ship made repeated voyages in European waters. In 1874 King Christian IX sailed aboard the frigate to Iceland, and in 1876 to St. Petersburg. Her last long voyage was to the West Indies in 1886—7 on which occasion Prince Charles, later King Haakon VII of Norway, was aboard as a volunteer cadet.

In 1892 the *Jylland* became a training ship and barracks, and on May 14, 1908 she was paid off. A tug had already reached Copenhagen to take her to a German ship-breaking firm when it was decided to keep her after all. Unfortunately by this time all the masts and spars had disappeared and the inadequate rig of the scrapped corvette *Dagmar* had to be used. The *Jylland* was then used to take various exhibitions round from port to port. In August 1912

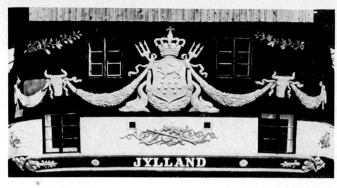

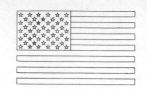

Alice S. Wentworth

she was bought by the property owner E. Schou and taken to Juelsminde where the 50th anniversary of the battle of Heligoland was celebrated on May 9, 1914.

During the First World War the frigate was again used for a while as a barracks. Until Schou's death she lay in Juelsminde and then in 1925 she was towed to Holmen. In 1926 the Committee for the Preservation of the Frigate Jylland was formed. Soon afterwards work began on restoration which was, unfortunately, interrupted later by the war. In 1935 she was taken to Copenhagen where from 1944—45 German refugees and later English troops lived aboard. In December 1947 she sprang a leak and sank.

After the war restoration was restarted and since 1957 the National Museum has also been involved. Several Jutland towns competed for the *Jylland*. It was finally decided to exhibit her at Ebeltoft where she was towed, without her masts stepped, on September 20, 1960. About 60,000 people visit her annually during the months of May to August. It is intended to re-rig her and do a thorough overhaul at an estimated cost of about Kr 3 million.

---

ex *Lizzie A. Tolles*

Type: 2-masted gaff schooner, Wood
Country: U.S.A.
Owner: Mr. Anthony Athanas, Boston, Massachusetts
Location: Boston, Massachusetts, Pier 4
Year of construction: 1863
Builders: at South Norwalk, Connecticut
Tonnage: 68.57 tons gross, 65.12 tons net
Dimensions:

LOA	91 ft	
Length hull	72 ft	
Length between perpendiculars	66 ft	
Breadth extreme	24 ft	4 in
Depth in hold	7 ft	2 in
Present draft	6 ft	

Rig:
 four sails, 2 headsails, gaff sail on each mast
Masts and spars:
 height of mainmast over deck 76 ft
Engine: no auxiliary
Complement: 6 to 8 men under sail
Use: museum ship

The former *Lizzie A. Tolles* was probably built in 1863 and was considered a fast ship in her days. She carried bricks for the most part, but also coal and oysters in Long Island Sound until she was bought in 1903 by Captain Arthur Stevens of Wells, Maine. He rebuilt the schooner completely so that on her second launching she was virtually a new ship, now renamed after the Captain's niece, Alice Stevens Wentworth Pellitier. She spent 40 years trading along the New England coast, during which period her home port changed first to Vineyard Haven and then to New Bedford. Her third and best-known owner was Captain Zebulon N. Tilton. In 1939, due to financial difficulties, it appeared that the ship would have to be laid up, but many well-wishers, among them famous stars of stage and screen, helped her to a new start. In 1944 the *Alice S. Wentworth* was sailed alone from Nantucket to Gloucester by the famous single-handed sailor Captain Parker J. Hall—he was 84 years old at the time.

When the war was over merchant sailing was no longer a paying proposition and passenger-carrying showed a better profit. The schooner was owned successively by Captain Guild, Captain Hawkins and lastly Mrs. Anne White who sailed her in the waters of Vineyard Sound. In the autumn of 1962 the *Wentworth* was damaged during a hurricane in Vineyard Haven, and the following winter she sank at her winter berth in Woods Hole but was immediately raised. On June 16, 1965 Mr. Anthony Athanas of Boston bought her for $ 13,500. Since then she has been a floating museum and tourist attraction at Anthony's Pier 4 Restaurant in Boston. In the spring of 1966 she again went to the bottom but was raised.

Star of India

ex *Euterpe*

Type: bark. Iron
Country: U.S.A.
Owners:
   Maritime Museum Association of
   San Diego, California
Location: Embarcadero, San Diego,
   California
Year of construction:
   1863. Launched November 14, 1863
Builders:
   Gibson, McDonald & Arnold,
   Ramsey, Isle of Man, Great Britain
Tonnage:
   2200 tons displacement,
   1197 tons gross
Dimensions:

LOA	278 ft
Length hull	216 ft
Length between perpendiculars	110 ft
Breadth extreme	29 ft
Depth in hold	22 ft
Loaded draft	21 ft 7 in

Sail area: 22,066 sq ft
Rig:
   19 sails. 3 (4) headsails. Double topsails, single topgallants, royals
   Mizzenmast: spanker, gaff topsail
Masts and spars:
   fore and main masts with topmasts
   and topgallant masts, mizzenmast
   with one topmast
   Height of mainmast

over deck	124 ft 8 in
Length of main yard	72 ft 2 in
Length of main royal yard	39 ft 4 in

Engine: no auxiliary
Complement: originally 38
Use: museum ship

The British shipping company, Wakefield Nash & Co. of Liverpool, built the full-rigged ship *Euterpe* in 1863. She sailed twice to Calcutta under their flag, suffering considerable damage through collision and storms on each occasion. On her second voyage home her captain died on board. As the voyages proved unprofitable the company decided to sell her in 1861 to the East India merchant David Brown of London. Under her new owner *Euterpe* was again engaged in the Indian trade until she was sold to the shipping company of Shaw, Savill & Albion in 1871, under whose flag she spent the next 27 years. Most of her voyages were round the Cape of Good Hope to South Australia and New Zealand, often returning to Europe via the Pacific Coast of the U. S. A. and Cape Horn. One of the company's captains, Mr. T. E. Phillips, circumnavigated the world ten times in succession aboard her.

As well as freight she very often carried emigrants to Australia and New Zealand, but the ship never proved herself particularly fast. In 1899 J. J. Moore (Pacific Colonial Ship Co.) of San Francisco bought her and she spent the next two years under the Hawaiian flag carrying timber from the U. S. A. (Puget Sound) to Australia, generally returning laden with coal. Two timber ports were cut in her stern to enable her to ship the long balks and trunks. In the winter of 1901 the Alaska Packers Association added *Euterpe* to their 'Star' fleet, renaming her the *Star of India,* and she went to a shipyard for an extensive refit and conversion. She was converted from full-rigged ship to bark and accommodation was provided for the crew, which often numbered 200. The poop was enlarged almost to the mainmast, and the forward deckhouse broadened, which raised her gross tonnage to 1318 tons. As one of the 'Star' fleet the bark sailed each year to the big canneries at Bristol Bay in Alaska, carrying seamen, fishermen and cannery workers. Her last voyage under the Alaska Packers flag was in 1923. Mr. J. Wood Coffroth acquired the ship in 1926 for the Zoological Society of San Diego intending her to be the centrepiece of an oceanographic museum and aquarium in San Diego, but the world economic crisis of the twenties prevented this.

By the end of the second world war the ship had fallen into a very poor state. Her upper spars and yards had to be lowered on account of the volume of air traffic over San Diego, but this job was so badly carried out that later, when it came to restoring her, hardly any of her standing rigging could be used. In 1959 a group of San Diego men decided to restore the ship as an example of that particular era of sail, and they formed the Star of India Auxiliary. Restoration was completed for the most part for the ship's 100th birthday. Euterpe has been her figurehead ever since she was built. Today the ship lies on the Embarcadero in San Diego and houses an oceanographic museum in the tweendecks.

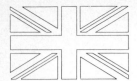

Carrick

ex *City of Adelaide*

Type:
formerly full-rigged clipper ship.
Composite construction

Country: Great Britain

Owner: Royal Naval Reserve Club

Location:
River Clyde, Clyde Street, Glasgow

Year of construction: 1864

Builders:
Pile of Sunderland, England

Tonnage: 791 tons gross

Dimensions:

Length between perpendiculars	176 ft	3 in
Breadth extreme	36 ft	
Depth in hold	18 ft	8 in

Rig:
originally double topsails, double
topgallants, royals

Masts: topmasts and topgallant masts

Engine: no auxiliary motor

Use: club headquarters

Only two composite clippers survive from the great days of the clipper ship, the *Cutty Sark* in London and the *Carrick* ex *City of Adelaide* in Glasgow. Although the well-known square-rig expert H. A. Underhill considers the hull of the *Carrick* to be the more elegant, the ships cannot now fairly be compared, for the *Cutty Sark* displays the full beauty of her rig, while the *Carrick* has become a hulk. Only the lowermasts and topmasts have been re-stepped and rigged up to now. No bowsprit completes the thoroughbred line of her bow, and a far from beautiful deck, or rather roof, covers everything except the poop and forecastle decks and disguises her elegant lines. She was built as a full-rigged ship for the Australian passenger line Devitt & Moore. For nearly 100 years she mostly carried emigrants to Adelaide, once making a record trip of 65 days from London to Adelaide. When passenger-carrying became unprofitable due to the preference for steamships, her owners diverted her to the wool trade. Shortly before the First World War the British navy took over the clipper and changed her name to H.M.S. *Carrick* after the area in south-west Scotland. During the war she was probably a hospital ship and was later converted to a depot and schoolship. She lay in the outer harbour at Greenock until 1947, first as Naval Gunnery School H.M.S. Carrick and later as headquarters ship of the Greenock Sub-Division R.N.V.R. In 1946 the Royal Naval Reserve (R.N.R.) were looking for a suitable place for their Officers Club and a year later the *Carrick* was selected and adapted. Since then she has lain on the Clyde in Glasgow, close to Clyde Street.

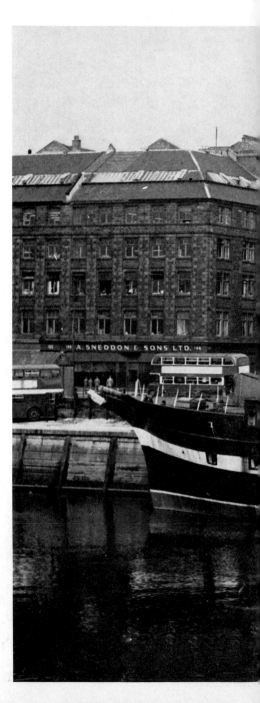

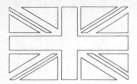

Cutty Sark

ex *Maria di Amparo*
ex *Ferreira* (= *El Pequina Camisola*)
ex *Cutty Sark*
Type:
full-rigged ship. Composite construction
Country: Great Britain
Owner:
Cutty Sark Preservation Society, London
Location:
in drydock at Greenwich, England
Year of construction:
1869. Launched November 23, 1869.
Builders:
Scott & Linton, Dumbarton.
Completed by Denny Bros.
Tonnage:
2100 tons displacement,
963 tons gross, 921 tons net
Dimensions:

LOA	280 ft
Length hull	224 ft
Length between perpendiculars	212 ft 6 in
Length of keel	210 ft
Breadth extreme	36 ft
Depth in hold	21 ft
Draft (heavy cargoes)	20 ft

Sail area: 32,800 sq ft
Rig:
34 sails. 4 headsails. All masts with double topsails, single topgallants, royals; mainmast: skysail; fore and mainmasts: studding sails
Masts and spars:

Bowsprit with jib-boom	67 ft 6 in
Foremast: from the deck to masthead	129 ft
Fore main yard	77 ft 9 in
Fore royal yard	37 ft 9 in
Mainmast: from deck to masthead	149 ft 4 in
Mainyard	77 ft 9 in
Main royal yard	37 ft 9 in
Main skysail yard	34 ft
Mizzenmast: from deck to masthead	108 ft 6 in
Cro'jack yard	66 ft 4 in
Mizzen royal yard	32 ft 10 in
Spanker boom	51 ft 10 in

Complement:
maximum 28. Usually 23—24 (the ship was also worked by 19 men)
Use: museum ship

In order to bring the Chinese tea-harvests ever quicker to Europe, and especially to England, the tea-merchants ordered faster vessels. At that time steamers could not attain such high speeds as the sharp-bowed elegant clippers, the 'racehorses of the oceans.' In 1869 the owner Captain John Willis had the clipper *Cutty Sark* built with a view to beating the year old *Thermopylae* in the tea race. The name *Cutty Sark* is of Scottish origin and means 'short shirt': it refers to a chemise worn by the witch Nannie in Burns' poem 'Tam O'Shanter'. Until 1877 the full-rigged ship sailed almost exclusively on the China Run, repeatedly making record trips and often reaching speeds of 17 knots. From 1877 on the *Cutty Sark* was mostly engaged in the Australian wool trade. Her sail area was considerably reduced in 1880, her lower masts being shortened by 10 feet, and she spent the next few years tramping, carrying coal, oil in drums, iron, etc. From 1884 to 1895 the ship was under the command of Captain Woodget, again mostly carrying wool from Australia. In 1895 she was sold to the firm of J. A. Ferreira in Lisbon. The name was changed to *Ferreira*, but mostly she was called *El Pequina Camisola*.

Little is known of her activities under the Portuguese flag. In 1916 she was dismasted in a storm due to badly stowed coal. The clipper ran for Cape Town and was rerigged there as a barkentine. In 1920 Ferreira sold her to the Cia. de Navegacao de Portugal in Lisbon, but voyages under this flag proved unprofitable and vain attempts were made to sell the famous ship back to England. Finally she went to Gibraltar as the *Maria di Amparo*. In 1922 she was bought by Captain Wilfred Dowman of Falmouth and at great expense the *Cutty Sark*, as she was again called, was restored as a full-rigged ship. She lay in Falmouth as a stationary training ship until Dowman's death in 1936. His wife gave the ship to the Nautical Training College Worcester in London in 1938.

In June of that year the *Cutty Sark* made her last journey in open seas under tow to London where she was moored at Greenhithe near the *Worcester*. During the war she was unrigged to her lower masts. In 1951 she had a thorough survey in the Millwall drydock and her condition was found to be faultless. The following year the National Maritime Museum in Greenwich decided to make her a permanent memorial to the great days of sailing ships and in 1953 her training ship days came to an end. The Cutty Sark Preservation Society was founded and necessary maintenance was effected in the East India Docks. On July 10, 1954 the *Cutty Sark* was towed to her dry berth at Greenwich where the Queen opened the ship on June 25, 1957. The figurehead had already been whittled away and the exact details of the original are not known. The present figurehead is that of the old witch Nannie. On open days and festive occasions a real horse's tail is often put into her outstretched left hand; according to the fable she tore it from Tam O'Shanter's horse Meg as he fled away. The hold now houses a museum with a display of many figureheads and is also used for instruction.

☆ ☆

Boys Marine Training Establishment

ex *El-Faroukieh*
ex *Hokki und Arselan*
ex *El-Kahira*
ex *Henny*
ex *Cape Finisterre*

Type: bark. Iron

Country: United Arab Republic

Owners:
Port and Lighthouse Administration,
Alexandria

Location:
West Harbour, Alexandria,
at Ras-El-Tin

Year of construction: 1874

Builders:
T. Wingate & Co., Glasgow, Scotland

Tonnage:
929.50 tons gross, 838.18 tons net

Dimensions:

LOA	221 ft 2 in
Length hull	196 ft 10 in
Length between perpendiculars	179 ft 6 in
Extreme breadth	33 ft
Depth moulded	21 ft 8 in
Depth in hold	18 ft 4 in
Draft (unladen)	7 ft 6 in

Rig: 19 sails

Masts:
Height of mainmast over deck 132 ft
Fore- and mainmasts with topmasts
and topgallant masts.
Mizzenmast with one topmast.

Engine: no auxiliary

Use: stationary schoolship

The bark *Cape Finisterre* was built in 1874 for A. Lyle & Sons of Greenock. Lyle owned a small fleet of freighters, all of which were called *Cape—*: *Cape York, Cape Clear* etc. She sailed under this flag until September 1891 when, with the new name *Henny*, she was acquired by the shipowners T. Handorff of Elsfleth on the Weser. In 1904, under the same name, she was bought by Prospero Razeto fu Francesco of Comogli near Genoa, where she was subsequently registered. In 1913 she was bought by the firm of J. S. Sorris & E. D. Tripcovich of the island of Santorin in Greece who changed her name to *Adriatico*. This was a one-ship tramp business, the owners living aboard and trading wherever the ship happened to be. In 1920 her name disappeared from the registers, presumably because she was no longer classified.

In 1923 she re-appeared as *El-Kahira* (Cairo) belonging to Mustapha Eff. Hokki E. Eff. Arselan af Alexandria who later changed her name to *Hokki and Arselan*. In 1930 the Egyptian Government bought the sailing vessel as a stationary schoolship for the education of Egyptian naval recruits, and she is still being used for this purpose today. At present the ship has no name: her title is *Boys Marine Training Establishment* ex *El-Faroukieh* and she lies in the western harbour of Alexandria off Ras-El-Tin.

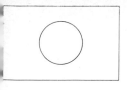

Meiji Maru

Type: full-rigged ship, Iron
Country: Japan
Owner:
    Mercantile Marine University, Tokyo
Location:
    drydock on the University campus,
    Tokyo
Year of construction: 1874
Builders:
    Robert Napier, Glasgow, Scotland
Tonnage: 1038 tons gross, 457 tons net
Dimensions:

LOA	31 ft	
Length hull	249 ft	4 in
Length between perpendiculars	239 ft	6 in
Breadth extreme	28 ft	
Depth moulded	25 ft	

Rig:
    26 sails (full-rigged ship). Double
    topsails, single topgallants, royals
Masts and spars: Height of mainmast

over deck	101 ft	9 in

    Bowsprit with jib-boom
Engine: 1530 hp piston steam engine
Use: museum ship

In March 1873 the Japanese Government instructed the firm of R. Napier of Glasgow to build a schooner-rigged steam-propelled lighthouse tender. *Meiji* (enlightened government) was the motto of Emperor Mutsuhito (1867 to 1912) under whose rule Japan became a great power. The emperor twice used the *Meiji Maru* for voyages; in March 1875 he sailed in her to Yokohama from Yokosuka after taking part in festivities connected with the naming of a man-of-war, and in July 1876 he returned to Yokohama in her from a tour of inspection in Northern Japan.

Meiji Maru was under the command of the Japanese lighthouse authorities until November 1897 when she was handed over to the Tokyo Marine Academy, forerunner of the present Merchant Navy University. She was altered and rigged as a full-rigged ship. From then on she lay in Tokyo Harbour as the Academy's stationary schoolship. In August 1927 her engines and boilers were removed. The Americans commandeered the ship in September 1945 and used her as a canteen for their troops. She was returned to the Academy in October 1951. Characteristics of this sailing ship are the through flush deck, with very little sheer, and the uninterrupted open guardrail. In March 1964 *Meiji Maru* was overhauled and brought to her present berth. There are plans to make her into a museum.

Joseph Conrad

ex *Georg Stage I*

Type: full-rigged ship. Iron

Country: U.S.A.

Owner:
Marine Historical Association Inc.,
Mystic, Connecticut

Location: Mystic Seaport, Connecticut

Year of construction: 1882

Builders:
Burmeister & Wain, Copenhagen,
Denmark

Tonnage:
203 tons gross, 187 tons net,
400 tons deadweight

Dimensions:
LOA	153 ft 7 in
Length hull	118 ft
Length between perpendiculars	100 ft 5 in
Breadth extreme	25 ft
Depth moulded	14 ft 9 in
Draft	11 ft 10 in

Rig:
20 sails, 4 headsails; low-setting single
topsails, single topgallants, royals,
studding sails on fore- and mainmasts

Masts and spars:
Height of mainmast from keel to
truck 98 ft 6 in. Masts, yards and
spars of wood. Bowsprit with jib-
boom

Engine: 265 hp diesel

Complement:
when sailing as a training ship:
captain, chief and second officers,
instructor, 5 petty officers, cook
and about 80 apprentices

Use: museum ship;
sationary schoolship

In 1882 the Danish shipowner Frederik Stage built a full-rigged ship, the *Georg Stage,* in memory of his son Georg. With his backing the Stiftelsen Georg Stages Minde was formed in Copenhagen, which still today owns the *Georg Stage II. George Stage I* was unusual for her time in that she had an auxiliary steam engine with vertical boiler, as well as a removable propeller. These were fitted because at that time a large number of the navy's sailing ships had an auxiliary engine, and boys had to familiarise themselves with this piece of ships' equipment during training.

The ship was and is still often described as an ex-steamer, but this is not right: she was a full-rigged ship and only used engines occasionally.

Georg Stage was built with a small high forecastle. The anchor windlass stood on the main deck and was worked by raising and lowering a lever, like a pumphandle. The bulwarks were doubled above the pin-rail, thus forming stowage space for the boys' rolled-up hammocks similar to the hammock nettings of older ships. Accommodation was on the tween-deck, hence the skylights and the companion-ways on the main deck. In course of time the wooden figurehead of Georg Stage had to be

replaced by a bronze bust because the boys had practised carving on it. Two small brass guns still stand on the poop and are used for saluting.

The ship was intended for use in the North Sea and the Baltic, and during the winter she was laid up in Copenhagen and unrigged by the boys themselves. On June 25, 1905 she was rammed at night in The Sound by the British steamer *Ancona of Leith*. The ship had no bulkheads and sank in less than three minutes with the loss of 22 boys.

After being raised she was repaired and altered, the old steam engine and detachable propeller being removed and four watertight bulkheads built. Thus she became a pure sailing ship. Not until 1916 was a 52 h.p. engine installed for use in harbour. In 1922 she was redecked and the old anchor windlass replaced by a capstan on the forecastle. In course of time she proved too small for the training programme: a new ship, *George Stage II* was in course of construction, so on August 29, 1934 *George Stage* was sold to Alan Villiers who fitted her out with a view to sailing round the world. Because she carried no cargo she was not a merchant vessel, and although many cadets sailed aboard her she was not an official training ship, so the Royal Harwich Yacht Club registered her under the name of *Joseph Conrad*.

Her great voyage began on October 22, 1934. She was damaged and nearly lost in New York. It was here that she was given a new figurehead, a bust of Joseph Conrad, her old figurehead going to *Georg Stage II*. The *Joseph Conrad* returned to New York on October 16, 1936, Villiers having covered 57,000 nautical miles in the meanwhile. On November 10, of that year she was sold to Mr. Huntington Hartford who fitted

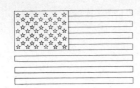

Falls of Clyde

her out as a luxury yacht, changing much of her interior and installing a 265 h.p. diesel. In 1939 Mr. Hartford presented the ship to the U.S. Maritime Commission and the *Joseph Conrad* was used as the seagoing training ship of the merchant navy until 1945, based in St. Petersburg in Florida, where she lay from 1945 to 1947 after being given to the Marine Historical Association. Since the summer of 1948 she has lain in Mystic Seaport in Connecticut as a museum ship. Courses for Sea Scouts and Sea Rangers are held aboard her.

Type: 4-masted, full-rigged ship. Iron
Country: U.S.A.
Owner:
Bernice P. Bishop Museum, Honolulu, Hawaii
Location: Honolulu, Hawaii
Year of construction: 1878
Builders:
Russel & Co., Port Glasgow, Scotland
Tonnage:
1195 tons displacement,
1809 tons gross, 1748 tons net
Dimensions:
LOA	about 323 ft
Length hull	about 280 ft
Length between perpendiculars	266 ft
Breadth extreme	40 ft
Depth moulded	23 ft
Depth in hold	23 ft
Draft (loaded)	21 ft

Rig:
32 sails (as full-rigged ship).
Double topsails, single topgallants, royals
Masts:
height of mainmast over deck 135 ft
Engine: no auxiliary
Use: museum ship

In 1878 the company of Wright & Breakenridge (later Wright, Graham & Co.) owned a fleet of nine large square-rigged vessels, the well-known Glasgow Falls Line. Six of them were four-masted full rigged ships, but the only one to survive today is the *Falls of Clyde*. Even before the turn of the century the ship sailed for a time under the Hawaiian flag, before being converted to a four-masted bark by Captain William Matson who bought her in 1900. The *Falls of Clyde* spent the next seven years carrying cargo and passengers between California and Hilo (Hawaii). In 1907 she was transferred to the ownership of Associated Oil (now the Tidewater Oil Company) and was converted into a sailing tanker. The next fifteen years were spent carrying cargoes of up to 19,000 barrels of oil between the west coast of America and Honolulu.

From 1926 to 1959 *Falls of Clyde* lay mastless as a fuel depot ship for the General Petroleum Company in Ketchikan Harbour, Alaska. A private buyer had her towed to Seattle hoping to form an organisation for her preservation, and several large west coast towns tried unsuccessfully to raise the necessary funds. Eventually an Alaskan Bank, which had put up the money for her purchase, decided that her hull should be sold on May 31, 1963 for $ 18,950, to be sunk as part of the Vancouver breakwater. Shortly before the completion date Karl Kortum, director of the San Francisco Maritime Museum, contacted Honolulu and immediately a fund-raising campaign was launched all over Hawaii. Contributions towards saving the ship, which had played such an important role in the more recent history of the island, came from industrialists, newspaper owners, several

trade delegations, but above all from the general public. In the meanwhile the Matson Navigation Company succeeded in negotiating a thirty-day postponement of the completion date. The collection raised not merely the $ 18,950, but also a further $ 5,000 for the transfer of the ship to Hawaii. At present she is in the hands of the B. P. Bishop Museum in Honolulu, who act as trustees. It is planned that she should become the property of the Museum. Preparations for restoration are under way and will probably be carried out by the Kapalama yard. The original figurehead, a female figure, has stayed in Seattle. When her restoration is complete the *Falls of Clyde* will be the only surviving four-masted full-rigged ship.

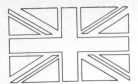

Dolphin

Type:
  at present a hulk, but formerly a bark.
  Composite construction
Country: Great Britain
Owner:
  The Dolphin Training Ship Society.
  Leith (Leith Nautical College)
Location: East Old Dock, Leith
Year of construction:
  1882/83. Launched December 9, 1882
Builders:
  Messrs. Dixon & Company,
  Middlesborough, England
Tonnage: 925 tons displacement
Dimensions:

Length between perpendiculars	156 ft 6 in
Breadth extreme	31 ft 10 in
Draft, foreward	11 ft 6 in
amidships	12 ft 2 in
aft	14 ft

Rig:
  deep setting single topsails, single
  topgallants, royals
Engine:
  750 hp triple expansion steam engine
Complement:
  as a warship under sail,
  100 to 115 men
Armament:
  originally 2 6-in and 2 5-in breach-
  loaders
Use:
  permanently moored training ship

Today it is hardly possible to imagine when you look at the hull of *Dolphin* that she was once rigged as a bark. Conspicuous is her almost vertical stem which, when *Dolphin* was in commission as a sailing ship, carried a very long almost horizontal bowsprit and jibboom. Four guns were carried, one to port and one to starboard at bow and stern in recesses in the low superstructure. After being commissioned *Dolphin* joined the Mediterranean squadron and was prominent when she raised the siege of the town of Saukin in the Red Sea which had been attacked and surrounded by the soldiers of the slave trader Osman Digna. In the following years she was engaged in chasing slave ships. In 1896 *Dolphin* returned to England and the following year her guns and steam engine were removed. That same year she went to Portland as sail training ship of the Sail Training Squadron.

By 1907 the composition of the British Fleet had changed considerably. There were now 30 submarines which were much too small to support their crews for long periods. *Dolphin* was therefore sent to Gosport and converted into the first submarine depot ship. In 1912 she became the flag-ship of Submarine Command at Fort Blockhouse, and the present shore establishment there bears the name H.M.S. *Dolphin*.

In 1924 the ship was put up for sale and bought by Sir Donald Pollock and Lieut-Commander J. M. Robertson, a Glasgow shipowner. They intended to moor her in Leith as a stationary recreation and club ship for youngsters, but while under tow the ship was severely damaged and dismasted in a storm. She had to be beached and only reached Leith five months later. After repairs *Dolphin* was converted at the shipyard in Rosyth belonging to Sir Donald Pollock. A lot of material from the battleship *King George V* which was being broken up there was used in her conversion. A large structure was built on the main deck to house instruction rooms. On completion *Dolphin* returned to Leith in 1928. Since the Second World War she has been used not only as a Club as originally planned, but also as an instructional ship for about 50 youngsters who for the most part live aboard while receiving basic instruction in nautical matters.

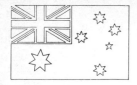

Polly Woodside

ex *Rona*
ex *Polly Woodside*

Type: bark. Iron

Country: Australia

Owners:
National Trust of Australia (Victoria);
The Polly Woodside Committee

Location: South Wharf, Melbourne

Year of construction: 1885

Builders:
Workman, Clark & Co. Ltd., Belfast

Tonnage: 694 tons gross, 610 tons net

Dimensions:

LOA	229 ft	8 in
Length hull	200 ft	6 in
Length between perpendiculars	191 ft	8 in
Breadth extreme	30 ft	3 in
Depth moulded	17 ft	
Depth in hold	16 ft	

Rig:
20 sails. Probably upper and lower topsails, single topgallants, royals

Masts:
Height of mainmast over deck 110 ft

Engine: no auxiliary

Complement:
between 11 and 15 (with deck boys)

Use: museum ship

Many large sailing vessels could have been preserved unaltered as museums at no great expense, but business considerations have doomed most cargo-carrying sailing ships to an inglorious end. At the last minute ship-lovers now are trying to save the few—even when, as in the case of *Polly Woodside,* no more than a mastless hulk survives.

Australia, which played so great a part in the great days of the sailing ship, has in *Polly Woodside* her last remaining large sailing vessel, so it was hardly surprising that the plan to restore her met with great enthusiasm in many circles.

The bark was built for W. J. Woodside (The Barque Polly Woodside Co. Ltd.) of Glasgow. It was said of her that she was the handsomest ship ever to be launched in Belfast. She spent many years carrying general freight for her owner. After running aground in New Zealand in 1903 she was bought by A. H. Turnbull & Co. of Lyttelton, New Zealand and renamed *Rona* (after Miss Rona Munro whose father was the marine superintendent of the Canterbury S.S. Co. New Zealand), operating as a freighter between New Zealand, the Pacific islands and Australia. On a voyage to the U.S.A. during the first world war she lost her bowsprit and figurehead in a collision in San Francisco harbour.

After the war the shipowners G. H. Scales of Wellington bought the bark. In 1921 she stranded on Barratt's Reef outside the entrance to Wellington harbour, and thereafter her masts were never restepped.

Rona was transferred to the ownership of the Adelaide Steamship Co. as a hulk in 1923, and was used as a coal lighter in Sydney until 1925, and then in Melbourne until 1953. Her last owners, who still used her for coal, were Messrs. Howard Smith of Melbourne.

In December 1967 the directors of this company presented the ship to the Australian National Trust (Victoria). In the meanwhile a committee had been formed which made many preparations for her restoration. After this is completed *Polly Woodside* will be moored permanently in the Yarra in Melbourne, and a museum will be housed in the tween-decks.

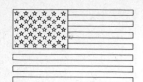

Balclutha

ex *Pacific Queen*
ex *Star of Alaska*
ex *Balclutha*

Type: full-rigged ship. Steel
Country: U.S.A.
Owner:
San Francisco Maritime Museum
Association, San Francisco, California
Location:
Pier 43 Fisherman's Wharf,
San Francisco, California
Year of construction:
1886. Launched December 9, 1886
Builders:
Charles Connell & Co, Glasgow,
Scotland
Tonnage:
1689 tons gross, 2660 tons burden
Dimensions:
LOA	256 ft	5 in
Length hull	244 ft	6 in
Length between		
perpendiculars	242 ft	10 in
Breadth extreme	38 ft	6 in
Draft	22 ft	8 in

Sail area: approx 20,452 sq ft
Rig:
25 sails. Double topsails,
single topgallants, royals
Masts:
all masts with one topmast.
Height of foremast		
over deck	140 ft	5 in
Height of mainmast		
over deck	143 ft	5 in
Height of mizzenmast		
over deck	128 ft	4 in
Main yard	86 ft	4 in
Main royal yard	40 ft	

Engine: no auxiliary
Complement: as a cargo ship, 26 men
Use: museum ship

Balclutha was built in Glasgow for Robert McMillan of Dumbarton on the Clyde. Her Gaelic name means Bal (town) on the Clutha (Clyde) and is the old name for Dumbarton. The ship was engaged in general trade—a true deepwaterman. Her maiden voyage was round Cape Horn to San Francisco, and altogether she rounded the Horn 17 times. *Balclutha* brought grain from California, guano from Chile, wool from New Zealand and rice from Rangoon to Europe, sailing under the British flag until 1899. From then until 1902, for a San Francisco Company under the Hawaiian flag, she took wood to Australia, returning to the U.S.A. with coal from Newcastle for the Southern Pacific Railroad. In 1902 she was bought by Pope & Talbot of San Francisco and since then has sailed under the American flag. She spent the next years in the salmon trade with a crew of sailors, fishermen and canners, often carrying as many as 300 men. These voyages lasted from spring to autumn and led her into Alaskan waters.
In 1904 she grounded near the Island of Kodiak and was severely flooded. The Alaska Packers Association bought the ship for $ 500 and undertook the difficult salvage operations, after which they added her to their 'Star' fleet, renaming her the *Star of Alaska*. Repairs were effected in San Francisco and her poop considerably lengthened to accommodate her large crew.
She was one of the fastest ships in the fleet and in September 1930 was the last vessel to return. But the days of the Alaska Packers were numbered and she spent three years laid up in the shallow bay of Alameda. In 1933 the film industry took her over and she was used in films as the *Pacific Queen*, calling at many ports as a pirate ship. In 1952 she was on the mud banks of Sausalito near San Francisco. Through the initiative of K. Kortum, director of the Maritime Museum of San Francisco, she was bought by them in 1954 for $ 25,000. Numerous firms gave services and materials free to restore her, otherwise costs would have run up to $ 250,000. After a year's work *Balclutha*, as she was again called, could be towed to her berth looking exactly the same as when she was built, with her typical broad white strake. The figure of a woman adorns her graceful bow.

51

Sigyn

Type:
barkentine. Wood. Constructed as a bark

Country: Finland

Owner:
"Sjöhistoriska Museet vid Åbo Akademi (Maritime Museum at Åbo Academy)

Location: Turku, Aura Quay

Year of construction: 1887

Builders: Gamla Varvet, Gothenburg

Tonnage:
359 tons gross, 301 tons net, 550 tons deadweight

Dimensions:
LOA	180 ft	6 in
(with original bark rig	193 ft	7 in)
Length hull	155 ft	10 in
Length between perpendiculars	139 ft	5 in
Breadth extreme	30 ft	6 in
Depth in hold	12 ft	6 in
Draft (fully loaded) about	13 ft	

Sail area:
with original bark rig, about 8611 sq ft

Rig:
as a bark, 20 sails; as a barkentine, 16 sails, 3 headsails, double topsails, single topgallants, royals, gaff sail and gaff topsail

Masts and spars:
masts, topmasts and spars of pitchpine. Foremast with topmast and topgallant mast, main and mizzen masts with single topmasts. Height of mainmast over deck 98 ft 6 in (as a bark, 105 ft). Bowsprit with jib-boom

Engine: no auxiliary

Complement:
as a bark, 11 men; as a barkentine, 8 or 9 men. In addition there were 2 to 4 apprentices

Use: museum ship

But few ships have changed hands as frequently as the *Sigyn*. She was built in 1887 as a wooden bark for A. Landgrens Enka of Göteborg. In 1905 she was bought by Anders Svensson of Halmstad, Sweden, who sold her in 1918 to C. T. Jonasson and Salsakers Angsags AB of Raa, Sweden. After 1921 she belonged to Salsakers Angsags alone. Siegfried Ziegler of Raa bought the ship in 1925, but sold her two years later to Arthur Lundqvist of Wardö, Aaland. In 1935 she was owned by Fredrik Eriksson of Wardö, and since 1939 she has belonged to the Sea History Museum of Abo Academy (Sjöhistorika Museet vid Abo Akademi).

Her maiden voyage was to China, after which she spent many years carrying freight all over the world. During a storm in 1913 *Sigyn* broke loose from her anchor off Kristiansand on the Norwegian coast and was severely damaged when she stranded. She was repaired and re-rigged as a barkentine. During the 1914—18 war she made several voyages across the Atlantic, the last of which was from Pensacola in Florida to Copenhagen. *Sigyn* then sailed mostly in the Baltic until 1937 when in the autumn she made her last voyage carrying freight from Frederiksund, Denmark to Wardö, after which she was laid up.

The Abo Academy bought the barkentine in the spring of 1939 to preserve her as a museum. She set sail again in September 1954 when she was used for filming, since when she has lain as a museum at the Aura Quay in Abo.

Sigyn *after a refit in 1967*

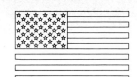

Wavertree

ex *Southgate*

Type: full-rigged ship (hulk). Iron

Country: U.S.A.

Owner:
South Street Seaport Museum, New York, New York

Location:
1968 still in Buenos Aires, Argentina, later in New York, New York

Year of construction: 1885

Builders:
Oswald Mordaunt & Co., Southampton, England

Tonnage: 2170 tons gross, 2118 tons net

Dimensions:

LOA	325 ft	
Length hull	293 ft	4 in
Length between perpendiculars	268 ft	5 in
Breadth extreme	40 ft	
Depth moulded	26 ft	7 in
Depth in hold	24 ft	3 in
Draft (loaded)	20 ft	4 in

Sail area: 31,495 sq ft

Rig:
28 sails. Double topsails, single topgallants, royals

Masts:

Height of mainmast over deck	140 ft	6 in

Equipped with top and topgallant masts

Engine: no auxiliary

Complement: 29

Use: museum ship

This merchant sailing ship was originally ordered as the *Southgate* by the Liverpool shipowners R. W. Leyland & Co., but changed hands while she was being built. On completion *Southgate* sailed in the Indian trade for the shipowners Chadwick Pritchard from 1886 until 1888. R. W. Leyland then bought her and under their 'hungry-goose' flag she made long voyages for the most part, usually carrying nitrate, sawn timber, barrel oil and jute to all parts of the world. In September 1910 *Southgate* was severely damaged in a storm off Cape Horn and returned to Montevideo for repairs.

In November of the same year, again off Cape Horn, she lost her main mast which broke off above decks. This time she put in to the Falkland Islands for refuge. Further repairs were obviously not worthwhile, so in April 1911 she was taken to Punta Arenas where she was used as a wool-store. In January 1948 she was towed to Buenos Aires to be broken up, but in the meanwhile Senor Alfredo Numeriani bought the ship and converted her into a sand lighter.

The South Street Seaport Museum, which was founded in 1966, now has a contract to restore the ship and to moor her in New York as part of the museum. It is to be hoped that the restoration of this large full-rigged ship to her old splendour, complete with her handsome figurehead and painted gun-ports, will be successful.

For pictures of Wavertree *see over*

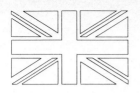

Wavertree *around 1890 in San Francisco (above) and in 1968 in Buenos Aires*

ex *Neptune (Delipa)*
ex *Pequod*
ex *Hispaniola*
ex *Ryelands*

Type: frigate (rig for filming). Wood

Country: Great Britain

Owner:
Mr. F. P. V. Latham, Morecambe, Lancashire

Location: Morecambe

Year of construction: 1887

Builders:
Glasson Dock, Lancaster, England

Tonnage:
158 tons gross (as topsail schooner *Ryelands*)

Dimensions: (as *Ryelands*)
LOA	130 ft
Length hull	102 ft
Length between perpendiculars	85 ft
Breadth extreme	22 ft
Depth in hold	12 ft
Draft	10 ft 9 in

Rig: (as *Moby Dick*) 11 sails

Masts:
Height of mainmast over deck	59 ft 9 in

Use: museum ship

Moby Dick

The *Moby Dick* cannot really be compared with the other sailing ships in this book, nor even with replicas such as the *Bounty,* but in her present condition she does at any rate give a rough impression of the appearance of an eighteenth century frigate. Even to the inexpert eye there are incongruities in her masting—her mizzen is stepped far too far forward and too close to the main mast, while her long jib-boom is at too sharp an angle. She does prove, however, that not all ships in historical sailing films are studio models, and that at least some effort is made to come somewhere near the original.

The *Moby Dick* was originally built as a three-masted double topsail schooner and was one of many English merchant sailers. She still had her original rig, and no auxiliary, in 1922. She was altered for the first time in 1950 for the film 'Treasure Island' when she was used as the *Hispaniola.* Due to the high stern superstructure and long jib boom her measurements altered appreciably. In 1953 *Hispaniola* lay in Scarborough for a short time as a floating aquarium until she was bought by Elstree Pictures Ltd. in 1954 for the film 'Moby Dick.' After further but rather inaccurate alterations she became the *Pequod* under Captain Ahab (alias Gregory Peck) during his hunt for the white whale. In 1956 the ship was transferred to Sapphire Films Ltd. and further alterations enabled her to take the parts of both *Neptune* and *Delipa* in the television film 'The Buccaneers.' She was then to have been broken up in Cornwall but her present owner managed to forestall this. He took her under sail back to her old home in Morecambe Bay. She has been given the name *Moby Dick* as a reminder of the second film in which she took part, which was filmed in the Irish Sea.

Af Chapman

ex *G. D. Kennedy*
ex *Dunboyne*

Type: full-rigged ship. Iron

Country: Sweden

Owner:
City of Stockholm (Svenska Turist-
föreningen)

Location: Stockholm, Skeppsholmen

Year of construction:
1888. Keel laid 1885. Launched
March 1888

Builders:
Shipbuilding Company, Whitehaven,
Cumberland, England

Tonnage:
2300 tons displacement, 1425 tons
gross, 1380 tons net

Dimensions:
LOA	280 ft	3 in
Length hull	257 ft	
Length between perpendiculars	233 ft	5 in
Breadth extreme	37 ft	5 in
Draft	18 ft	4 in

Sail area: 23,756 sq ft

Rig:
26 sails. 4 headsails. All masts have
double topsails, single topgallants,
royals

Masts and spars:
Height of mainmast over deck	136 ft	6 in
Length of mainyard	84 ft	4 in

Engine: no auxiliary

Complement:
as naval training ship, 50 permanent
crew and 200 cadets

Use: youth hostel

Due to a shipbuilding crisis, construction was spread over three years, and it was only at the end of this time that a buyer could be found for this ship. She sailed as a merchantman, mostly on the Australian run, under the name of *Dunboyne,* for her owners the Dublin firm of Charles E. Martin & Co. from 1888—1908. The full-rigged ship was bought in 1909 by the Norwegian shipowners Leif Gundersen of Porsgrund who did not change her name and continued to use her as cargo-ship. Before the end of the 1914—18 war she was owned for a short while by Emil Knutsen of Lillesand.

On July 30, 1915 she was sold to the Swedish shipowners A.-B. Transatlantik of Göteborg for £ 8,300. Under the new name of *G. D. Kennedy* her owners used her as a freight-carrying training ship for 30 boys, having equipped her with modern technical aids for this purpose. The Swedish Crown bought the ship in November 1923 for Kr 128,000, altering the interior completely to convert her into a pure training ship for the Swedish Navy. As no freight was to be carried, quarters for 200 cadets were made in the tween deck, which was lit by many portholes cut in the topsides. She was given the name *Af Chapman* after Frederic Henric af Chapman (1721—1808) who was a naval architect and Vice Admiral at Karlskrona. His important publication *Architectura Navalis Mercatoria* first appeared in 1786. Until 1937 the training ship made many voyages in all waters, her last major ocean voyage being in 1934.

In 1937 *Af Chapman* was paid off as a training ship and until 1947 served as a naval barracks in Stockholm. She was then bought by the City Museum of Stockholm and the Svenska Turist Foreningen (Swedish Tourist Board) used her as a hostel. She has been used in this way since the spring of 1949. Alterations made for this purpose scarcely affected the exterior: each mast still carries lower-, topsail- and topgallant-yards. The ship is not only a youth hostel but can be used by visitors of all ages.

Below: ships bell on the forecastle

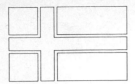

Fram

Type: 3-masted topsail schooner. Wood

Country: Norway

Owner and location:
Fram Museum, Oslo-Bygdøy

Year of construction: 1892

Builders:
Colin Archer's Yard, Rekevik, near
Larvik. Designed by Colin Archer

Tonnage:
800 tons displacement (fully
equipped), 402 tons gross, 307 tons
burden

Dimensions:
Length hull	117 ft
Length waterline	113 ft 2 in
Length keel	101 ft 9 in
Breadth extreme (without external ice protection)	36 ft
Depth in hold	17 ft
Draft (fully equipped)	15 ft 6 in

Sail area: 6,458 sq ft

Rig:
7 sails. 2 headsails.
Foremast: running squaresail, single
topsail, gaff sail. Main- and mizzen
masts: gaff sails

Masts:
fore- and mainmasts with snowmasts
(trysail masts), mainmast with one
topmast. Height of mainmast over
keel 131 ft 3 in

Engine:
220 hp (rated) triple expansion steam
engine. Speed under power 6 to
7 knots

Complement:
on Nansen's Polar Expedition a total
of 13 men

Use: museum ship

Although *Fram* (wich means 'forwards')
was built specifically as an expedition
ship and cannot therefore be classified
as one of the ships of the 'great days of
sail,' she does nevertheless warrant
inclusion on account of her rig. She
was built to sail in polar waters which
explains her small size and her lines.
Everything was designed to offer
minimum resistance to anticipated ice-
pressure. The proportion of her length to
to her breadth is about 3 to 1, her
sections are round and smooth and her
keel extends less than three inches below
her hull.

Naturally the hull itself was particularly
strongly built with a large number of
beams, supports and diagonal struts to
absorb and distribute the ice-pressure.
Her sides, made of several thicknesses
of planking, are up to 30 inches thick
and the whole of the hull is covered on
the outside by a 6-inch sheathing. It was
possible to raise both rudder and
propeller into a shaft to protect them
from damage by ice during the voyage.
The poop extends forward almost to
the mainmast; below its strong deck are
cabins for all the expedition members.
Many of the cabin walls, decks and
floors are covered with several layers
of insulating material. Even when she
was built the ship had electric light
provided by a dynamo driven either by
the steam engine or by a large windmill
on the main deck. Eight boats were
carried, the largest two being 29 feet
long and 7 feet in beam. The ice look-
out barrel on the mainmast was
originally over 100 ft above the waterline.

The ship became famous through the
great Norwegian polar expedition led
by Fritjof Nansen from 1893 to 1896,
for which she was built. A second
voyage into northern waters followed.

From 1910 to 1912 *Fram* was Roald
Amundsen's expedition ship in the
Antarctic when he reached the South
Pole in 1911. She has pressed further to
both north and south than any other
vessel. In Oslo-Bygdøy a special building
has been erected to house her — the
Fram museum.

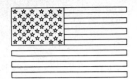

C.A.Thayer

Type: 3-masted gaff schooner. Wood

Country: U.S.A.

Owners:
State of California, San Francisco.
Maritime State Historic Park

Year of construction:
1895. Launched July 9, 1895

Builders:
Hans Bendixen, Eureka, California

Tonnage: 452 tons gross, 390 tons net

Dimensions:
LOA	218 ft 6 in
Length between perpendiculars	155 ft 6 in
Breadth extreme	36 ft 5 in
Depth in hold	11 ft 6 in
Draft	7 ft 10 in

Rig:
9 sails. Fore- and mainmasts with gaff courses and gaff topsails, mizzen mast with bermudan sail

Masts:
height of mainmast over deck 94 ft 10 in

Engine: no auxiliary

Complement:
8 to 9 men in the timber trade,
30 to 40 men when engaged in fishing

Use: museum ship

The extraordinarily rapid settlement of California at the end of the last century and the enlargement of the existing towns and villages meant that large quantities of building timber were required, which the country itself could not provide. Almost all the houses in this flourishing area were built entirely of timber, most of which was brought by ship to California. Trees were felled in the northwestern states, sawn in timber-mills by the sea and transported to the south by a fleet of more than a hundred schooners like the *C. A. Thayer.*

The ship was originally built for the E. K. Wood Lumber Company and was named after their secretary Clarence A. Thayer. She spent 17 years carrying nothing but timber before being sold to Mr. Peter Nelson in 1912. The *C. A. Thayer* then sailed to Alaska for salmon during the summers. Her big deckhouse, built well forward, dates from this period in her career. In 1925 she changed hands again and sailed on year-long voyages to the Bering Sea with one-man dories line-fishing for cod.

From 1942 to the end of the war she was used as a lighter before being fitted out again as a fisherman, and made her last voyage to the Bering Sea in 1950. After being laid up for seven years the Government was persuaded that *C. A. Thayer* was of historical importance and she was then thoroughly restored. She now lies as a museum ship near other trading vessels in San Francisco.

The C. A. Thayer *in 1951 (right) and 1964 (above).*

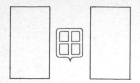

Giorgio Cini

ex *Fantome II*
ex *Belem*

Type: barkentine. Steel

Country: Italy

Owner: Mercantile Marine,
Centro Marinaro del Instituto 'Scilla'
della Fondazione Giorgio Cini

Home port:
Isola di S. Giorgio Maggiore, Venice

Year of construction: 1896

Builders: A. Dubigeon, Nantes

Tonnage:
562 tons gross, 611 tons Thames
Measurement

Dimensions:

Length between		
perpendiculars	167 ft	4 in
Breadth extreme	28 ft	7 in
Depth in hold	15 ft	

Rig:
13 sails (today 6 fore and aft sails are
set at the most). 2 headsails.
Foremast: fore course, upper and
lower topsails, single topgallants,
royal
Mainmast: main course, topsail, staysail, topmast staysail, topgallant
staysail
Mizzen mast: spanker (no mizzen
topsail because of the engine exhaust)

Masts and spars:
Lower masts, mizzen topmast, booms
all steel. Yards, fore and main topmasts and all other spars in wood.
Mizzen lower mast acts as an exhaust
pipe for the auxiliary. Hoisting main
gaff

Engines: 2 300 hp diesels

Use: sail training ship

This ship was built as the bark *Belem* (Bethlehem) for the shipping company Denis Crovan & Co. Her main cargo was cocoa beans which she carried from Pará (or Belem, Brazil) to Nantes for a Parisian chocolate factory. Later she sailed under the flag of H. Fleuriot & Co (Societé des Armateurs Coloniaux). In 1913 she was sold for £ 1,500 to the Duke of Westminster who converted the bark into a sea-going yacht without changing her name. Extensive alterations included auxiliary motor, electric light and an enlarged deckhouse. The iron poop rail was replaced by a rather unwieldy teak guardrail, and only teak was used for alterations to the decks and deck-fittings. The broad white strake was retained but painted just below the decks in the English manner. In 1921 *Belem* was sold to Sir A. E. Guinness who sailed her as a yacht under the name *Fantome II*. On her owner's death in 1950 she was put up for sale and bought the following year by the Italian foundation 'Giorgio Cini' after which she was renamed. As *Giorgio Cini* she was then re-rigged as a barkentine, although today she no longer sets her square-sails. For instructional purposes navigation instruments are provided and the ship carries an anchor winch on the fore-castle, patent anchors and boats in davits. A deckhouse amidships carries a smaller charthouse on top of it. This deckhouse extends to the sides making a sort of upper deck from which the ship is helmed. There is an emergency wheel on the poop.

Primarily the foundation caters for the orphans of seamen and fisherman, but it is up to the boys themselves whether they later choose to make the sea their career. They wear uniforms similar to those of the Italian Navy. The shorter voyages of the *Giorgio Cini* are mostly in the Adriatic, and she is berthed close by the school buildings on the island of San Giorgio in the school's own basin.

Santo André

ex *Sagres I*
ex *Flores*
ex *Max*
ex *Rickmer Rickmers*

Type: bark. Steel

Country: Portugal

Owners:
Portuguese Navy. Escila de
Marinharia de Armada

Location: Alfeite, near Lisbon

Year of construction: 1896

Builders: at Bremerhaven

Tonnage:
3067 tons displacement, 1980 tons
gross

Dimensions:

LOA	318 ft	3 in
Length hull	282 ft	2 in
Length between		
perpendiculars	259 ft	3 in
Depth in hold	25 ft	3 in
Draft	19 ft	8 in

Sail area: 37,675 sq ft

Rig:
24 sails. 4 headsails, double topsails,
double topgallants, royals. Mizzen
mast: spanker, gaff topsail

Masts: fore and mainmasts with topmasts
and topgallant masts. Mizzen mast has
one topmast

Engines:
2 350 hp Krupp diesel engines. Speed
under power about 10 knots

Complement:
as training vessel, 12 officers,
22 warrant officers, 140 crew and up
to 200 cadets

Use: stationary depot ship

This bark, which has had a varied career, was built as the full-rigged ship *Rickmer Rickmers* in 1896 for the shipowners Rickmers. She was used as a merchantman, mostly in the Far Eastern trade, usually carrying coal outward and rice and bamboo on the return trip, the latter being much in demand at the time. Later she also sailed as a nitrate trader. In 1905, after a storm in which she suffered severe damage aloft, she was re-rigged as a bark for reasons of economy. An unusual feature about her are her very high bulwarks, almost level with the poop and forecastle, and a rail that runs unbroken from bow to stern. This gives her a smooth sheer and very graceful looks.

In 1912 Rickmers sold the bark to the shipowners C. Krabbenhoft of Hamburg, from which port she sailed exclusively as a nitrate trader under the name of *Max*. When Portugal entered the war against Germany in 1916 she was caught with a cargo of nitrate in the Portuguese harbour of Horta in the Azores whilst on her homeward voyage, and became a Portuguese prize. Renamed *Flores* she carried war materials across the Atlantic until the end of the war.

In 1924 she was converted into a training ship for the Portuguese Navy and renamed *Sagres*. The figurehead, formerly the late Mr. Rickmers, was replaced by one of Infanta Henry the Seafarer, and all the square-sails and the spanker were emblazoned with a large red cross on a white ground. Her large permanent crew as a naval training vessel is explained by the fact that instruction was provided in all branches of the service. Orders were often given over loudspeakers. She was equipped with a complete range of modern navigation instruments for instructional purposes.

In 1931 two diesel auxiliaries were installed. She took part in the Tall Ships Races of 1956 and 1958. In 1962 *Sagres I* was replaced by *Sagres II*, ex *Guanabara*, ex *Albert Leo Schlageter*. She was renamed *Santo André* and at present lies in Alfeite harbour serving as supply and depot ship of the Escola de Marinharia da Armada.

Galatea

ex *Clarastella*
ex *Islamount*
ex *Glenlee*

Type: bark. Steel

Country: Spain

Owners:
Spanish Navy. Escuela de Maniobra "Galatea"

Home port: El Ferrol del Caudillo

Year of construction:
1896. Launched December 1896

Builders: A. Rodgers, Glasgow

Tonnage:
2700 tons displacement, 2800 tons gross

Dimensions:

LOA	310 ft 4 in
Length hull	272 ft 7 in
Length between perpendiculars	245 ft 8 in
Breadth extreme	37 ft 5 in
Depth in hold	24 ft 5 in
Draft, forward	17 ft
aft	20 ft 4 in

Sail area: 30,140 sq ft

Rig:
21 sails. 5 headsails, double topsails, double topgallants, courses, no royals (baldheader)
Mizzenmast: spanker, gaff topsail

Masts and spars:
Height of mainmast over deck 140 ft. Long bowsprit with jib-boom; 3 bowsprit nets, one behind the other

Engines:
2 four-cylinder, two-stroke Polar diesel engines totalling 1560 hp

Complement:
75 permanent crew, 150 cadets

Use: sail training ship

This bark was built in 1896 as the merchant sailer *Glenlee* for R. Ferguson & Co. of Port Glasgow. In 1899 she changed hands for the first time being transferred as *Islamount* to R. Ferguson & Co. of Dundee. She was sold again in 1905 to the Flint Castle Shipping Co. of Liverpool under whose flag she sailed until 1918. Like many another sailing vessel the *Islamount* was commandeered by the Government during the war, but instead of being stripped and used as a mastless hulk as most of them were, she was transferred to the shipowners J. Stewart & Co and continued to sail with freight. After the war she was sold to the Societa Italiana Di Navigazione 'Stella d' Italia' and when she had been completely modernised with two auxiliaries, electric light and up-to-date navigation instruments she was registered as *Clarastella* in 1920 with Genoa as her home port. On March 29, 1922 she was sold to Spain after being fitted out as a schoolship at the Cautieu Navale Triestino yard in Monfalcon, Trieste. Under the name of *Galatea*—one of the Nereides—she became the training ship for seamen of the Spanish Navy (Escuela de Maniobra).

Above decks she has been much altered since her days as a cargo carrier. A large deckhouse has been erected between her fore- and main masts, and aft of the main mast is the entrance to the engine-room on top of which her boats are lashed. There is a small bridge forward of the mizzen from which the vessel is steered, while the old wheel on the poop remains for emergency steering. In the tween-decks there are accommodation and instruction rooms for the boys, as well as workshops. A female figure graces the bow. *Galatea* operates mostly under sail, only using her engines in harbour and when the wind is adverse.

Najaden

Type:
full-rigged ship. Composite construction

Country: Sweden

Owner: town of Halmstad

Location:
at Halmstad in the R. Nissan, Slottskai (Castle Quay)

Year of construction:
1897. Launched February 12, 1897

Builders:
Royal Naval Shipyard, Karlskrona

Tonnage:
350 tons displacement (fully equipped)

Dimensions:
LOA	160 ft	1 in
Length hull	131 ft	5 in
Length between perpendiculars	111 ft	5 in
Breadth extreme	27 ft	6 in
Daft (equipped)	12 ft	2 in

Sail area:
originally 7,965 sq ft (without studding sails)

Rig:
originally 17 sails (excluding studding sails). 4 headsails; single topsails, single topgallants, royals; mainmast: gaff sail without boom (a Spencer).
Studding sails on fore and main masts

Masts and spars:
topsail and topgallant yards. Bowsprit with jib-boom, angled spritsail yard, dolphin-striker.
Height of mainmast over deck 82 ft (the topmasts have been shortened)

Engine: no auxiliary

Complement:
3 officers, doctor, 2 senior warrant officers, 6 warrant officers, 10 sailors, 100 boys

Use: museum ship

Najaden was built as a training ship for the Swedish navy, her design being based on the typical nineteenth-century sailing frigates. As such is one of the smalest full-rigged ships to have been built. Originally her hull was painted black with a broad white strake. When her rig was cut down in the thirties her royals were removed and the topgallant masts considerably shortened. Her fore- and main-topsails had three rows of reefpoints, the mizzen-topsail only two rows. The standing rigging was set up to outside chain-plates with deadeyes and lanyards. Due to her small size the boats were carried outboard, one on either side outside the mizzen rigging and one in davits across the stern. The two stocked anchors were also stowed outboard due to lack of deckspace. As in most of the nineteenth-century fighting ships hammocks were stowed between the inner and outer bulwarks. The nicely carved bow ornament is a coat of arms bearing the three Swedish crowns. In 1900 a sister ship, the *Jarramas*, was built, but unlike the *Najaden* she was of iron, nor did she have her older sister's raised quarterdeck. Both vessels sailed almost exclusively in the North Sea and the Baltic.

Najaden was an active training ship until the summer of 1938 after which she was unrigged in the autumn. During the war she was probably a houseboat and in 1945 lay as a hulk in very bad condition in Torekov where she was to have been broken up. The town of Halmstad came to her rescue, restored her completely and re-rigged her at the Karlskrona shipyard. She was towed to Halmstad on July 29, 1946 and moored there in her berth in the Nissan, attracting much public interest. In winter she is used as an art school and in the summer as a cafe.

Presidente Sarmiento

Type: full-rigged ship (frigate). Steel

Country: Argentina

Owners:
Argentine Navy. Maritime Museum Ship (Buque-Museo Fragata A.R.A. Presidente Sarmiento)

Location: Buenos Aires

Year of construction:
1898. Launched August 31, 1897. Commissioned July 20, 1898

Builders:
Cammell Laird, Birkenhead, England

Tonnage: 2750 tons displacement

Dimensions:
LOA	279 ft	
Length hull	251 ft	
Length between perpendiculars	238 ft	2 in
Breadth extreme	43 ft	8 in
Depth moulded	24 ft	

Sail area:
36,155 sq ft (with studding sails)

Rig:
23 sails, of which 12 studding sails, 4 headsails. Typical naval rig: single topsails (very low setting), single topgallants, royals. Fore- and mainmasts: in place of the topmast staysails there were gaff sails (Spencers) without booms

Masts and spars:
Height of mast over deck 163 ft. Bowsprit with jib-boom and outer jib-boom

Engine:
2800 hp steam engine with four boilers. Speed under power 15 knots

Complement: up to 400 men under sail

Armament:
2 7.6 cm Nordenfeldt guns, 2 5.7 cm Nordenfeldt guns, 4 4.7 cm Hotchkiss guns, 4 4.8 in Armstrong guns and 3 torpedo tubes

Use: museum ship

Government training ships do not only educate cadets, but are used to a great extent as ambassadors to represent their countries abroad and 'show the flag.' Very few training ships have done this so intensively or for so many years as the Argentinian *Presidente Sarmiento* during her 63 years of active service. Whenever she sailed into a foreign port kings, emperors and presidents came aboard as guests. She was present at the coronation celebrations of Edward VII and George V of England and Alfonso XIII of Spain, as well as the inaugurations of Presidents Taft of America, Alessandri of Chile and Alvaro de Obregon of Mexico.

In 1894 the Argentinian Captain D. Martin Rivadavia suggested to the President that a modern training ship should be built for the education of officer cadets. The sailing corvette *La Argentina* which had been built in Trieste had been used for this purpose from 1884 to 1891, but she had made only five voyages.

In accordance with President Luis Sáenz Peña's decision, a commission of naval officers planned the building of a new sail training ship and an English shipyard was given the job of building her. She was named after President D. Domingo Faustino Sarmiento (February 13, 1811—September 12, 1888), President from 1868—1874, who had taken a special interest in naval training and had founded the naval academy. On his death the biggest ship in the Argentinian Navy, the cruiser *Los Andes,* was to have been named after him, but instead it was decided to give his name to the new training ship.

The *Presidente Sarmiento* is typical of the large steam-powered corvettes of the nineteenth century with her baroque bow and stern decorations and her galleries accessible only from the officers' cabins. The poop reaches right amidships in order to accommodate the large crew, and the long forecastle extends to aft of the foremast. The hull is actually made of steel, sheathed in teak, which itself has a further sheath of copper below the water line to prevent teredo attack. One of the torpedo tubes opens just above the water line in the stem.

On July 20, 1898 the Argentinian flag was flown for the first time. Sub-Lieutenant D. Enrique Thorne was in command for the crossing to Argentina and on September 10, 1898 the *Presidente Sarmiento* sailed into Buenos Aires. Her first long voyage lasted from January 12, 1899 until September 30, 1900 under the command of the then Frigate Captain D. Onofre Betbeder, sailing round the world and covering 49,500 miles. In the years up to December 1938 she made 37 long voyages and covered a total of 576,770 miles, during which time over 1,500 naval officer cadets, all of them in their last year at the Naval Academy, trained aboard her. In 1938 the first phase in her life as a training ship came to an end. From then on, with the exception of two long voyages, she only made short trips and carried recruits as well as officer cadets.

With 1,100,000 miles behind her, the ship was taken out of active training service on January 26, 1961. Her successors today are the full-rigged ship A.R.A. *Libertad,* and the cruiser A.R.A. *La Argentina.* She lies now in Buenos Aires harbour as a national and cultural memorial: not without reason is she considered a 'reliquia histórica' by the Argentinians.

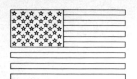

Wawona

Type: 3-masted gaff schooner. Wood

Country: U.S.A.

Owner:
"Save Our Ships" Inc., Seattle, Washington

Location:
Lake Union, Seattle, Washington

Year of construction: 1897

Builders:
Hans Bendixen, Fairhaven, California

Tonnage:
630 tons displacement, 468 tons gross, 413 tons net

Dimensions:
Length between perpendiculars	156 ft
Breadth extreme	36 ft
Depth moulded	12 ft 3 in

Rig:
7 sails. 4 headsails (staysail with boom), one gaff sail per mast

Masts and spars:
all masts the same height; height above deck 114 ft; without separate topmasts. Hoisting gaffs

Engine: no auxiliary

Complement:
8 men when used in the timber trade; over 30 as a cod fisher

Use: museum ship

For some years now, interested groups in Seattle have been actively engaged in the restoration and maintenance of the *Wawona*. As a thorough overhaul, complete with renewal of the masts, is necessary a large sum of money must be raised. The schooner was built for the lumber trade in 1897 for Dolbeer & Carson of Eureka and San Francisco. The large loading ports below the starboard hawse-pipe bear witness of her former employment when long balks of timber were shipped through them. The ship could carry about 630,000 board feet of timber (about 20,000 cubic yards).
In 1913 *Wawona* was converted into a cod fisherman by the provision of stowage space for fish and additional accommodation for the enlarged crew. It is very possible that this schooner made the world's record catch for ships of this type. Her last fishing voyage was in 1947. During the war she was chartered by the Government to carry timber.
The name *Wawona* is Indian and is the name of a tree which is native to California.

Jarramas

Type: full-rigged ship. Iron

Country: Sweden

Owner: town of Karlskrona

Location:
Borgmästarekajen, Karlskrona

Year of construction:
1899. Keel laid March 18, 1899.
Launched in February 1900.

Builders: Polhamsdocken, Karlskrona

Tonnage:
350 tons displacement (fully
equipped)

Dimensions:

LOA	160 ft	9 in
Length hull	128 ft	5 in
Length between perpendiculars	109 ft	3 in
Breadth extreme	27 ft	6 in
Depth in hold	13 ft	
Draft (without equipment)	10 ft	6 in

Sail area:
originally about 8,610 sq ft (excluding
studding sails)

Rig:
originally 17 sails (excluding studding
sails). 4 headsails. Single topsails,
single topgallants, royals.
Mainmast with gaff sail without
boom (Spencer). Studding sails on
fore- and mainmasts

Masts and spars:
topmasts and topgallant mast, bowsprit with jib-boom, dolphin striker.
Height of mainmast over deck
82 ft 10 in

Engine: no auxiliary

Complement:
3 officers, doctor, 7 warrant officers,
10 petty officers, 100 boys between
the ages of 13½ and 15

Use: museum ship

The first *Jarramas* was a fregate built by Charles XII of Sweden in 1716 in memory of a fierce battle against the Sultan of Turkey which had earned him the title of 'Illerim and Jarramas' (Thunder and Lightning) from the Turks. This fregate remained in service long after Charles' death, but her eventual fate is unknown. From 1825 to 1859 the Swedish Navy had a corvette called *Jarramas*.

The present iron *Jarramas* was built as a second training ship for the Swedish Navy at the turn of the century, soon after the wooden *Najaden*. They are sister-ships with many details in common. Both, originally, had a black hull with painted ports on a white strake. The rig of *Jarramas*, too, was altered in the thirties and her topgallant masts considerably shortened. The fore- and main-topsails had three rows of reef points, the mizzen-topsail only two. Her standing rigging was set up to outside channels with dead eyes and lanyards. Due to her small size the boats were carried outboard, one on either side outside the mizzen rigging and one in davits across the stern. The two stocked anchors were also stowed outboard due to lack of deckspace. As in most nineteenth-century fighting ships hammocks were stowed between the inner and outer bulwarks. In contrast to *Najaden* the *Jarramas* has a completely uninterrupted main deck. Both ships sailed in the North Sea and the Baltic, and *Jarramas*' last voyage was round Sweden in 1946. In 1950 the town of Karlskrona bought the sailing ship, and today she is a museum with a cafe on board. These full-rigged ships were replaced in 1947 by the schooners *Gladan* and *Falken*.

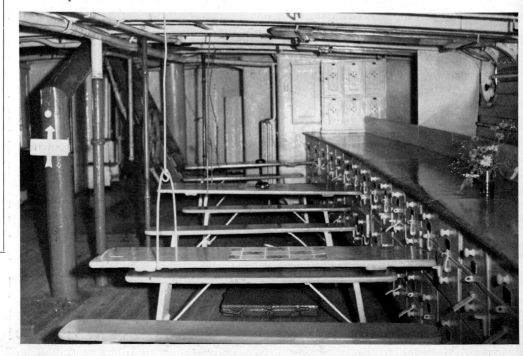

Right: cadets accommodation under the main deck (in the hold) when Jarramas *was a sail training vessel*

Kaiulani

ex *Star of Finland*
ex *Kaiulani*

Type: bark. Steel

Country: U.S.A.

Owner:
National Maritime Historical Society,
Washington D.C.

Location:
Washington Channel, Maine Avenue,
Washington D.C.

Year of construction:
1899. Launched July 2, 1899

Builders: A. Sewall & Co, Bath, Maine

Tonnage:
1699 tons gross, 1425 tons net

Dimensions:

LOA	310 ft
Length hull (no figurehead)	250 ft
Length between perpendiculars	225 ft
Breadth extreme	42 ft
Depth moulded	21 ft 6 in
Depth in hold	20 ft
Draft loaded	16 ft

Sail area: 25,995 sq ft

Rig:
24 sails. 4 headsails, double topsails,
double topgallants, royals
Mizzen mast; spanker, gaff topsail

Masts:
Height of mainmast over deck 164 ft
Fore- and mainmasts with topmasts

Engine: no auxiliary

Complement:
under sail, 18; 3 officers, 12 seamen,
deckboy, carpenter and donkeyman

Use: museum ship

This bark was built for the shipowners Williams, Diamond & Co. of San Francisco and until 1910 was engaged in the sugar trade between the Hawaiian Islands and the west coast of the U.S.A. Her name is that of a Hawaiian Princess, Kaiulani (meaning child of heaven) who was the last heir to the crown of the Hawaiian royal family, and who died aged 24 on March 6, 1899.

Kaiulani proved herself one of the fastest ships in the Pacific during her many voyages, and is now the last surviving sailing merchantman that was built in the U.S.A. (The total of square-rigged sailing ships of American origin is estimated at about 17,000.)

In 1910 *Kaiulani* was sold to the Alaska Packers Association of San Francisco and renamed *Star of Finland*. (Every ship in this fleet was called 'Star'.) Her poop was extended to the mainmast to accommodate the large crew of seamen, fishermen and cannery workers. Until 1927 the *Star of Finland* sailed regularly with the large fleet engaged in salmon fishing in Alaska. Then she was laid up with many other sailing vessels in Alameda near San Francisco until 1936 when she set sail again for a short time and 'played' the *William Brown* in the film 'Souls at Sea.'

In 1941 she was thoroughly overhauled in Alameda. She reverted to the name *Kaiulani* with the Hammond Lumber Company and under the Panamanian flag sailed on September 5, 1941 with a cargo of sawn timber from Port Aberdeen, Washington. After calling at Pitcairn Island she rounded Cape Horn on December 17 and reached Durban in South Africa on January 29, 1942. Her last voyage under sail took her from Durban to Hobart, Tasmania.

As no new crew could be engaged her owners were forced to sell her. The bark was towed to Sydney, stripped and equipped with an auxiliary engine. She lay as a coal hulk until she was sold to Vincente Madrigal in 1948 for $ 18,250, after which she carried lumber in Philippine waters.

On October 5, 1964 the Philippine President Diosdado Macapagal presented her to the American Government. President Johnson entrusted the National Maritime Historical Society with her restoration. Funds were and are being collected from all parts of the United States for this purpose and the ship will be restored at a yard in Manila. The *Kaiulani* will eventually round Cape Horn under sail in her original condition en route to her final resting place in Washington, D.C.

Andalucia

ex *Ville de Mulhouse*

Type: four-masted bark (hulk). Steel
Country: Chile
Owner: Chilean Navy
Location: Punta Arenas
Year of construction:
1899. Launched April 27, 1899
Builders:
Forges et Chantiers de la
Méditerranée, yard at Graville,
nr Le Havre
Tonnage: 3110 tons gross, 2798 tons net
Dimensions:
Length between
perpendiculars   311 ft
Breadth extreme   45 ft
Depth in hold   24 ft 3 in
Rig:
double topsails, double topgallants,
royals
Engine: no auxiliary
Use: depot ship

Ville de Mulhouse was the first ship to be built for the Société des Voiliers Havrais. Both she and a second four-masted bark belonging to the same company could easily be recognised from afar, for the poop deck was brought forward as far as the mizzen while the forecastle extended aft as far as the mainmast, leaving only a relatively small part of the main deck open.

The *Ville de Mulhouse* mostly carried nickel ore from New Caledonia to Glasgow or Le Havre. Her maiden voyage was on July 7, 1899 from Le Havre, and she reached Muéo in New Caledonia in 84 days. All her voyages were without untoward incident, until one from Antwerp to Los Angeles which lasted a full 185 days.

In April 1909 the French Government purchased the four-masted bark and used her as a troop transporter until the end of the war.

In 1926 she sailed through the Magellan Straits to Punta Arenas where she was unrigged and moored as a coal store, leaving only her lower masts and yards standing, the condition in which she is today. She has been given the name of *Andalucia* and at present is used as a depot ship by the Chilean fleet. In about 1970 she is to be given to the town of Punta Arenas, when she will be turned into the club ship of various nautical organisations such as the Caleuche, a club for retired officers, the Hermandad de la Costa Yacht Club and the Life Boat Institution.

Andalucia *today*

Types of sailing ships

This short summary only deals with basic types which are still found today and which are illustrated in this book. Square-rigged ships are distinguished by the number of their masts and the arrangement of their yards. The three-masted, full-rigged ship became the classical type of square-rigger. In it each of the three masts carries a complete set of square sails. So much did it come to typify the sailing ship as such that it is often simply called 'a ship'. An even larger type was the four-masted ship, and the largest ship ever built was the five-masted *Preussen* of 5,081 tons gross. A full-rigged ship needed a very large crew in relation to her profitability, which is why shipowners preferred the bark. In this type the aftermost mast, the mizzen mast (or the jigger mast in the case of a four-masted bark) was fore-and-aft rigged, usually with gaff sails, which could be handled by a few men. There was the additional advantage that the fore-and-aft mizzen sails make a bark easier to steer and steady, their effect being similar to that of the tailplane in an aircraft.

The navy had no need to practise economy in the size of crews. There were always enough men to run full-rigged ships (*Constitution*, page 16, *Victory*, page 12). Apart from three-masted barks, which have become known simply as barks, it was the large four-masted barks which were prominent in promoting world trade and linking the continents at the end of the last century. The large fleet of Flying-P-Liners of the Hamburg shipowner Ferdinand Laeisz played a leading part in this. Their last remaining vessel still under German ownership is the four-masted bark *Passat* (page 110) which is now moored at Travemünde. The largest sailing ship ever was the five-masted

bark *France II* owned by Antonin Dominique Bordes of Bordeaux. She measured 5,633 tons gross.

A ship with a square-rigged foremast and at least two other masts which are fore-and-aft rigged is called a barkentine. A type not often met with was the four-masted barkentine, and there were even six-masted barkentines like the *E. R. Stirling* (1883). However, this clumsy rig deprived the ships of all their elegance. Among the smaller types of square-rigged vessels was the two-masted brig, in which both masts are square-rigged, and the brigantine, in which only the foremast is square-rigged. The fine-looking brigs have, unfortunately, disappeared altogether from the oceans of the world. The last remaining example, the fighting brig *Niagara*, has been preserved as a museum in Erie, Pennsylvania.

Another large group of big sailing ships are the schooners. In this type all masts are fore-and-aft rigged. The sails may be gaff, Bermudan or staysails. The basic type of schooner is a two-masted vessel in which the after mast is the taller of the two and gaff-rigged.

In order to make better use of following winds some schooners set square topsails on the foremast instead of fore-and-aft topsails. They are known as topsail schooners. The main difference between a topsail schooner and a barkentine is the absence of any fore-and-aft sails on a barkentine's foremast.

The largest fore-and-aft schooner ever built was the *Thomas W. Lawson* of 5,218 tons gross. She was sailed with a crew of only sixteen. This illustrates one of the most important advantages of the schooner: even a large sail area can be handled by a comparatively small crew, because most of the work can be done from the deck. With a trading ship,

where profitability counts, this was a vital consideration. Modern sail training vessels, on the other hand, are almost exclusively square-rigged, because the size of crew is no problem. The object, quite on the contrary, is to have as many places as possible for hands to be trained.

The various types of schooners frequently set a running square sail on the foremast. This is usually cut deeper than a normal foresail. Staysail schooners set staysails on the lower stays only, and they are usually boomed. The triangular space between each lower stay and the mast forward of it is filled with a trysail. There is an unusual feature about the rig of the Polish three-masted staysail schooner: each of the two trysails is set between two curved gaffs to make them set better. This is known as a wishbone-rig, possibly because the former Brazilian Navy training vessel *Albatroz*, ex *Wishbone*, used it. Orignally it was introduced in the United States.

In a ketch the after mast, i. e., the mizzen mast, is the shorter of the two.

The tonnage and measurement of ships

To complete the description of types of ships, the following list refers to illustrations in this book which clearly show the main characteristics of each particular rig:

Full-rigged ship: *Georg Stage*
Four-masted bark: *Krusenstern*
Bark (three-masted): *Gorch Fock*
Four-masted barkentine: *Esmeralda*
Three-masted barkentine: *Palinuro*
Brig: *Niagara*
Brigantine: *Wilhelm Pieck*
Four-masted topsail schooner:
Juan Sebastian de Elcano
Three-masted topsail schooner:
Eugen Eugenides
Two-masted topsail schooner:
La Belle Poule
Four-masted Bermudan-rigged schooner:
Albatross
Four-masted gaff schooner: *Argus*
Three-masted gaff schooner: *Bel Espoir*
Two-masted gaff schooner: *Falken*
Three-masted staysail schooner:
Zawisza Czarny
Ketch: *Seute Deern II*
Lateen rig: *Mayflower II*

While every man still had to make his own tools and gear (and was still capable of doing so) he was independent of designers, factories, market prices and other aspects of an organised economy. This applied equally to ships and boats, especially to smaller vessels used for hunting. There was no need to calculate the size of these craft in any way, not even if they were built jointly by, or for the joint use of, a community. They were purely for private use, and their size was determined by the purpose to which they were put, the skill of the builder and the material available. Even today ships and boats in some countries are built by the users themselves. Only when shipyards were established that would build ships to order and for payment did it become necessary to stipulate a precise size in order to fix a purchase price. If the ship was a trading ship intended to make a profit, its capacity for cargo was an additional consideration.

In modern shipping the measurement of vessels has become a necessity. Insurance premiums, canal and harbour dues and so on are dependent on the size of a ship. In very busy ports a ship cannot be allocated a berth unless her length, breadth and draft are known.

In the course of time various ways of measuring ships have evolved. They frequently lead to ambiguities, because it is not always clear whether a measurement is based on the metric or the English system of measurements. Another source of discrepancy are the points of reference on which certain dimensions are based. For example, the 'length over all' (abbr. LOA) of a ship, and this applies especially to sailing ships, may differ considerably from one source of reference to another depending on which two points are chosen as extremities. This is all the more puzzling because this dimension, at least, would appear to be clearly defined by its very name.

A very old measure for the cargo capacity of ships, widely used in the Middle Ages, is the 'tun' (= wine cask) which equalled 252 gallons. It was purely a measure of capacity, and it was not till much later that the 'ton' became a measure of weight. In the metric system 1 ton equals 1000 kg, whereas the English ton (long ton) equals 2240 lb or 1016 kg. The 'ton register' has become an international unit for measuring the internal capacity of ships.

The different ways of expressing the size and freight carrying capacity of a ship are listed below in detail.

Register tonnage. Measure of internal cubic capacity of seagoing ships, mostly cargo carriers. 1 ton register equals 100 cub.ft or 2.832 cub.metres.

Gross register tonnage. This measures all spaces below the main deck plus the parts of the superstructure carried out to the sides. Expressed in tons gross.

Net register tonnage. This is the gross tonnage minus all the spaces occupied by crew accommodation, mess rooms, galley, food stores, fresh water tanks, engine and navigation rooms, bunkers, oil tanks, ballast and store rooms for rope, sails and paint. In other words, net tonnage measures the space which 'earns money'. This includes passenger accomodation. It is expressed in tons net.

Burden. Old term for ship's carrying capacity. The amount of cargo, by weight, which a ship could load to reach her maximum permissible draft.

Load. Loading capacity. The amount of cargo, by volume, which a ship can load. Usually expressed in registered tons.
Deadweight. The carrying capacity of a ship including bunkers and ship's stores. It may be expressed in metric tons or long tons.

Displacement. The weight of water displaced by the ship's underwater body. It may be expressed in long tons or metric tons, in the metric system also by cubic metres.

Ship's weight. Same as displacement.

Thames Measurement. Measurement applied mainly to yachts, based on a formula used in similar form by the Admiralty in the 14th century:

$$\text{Tons T.M.} = \frac{(L-B) \times B \times \frac{1}{2}B}{94}$$

The formula used to be length × beam × moulded depth over 100. Today ½ breadth is used instead of moulded depth and the whole divided by 94.

The tonnage of warships is usually given in tons displacement (long tons). It is frequently expressed by two figures separated by a fraction line. The upper figure represents the displacement of the vessel fully equipped but without fuel, the lower figure the additional displacement after bunkering. Occasionally the tonnage of warships is given in 'tons standard displacement', which are, again, long tons.

Until some way through the 17th century ship building was a craft which depended solely on the skill and experience of the builder. There were no plans on which to base either design or construction. Sometimes a model was built to give the customer an approximate idea of what the finished ship would look like, but this was never binding. The final dimensions of a vessel were not known until it was finished. Gradually builders learnt to draw up building plans beforehand. The various types of ships had to stand up to greater demands, and they steadily increased in size. Seagoing ships were now designed and proper building plans drawn up for the shipyard. Thus, shipbuilding developed into a technical process of the

first order. The projection of the three principal planes, the so-called lines drawing, became the basis of hull design. A lines drawing contains:

1. the profile or sheer plan
2. the waterline plan
3. the body plan.

This three-dimensional plan enables every line and every point of the hull to be fixed. The well-known work *Architectura Navalis Mercatoria* by the Swedish shipwright Frederik Henrik af Chapman, which was published in Stockholm in 1768, is an outstanding example of the amount of design work which went into the building of a ship in those days.

A number of hull dimensions are of particular importance in designing a ship and generally calculating its dimensions. They enable us to picture the size and approximate shape of a vessel. The points of reference of the dimensions are fixed by the lines and extremities of the hull. In sailing ships, of course, the hull alone does not determine the size of the vessel. Quite apart from the masts and spars, there are the bowsprit and mizzen boom to be considered.

The profile plan is developed from the base line, which marks the floor. The waterlines are drawn horizontally one above the other. One of them is the load waterline (L.W.L., also called designed waterline — D.W.L.). This is the line, or rather the plane, on which the ship floats when fully laden (or fully equipped in the case of warships or training ships). In cargo-carrying vessels the actual load waterline at any time need not be identical to the designed waterline, because the specific weight of

water varies with its salinity and temperature. This affects a vessel's draft and thus its waterline.

Cross-sections of the hull perpendicular to the waterlines make up the body plan. In very large sailing ships with a vertical stern post, the first and aftermost section is made to coincide with the after edge of the stern post, in motor vessels with the forward edge of the rudder post. The last and most forward section cuts the stem post on the D.W.L. There are thus two perpendiculars whose position is fixed on the base line: the fore and after perpendiculars. The distance between the two is termed the 'length between perpendiculars' and is one of the principal dimensions used in measuring ships. In smaller ships with a raked stern post the after perpendicular intersects the stern post on the D.W.L. The length between perpendiculars does not take into account the length and shape of the rudder blade. In many cases where 'length waterline' is given this includes the rudder blade.

'Length hull' is a term designating the length of the hull from figurehead to taffrail. Instead, 'length over all' (abbr. LOA) is often used. But 'length over all' in sailing ships should stand for the total length of the vessel, i.e. from the forward end of the bowsprit or jib-boom to the after end of the mizzen boom, or, if this does not project outboard, to the taffrail.

'Breadth extreme' means the maximum breadth of the hull measured to the outside of the planks. Old sailing ships usually had their maximum breadth at half the moulded depth because the hull had a pronounced tumble-home. This was to prevent the crew of another ship that might come alongside in battle from boarding and to enable the guns to remain in action.

'Depth moulded' is measured amidships between the lower surface of the frame on the centreline (in steel vessels) or the outer edge of the keel rabbet (in wooden vessels) to the top of the upper deck beam at the gunwale.

'Depth in hold' describes the height of useful interior space. It is measured amidships between the upper surface of the floor to the top of the uppermost deck beam. In old, multi-decked warships 'depth in hold' measures only the space between the floor and the top of the deck beam of the lowest deck.

'Draft' is the distance between the load waterline and the lowest point of the keel. In larger ships draft marks are painted on both the stem and stern posts. These are in Roman numerals six inches high and indicate the depth in feet.

Glossary of common nautical terms

A

Abeam. On the side, or beam, of the vessel at right angles to the fore-and-aft line.
Aft. Near, or towards the stern, or behind e.g. aft of the mast' or 'abaft the mast'.
Amidships. In the centre of the ship, with reference to either length or breadth.
Athwartship. Across the fore-and-aft line.

B

Backstays. Standing rigging staying the mast, running from the masthead to the vessel's sides aft of the shrouds.
Baggywrinkle (or bag o'wrinkle). A tufted braid made from chopped rope strands which is wound round stays and shrouds to prevent chafing of sails.
Bald-headed. Said of a square-rigged vessel without royals or a schooner without topmasts.
Ballast. Heavy material, such as sand, stone, water, placed in the bottom of a ship to give her stability. Particularly important when no cargo is carried.
Bark, or barque. Originally a three-masted vessel with her fore and main masts square-rigged and the mizzen mast fore-and-aft rigged. Later also used to describe a four- or five-masted vessel with all but her aftermost mast square-rigged.
Barkentine, or barquentine. A three-masted vessel with her foremast square-rigged, her main and mizzen masts fore-and-aft rigged.
Belay. To make a rope (sheet, halyard etc) fast to a cleat, pin, bollard etc.
Bend. To bend a sail is to make it fast to a spar (mast, yard, boom, gaff).
Bilge. The curved part of a ship's hull where the sides and bottom meet. Also the inside of the hull below the cabin sole where the bilge water collects.
Bilge keel. Longitudinal timber fastened along the bilges of some large flat-bottomed ships to reduce rolling.
Boom. A spar holding the foot of a fore-and-aft sail.
Bow. The forward end of the hull.
Bowsprit. A spar, firmly secured to the hull, which projects forward of the bow and carries the forestays on which the staysails are set.
Braces. Ropes made fast to the yard-arms by which the angle of square-sails to the fore-and-aft line can be changed.
Brail. Haul up the body of a square-sail to the yard with the help of buntlines.
Brig. A two-masted vessel in which both masts are square-rigged.
Brigantine. A two-masted vessel in which the foremast is square-rigged, the mainmast fore-and-aft rigged. The correct name for this type is hermaphrodite brig, but it is just as often referred to as brigantine. The true brigantine sets a square topsail and topgallant on the mainmast.
Bulkhead. Partition, athwartships or fore-and-aft, to separate one part of the hull from another.
Bulwarks. Woodwork around a vessel above deck level.
Buntlines. Ropes used for hauling up (brailing) the body of a sail.

C

Cap. A fitting of wood or iron with two holes in it used to connect the head of one mast with the lower part of the next mast above it.
Capstan. A revolving machine with a perpendicular axis used for hoisting and heaving. Worked by crew walking round pushing horizontal bars.
Catheads. Short horizontal beams on either side of ship's bow for raising and stowing anchor.
Chafe. Rubbing of the surface, particularly of sails against shrouds stays etc.
Chain-plates. Plates of iron bolted to a ship's sides to which shrouds are made fast.
Channels. Pieces of plank bolted to the outside of the hull, below the shrouds, across which the shrouds are led to the chain-plates.
Chocks. Shaped wedges between or upon which things are stowed on deck, e.g. boats.
Classification. Any larger vessel is classified following a survey to determine to what standard it has been built or in what condition it has been maintained.
Clewline. Rope which hauls up the clew, i.e. either of the lower corners, of a square-sail.
Clipper. Swift sailing ships with sharp bows and fine lines that originated in the United States. Term later used generally for fast sailing ships, even four-masted barks.
Coamings. Raised works round hatches to prevent water getting in.
Composite construction. Wooden planking on a metal frame and keel.
Corvette. Type of warship smaller than a frigate. Usually rigged as ship, with guns mounted on the upper deck. Mainly used for scouting, convoying and privateering.
Courses. The (square) sails that hang from ship's lower yards, i.e. forecourse, maincourse, mizzen course.
Crossjack (pro. cro'jack). Another name for the mizzen course.
Cross-trees. Pieces of timber or metal at the masthead to spread the shrouds and backstays.
Crowsnest. Barrel-like look-out post high up on the mast.
Cutter. A naval pulling boat. Also a single masted sailing boat.

D

Davits. Cranes fitted in pairs in which a ship's boats are carried. Can be swivelled for lowering and hoisting.
Deadeye. A circular block of wood with a groove round it and three holes in it. Used in pairs, with lanyards rove through them to make a tackle, for setting up rigging.
Deck beams. Lateral beams, spanning the hull over the heads of the frames, on which the deck rests.
Dhow. Arabian sailing vessel with two or more masts rigged with lateen sails. The name is not used by the Arabs themselves.
Dinghy. Small open boat which can be handled by one man.
Displacement. The weight of water displaced by a vessel.
Dolphin striker. A wooden or iron spar projecting down from the bowsprit end to spread the stays that run out to the jib-boom end.
Donkey boiler. Boiler to provide steam power for heavy-duty winches, windlasses etc.
Dory. Small flat-bottomed rowing boats manned by one or two fishermen, used for catching cod off Newfoundland. The name is derived from the Portuguese pescadores meaning fishermen.
Draft marks. Numerals painted on the stem and stern post of ships which mark the draft in feet.
Dromon. Byzantine warship with two banks of oars on each side.

F

Fiddlehead. Carvings at a ship's bow in the absence of a figurehead proper.
Figurehead. A carved figure, or head, under a ship's bowsprit. Made to look as though growing of the stem. Usually in some way connected with the name of the ship.
Floors. Transverse timbers, placed across the keel, which reinforce the frames.
Flush deck. An upper deck without any superstructure.
Foot. The bottom edge of a sail.
Fore-and-aft. Lengthwise with the ship, parallel to her centreline.
Fore-and-aft rig. In which the sails set thus.
Forecastle. That part of the upper deck forward

of the foremast, also the accommodation of the crew beneath this deck.

Foremast. First mast in all two- and more-masted vessels, except yawls and ketches.

Foresail. In square-riggers the lower sail on the first mast. In schooners the lower sail set abaft the foremast.

Full-rigged ship. Originally a three-masted ship in which all masts were fully square-rigged. Later also square-rigged ships with more than three masts.

Full sail. To carry full sail means to have all available sail set.

G

Gaff. Spar to which the head of a fore-and-aft sail is bent. Its lower end seizes the mast in a kind of fork.

Galeas. Two-masted gaff-rigged Baltic trader.

Genoa. Large triangular headsail set on the forestay of yachts.

Gig. Light, narrow ship's boat.

Gun ports. Openings cut into the sides of a ship through which the guns are fired. In the old warships these could be closed from the outside with gun-port covers. In more recent times ships have frequently been painted with imitation gun-ports. i.e. black squares on a band of white or yellow just below deck level.

H

Halyards, or halliards. Ropes for hoisting and lowering yards, gaffs and sails, often with the help of halyard winches.

Hawse-hole, or hawse-pipe. Hole or pipe in ship's bows, or on deck, through which the anchor cable runs.

Headsails. All sails set on stays before the foremast.

Hoop. Iron or wooden rings sliding along masts, gaffs, booms etc. to which sails are bent.

Hulk. Hull of dismantled ship, frequently used as store vessel.

Hurricane deck. Flush upper deck above the main deck. The bulwarks are taken up to this all round; this results in one long, continuous superstructure.

J

Jacob's ladder. A rope ladder with wooden rungs used for climbing aloft.

Jib-boom. Boom rigged out beyond the bowsprit. Contrary to the bowsprit itself it can be unrigged. In some vessels extended by an outer jib-boom with the object of spreading out the jibs and staysails and thus making them more efficient on the wind.

Jigger. Fourth mast in square-rigged vessels or schooners. It is always fore-and-aft rigged.

Jollyboat. Small, light ship's boat with transom stern.

K

Keel. The 'spine' of the hull, running fore-and-aft its entire length and supporting the frames.

Knot. See 'Nautical mile'.

L

Laid up. Temporarily taken out of service.

Lateen sail. A triangular sail bent to a long yard set at an angle of 45° to the mast. Probably originated in the Mediterranean.

Leach, or leech. The after edge of a sail.

Lee. Downwind; the side opposite to that from which the wind blows.

Log. To measure the speed of a vessel from on board. Also the ship's diary.

Long-boat. The largest of a ship's boats. Always carried on deck.

Luff. The forward edge of a sail. Also the action of bringing the vessel up into the wind.

M

Mainmast. Second mast in vessels with two or more masts, except yawls and ketches.

Mainsail. The lower sail set on that mast. In square-riggers also called the main course.

Mess. Living and dining room on cargo- and warships.

Mizzen mast. The third mast in vessels with three or more masts. In a yawl or ketch the shorter, after mast.

Mizzen sail. The lower sail set on that mast. In square-riggers also called the mizzen course or, more commonly, the crossjack (pron. cro'jack).

Moonsail. A triangular sail set above the sky-sail in square-riggers.

N

Nautical mile. One nautical mile is a sixtieth of a degree of latitude measured at the equator. It equals 6080 ft or 1852 metres. A speed of 1 nautical mile per hour is 1 knot.

P

Pin-rails. Wooden ledges bolted inside a ship's rails, in the shrouds and around the mast.

They hold the belaying pins on which the running rigging is belayed.

Pole mast. A mast which is made in one piece; not having a separate topmast.

Port. The left hand side of a vessel when facing forward.

Pram dinghy. A small, box-like boat with a transom stern and flat bow.

Q

Quarter. Either side of ship aft of main shrouds, e.g. 'on the quarter' meaning between abeam and astern. A 'quartering sea' (or wind) approaches the ship on the quarter.

Quarterdeck. That part of the upper deck aft of the mainmast.

R

Rabbet. A groove on either side of the keel and stem to receive the edges of the planks.

Rail. The top of the bulwarks. 'Guardrails' or 'lifelines' are a fence of wires and stanchions surrounding the deck.

Reef. To shorten sail.

Reef points. Rows of small ropes on a sail, parallel to the yard or gaff, with which the sail is tied up when it is reefed.

Rig. The whole of a ship's masts and sails and the way they are arranged.

Rigging. A general term for all the ropes and wires used to work and stay a vessels spars and sails. See 'running rigging' and 'standing rigging'.

Royal. A square sail set above a topgallant sail.

Running rigging. All ropes and wires used to work sails, yards, gaffs, booms.

Running square-sail. A large, deep-cut square-sail set on the fore lower yard by many topsail schooners when running before the wind.

S

Schooner. A sailing vessel with two or more masts none of which is fully square-rigged. See 'staysail schooner' and 'topsail schooner'.

Shrouds. Standing rigging supporting the mast on either side.

Sheathing. Covering of a ship's bottom against teredo (copper) or damage from ice in Arctic waters.

Sheet. A rope made fast to the clew of a fore-and-aft sail (or its boom) to control the way it sets.

Skysail. A square sail set above a royal.

Sloop. A small fore-and-aft rigged vessel with one mast.

Snowmast. A light mast, immediately aft of the

mainmast (usually in a brig) on which a gaff sail is set. Also called trysail mast.

Sound. To measure the depth of water.

Spanker. Gaff sail set on the aftermost mast of a ship or bark.

Spars. General term for masts, booms, yards, gaffs.

Spencer. A gaff sail without a boom set aft of the fore and mainmast of a square-rigger.

Spinnaker. A light, deep-cut sail set on yachts which was set on a yard below the bowsprit.

Spritsail. On the old sailing ships a square sail when running before the wind.

Spritsail topsail. Square sail set above the spritsail on a yard from the spritsail topmast, a small mast mounted on the bowsprit. Found in old warships.

Stability. The ability of a vessel to counteract heeling.

Standing rigging. All ropes and wires which support the masts and are not 'moved'.

Starboard. The right side of a vessel when facing forward.

Stays. Ropes of the standing rigging which support the mast, leading forward (forestays) and to the sides (backstays).

Staysail. A triangular fore-and-aft sail set from a stay.

Staysail schooner. A schooner rigged with fore-and-aft sails only, most of them setting on stays.

Stem. Continuation of keel forward, sweeping upwards to the bowsprit.

Stern. After end of a vessel (round stern, transom stern, etc.)

Stern post. Continuation of the keel aft, sweeping upwards to the deck.

Stock anchor, or old-fashioned anchor. The traditional anchor which has a fixed stock at right angles to the shank.

Stockless anchor, or patent anchor. An anchor in which the flukes can be folded and the shank hauled up into the hawse-pipe.

Studding sails. Additional panels of cloth set on either side of a square-sail on booms rigged out beyond the yard. Set when running in light winds.

T

Tack. The forward lower corner of a sail. Also to alter course by putting the ship's bow through the eye of the wind.

Tackle. Purchase formed by a rope rove through one or more blocks.

Tiller. A horizontal bar fitted into the head of the rudder by which the vessel is steered. Large vessels have a wheel instead.

Top. Platform at the head of a mast, resting on the trestle-trees.

Topgallant sail. Single or double square-sail set above the topsail(s) on a square-rigged mast.

Topmast. The second mast above the deck, next above the lower mast.

Topsail. In square-riggers, the single or double square-sail(s) set above each course (lower sail). In topsail schooners the square-sails set above the gaff foresail. In fore-and-aft schooners the triangular sails set above all lower gaff sails.

Topsail schooner. A schooner which sets one or more square-sails on the foremast above the gaff sail.

Tramp. Cargo ship which does not run on a regular line but picks up cargo where it can get it. (opposite: liner)

Trestle-trees. Strong lateral and longitudinal pieces of timber at the masthead to support the top in square-riggers and large schooners.

Transom stern. A flat stern.

Trim. To arrange cargo and gear in such a way that the vessel floats as she should (i.e. not down by the head or stern). Also to set the sails at the most favourable angle to the wind.

Trireme. A Greek galley with three banks of oars.

Tweendeck. Any deck between the maindeck and the ship's bottom. In sailing ships usually one only.

W

Wales. Strong, raised planks along the length of a ship's sides. They contribute to stiffness and protect the sides from damage by ships coming alongside.

Warp. To move a vessel from one place to another by means of a warp (= rope). It can be done with the help of a kedge anchor which is let go, in which case it is called kedging.

Windlass. A revolving machine with a horizontal spindle used to weigh anchor.

Winch. A cranked revolving spindle, vertical or horizontal, to provide extra power in sweating up halyards, sheeting in sails etc.

Windward. The side from which the wind blows.

Y

Yard arms. The extremities of a yard.

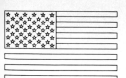

Victory Chimes

ex *Edwin and Maud*

Type: 3-masted gaff schooner. Wood

Country: U.S.A.

Owner:
Capt. Frederick B. Guild, Maine
Coast Cruises, Castine, Maine

Home port: Castine, Maine

Year of construction:
1900. Launched April, 1900

Builders:
J. M. C. Moore, Bethel Shipyard,
Bethel, Delaware

Tonnage:
208.48 tons gross, 178 tons net

Dimensions:
LOA	170 ft	
Length on deck	131 ft	7 in
Length between perpendiculars	126 ft	
Breadth extreme	24 ft	
Depth in hold	8 ft	6 in
Draft	7 ft	

Sail area: 7,500 sq ft

Rig:
6 sails, 3 headsails. All masts with
gaff sails only

Masts:
Height of mainmast over deck 83 ft
(all masts equal height). One-piece
masts

Engine: no auxiliary

Complement: 9 men, 43 passengers

Use: private charter vessel

While the victory bells were ringing in America at the end of the First World War, a three-masted schooner was being launched by a yard in Nova Scotia. Her owner named her *Victory Chimes* to celebrate the day and the present sailing vessel was given the same name in memory of the earlier schooner. The ship was built as the *Edwin and Maud* in the year 1900 as a freighter to be used for carrying lumber. Ships of this type were rigged as bald-headed schooners, that is to say they carried only gaff sails and no topmasts. Their maximum breadth was 25 feet and they were flat-bottomed so as to be able to use the Chesapeake and Delaware Canals. They were, nevertheless, very seaworthy and more than capable of crossing the Atlantic.

In 1954 the *Edwin and Maud* was converted to a passenger-carrying sailing ship. She went to Rockland, Maine and was given the name *Victory Chimes*, cruising under the command of Frank Elliott. Now she belongs to Captain F. B. Guild of Castine, Maine and is the largest American passenger-carrying sailing ship, and the only existing three-masted schooner with no auxiliary engine. She is equipped with electric light, air conditioning and running water in all the cabins. There are thirteen two-berth, one three-berth and three four-berth cabins for passengers. From the middle of June to the middle of September the schooner sails on weekly cruises in the waters off Maine.

Duchesse Anne

ex *Grossherzogin Elisabeth*

Type:
built as full-rigged ship. Steel.
At present a hulk (garrison ship)

Country: France

Owner: French Navy

Location: Brest

Year of construction:
1901. Launched March, 1901

Builders: J.C. Tecklenborg, Geestemünde

Tonnage: 1260 tons gross, 721 tons net

Dimensions:

LOA	approx 301 ft 10 in
Length hull	approx 262 ft 6 in
Length between perpendiculars	226 ft 5 in
Breadth extreme	39 ft
Depth in hold	20 ft 8 in

Rig:
formerly 24 sails, 3 headsails.
Double topsails, single topgallants, royals

Masts and spars: formerly

Height of mainmast over deck	131 ft 3 in
Length of main yard	72 ft 2 in
Length of main royal yard	37 ft 9 in

Bowsprit with jib-boom (today removed)

Engine: no auxiliary

Complement:
under sail, a total of 180 to 200

Use: garrison ship

Until the end of the First World War the Deutsche Schulschiff-Verein (German Schoolship Association), which had been founded in 1900, owned three sail training ships all of which had been built for the association. These ships were purely for training and carried no cargo. They were named after members of the family of the House of Oldenburg whose Grand Duke had so generously sponsored the training of naval cadets in sailing ships. The first of these vessels was the *Grossherzogin Elisabeth* (now *Duchesse Anne*) which was launched in 1901. She was followed in 1909 by the *Prinzess Eitel Friedrich* (now *Dar Pomorza*) and in 1914 by the *Grossherzog Friedrich August* (now *Statsraad Lehmkuhl*).

Grossherzogin Elisabeth was one of the first sail training ships not to carry cargo, and she was designed to accommodate a large number of boys.

All the German training ships were painted with the same colour scheme: a white hull topped by a light ochre poop and forecastle, which made them look very elegant, because it clearly defined the unbroken sheer line. The presentday *Gorch Fock* also uses this colour scheme.

Grossherzogin Elisabeth served as a training ship for 44 years making short voyages in the summer, mostly in the North Sea and Baltic, interspersed with winter voyages usually to South Africa, South America and above all the Caribbean. In 1928 a fire in the sail locker damaged the ship considerably. A second incident occured in 1931 when the sailing ship was in collision with the Latvian sailing vessel *Evermore,* both ships being damaged above the waterline. Shortly before the Second World War the *Grossherzogin Elisabeth* was transferred under the same name to the Deutsche Seemansschule (German Seamen's School) in Hamburg. In 1945 she had to be handed over to the French as war reparations. To start with it appeared that under her new name *Duchesse Anne* she would continue to sail as a training ship, but later plans were made to use her as a stationary training ship in Lorient, Brittany. These, too, came to nothing, and in 1946 she was unrigged down to her lower masts, remaining idle until 1951, at the end of which year she was towed to Brest. There the *Duchesse Anne* lies today as a barracks for the French Navy. The solidity of her construction would certainly permit her to be rerigged without much difficulty.

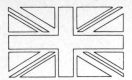

Discovery

Type: bark. Wood

Country: Great Britain

Owners:
London Division, Royal Naval Reserve. Royal Navy Recruiting Headquarters

Location:
Victoria Embankment, London

Year of construction:
1901. Launched March 21, 1901

Builders:
Dundee Shipbuilder's Company, Steven's Yard, Dundee, Scotland. Designed by W. C. Smith

Tonnage:
1620 tons displacement, 736 tons gross

Dimensions:
Length between perpendiculars	171 ft 4 in
Breadth extreme	33 ft 10 in
Draft	15 ft 9 in

Sail area: 12,315 sq ft

Rig:
18 sails, 3 headsails, double topsails, single topgallants, royals. Note: the sailplan did not remain constant

Masts and spars:
fore- and mainmast: topmasts and topgallant masts.
Mizzen mast: topmast only. Bowsprit with jib-boom

Engine:
450 hp triple expansion steam engine

Complement:
on Scott's Expedition, without scientists, 38

Use: museum ship

The main topic under discussion at the Berlin International Geographical Congress of 1899 was the exploration of Antarctica, and those attending the congress agreed on greater international co-operation. Following this, the Royal Geographical Society commissioned the building of the *Discovery* for the proposed British Royal Antarctic Expedition.

In order to cope with the particular problems of sailing in Polar waters, special plans were drawn up. The ship was given a double skin and, because of the danger of sticking fast in the ice, there were no bilge keels. The great disadvantage of this was that the ship was liable to roll heavily. So as to help break a passage through the ice, the stem was sharply raked, as was the stern with a view to protecting the rudder and propeller from damage by ice. The rudder blade could be replaced at sea from on deck, and it was also possible to remove the propeller and house it in a vertical shaft above. Spars and sails on the two forward masts were interchangeable. The shrouds and backstays were set up to outside channels with deadeyes and lanyards. On her great voyage the ship carried five 26 ft whaling boats and two Norwegian prams aboard, and she could carry stores and provisions for two years. The ice look-out barrel hung at the mainmast truck. Her only ornamentation were beautifully carved scroll-boards at the bow flanking the British coat-of-arms.

On July 31, 1901 the *Discovery* left London, carrying five scientists among her crew, which consisted of members of the Royal Navy, mostly volunteers. Her Commander was Robert Falcon Scott, himself a Naval Officer. She did not prove to be very fast, for her sail area had deliberately been kept small. The expedition lasted until September 1904.

On her return the ship was sold to the Hudson's Bay Company who used her as a supply vessel operating between Great Britain and North America. She was laid up in 1912, but in 1914 the bark was chartered to the French Government to carry ammunition to Russia. She was laid up again from 1920 to 1923 in which year she was bought by the Discovery Committee and re-equipped for use in the Antarctic. From 1925 to 1927 she was used for research in the whaling grounds off South Georgia and the Southern Orkneys. In 1928 she was once more fitted out for a great Polar voyage and sailed with Sir Douglas Mawson on his South Pole Expedition until 1931. From then until 1937 she lay idle in the East India Docks in London, before being handed over to the Boy Scouts Association as a stationary training ship. In 1955 the *Discovery* became the training ship of the Royal Naval Volunteer Reserve, London Division, and since 1958 that of the Royal Naval Reserve as well as being the Headquarters of the Royal Naval Recruiting branch and the Scott Museum. The masts and spars remain standing, but the yards have been lowered.

Suomen Joutsen

ex *Oldenburg*
ex *Laennec*

Type: full-rigged ship. Steel
Country: Finland
Owner:
Merchant Navy Seamans School, Turku
Location: Turku, Aura Quay
Tonnage:
2900 tons displacement, 2260 tons gross
Dimensions:

LOA	315 ft
Length hull	291 ft
Length between perpendiculars	262 ft 6 in
Breadth extreme	40 ft 4 in
Draft	17 ft

Sail area: 24,220 sq ft
Rig:
27 sails, 4 headsails, Fore- and mainmasts: double topsails, double topgallants, royals. Mizzen mast: double topsails, single topgallant, royal
Masts and spars:
all masts with top and topgallant masts. Height of mainmast over waterline 170 ft 7 in. No gaff on the mizzenmast, but small gaff on crosstrees used for signalling
Engines:
2 200 hp Scandia diesel engines. Speed under power about 6 knots
Complement:
as a stationary schoolship 150, including cadets
Use: stationary schoolship

This full-rigged ship was built as the *Laennec* for the Société des Armateurs Nantais to carry nitrate and other cargo. She was accident-prone, even under her first owners, and continued to be so throughtout her sailing life. In 1921 she was laid up by the company in La Martinière near Nantes due to lack of freights.

Two years later she was bought by the shipowners H. H. Schmidt of Hamburg and renamed *Oldenburg*. A a cargo-carrying schoolship she was again mostly engaged in the nitrate trade. She was bought by the Bremen sailing-ship company "Seefahrt" in 1928 and continued as a cargo-carrying school-ship under the same name until 1931 when the Finnish Government acquired her. They renamed her *Suomen Joutsen,* meaning Swan of Finland, and converted her into a training ship for the Finnish Navy. Accommodation for 80 to 90 cadets was provided in the tweendecks and portholes were cut in the topsides. Due to the alterations her freeboard was considerably increased, but the major change was the installation of two auxiliary motors. She made regular training voyages until the outbreak of war when she was unrigged and used as a barracks. After peace was declared *Suomen Joutsen* made several more voyages, and today she is the stationary training ship of the Finnish Merchant Navy.

A peculiarity which dates from the original plans is the single deck which joins the long forecastle and the forward deckhouse. These, in turn, are linked with the deckhouse aft of the mainmast and the poop by catwalks.

Originally the crew lived in the forward deckhouse in which, apart from the galley and donkey boiler, a seamen's mess was installed—an unusual feature at that time.

Pommern

ex *Mneme*

Type: four-masted bark. Steel

Country: Finland

Owners:
    town of Mariehamn on the Åland
    Islands. Ålands Maritime Museum

Location: Mariehamm

Year of construction: 1903

Builders:
    J. Reid & Co Ltd., Whiteinch,
    Glasgow

Tonnage:
    2376 tons gross, 2144 tons net

Dimensions:

LOA	349 ft	6 in
Length hull	315 ft	
Length between		
perpendiculars	287 ft	
Breadth extreme	43 ft	4 in
Depth in hold	24 ft	7 in
Draft approx	21 ft	4 in

Rig:
    27 sails. 4 headsails; double topsails,
    double topgallants, no royals
    (baldheader). Jigger mast: spanker,
    gaff topsail

Masts and spars:
    all square-rigged masts are the
    same height.

Height of mainmast	
over deck	152 ft
Length of mainyard	91 ff
Length of main upper	
topgallant yard	58 ft

Engine: no auxiliary

Use: museum ship

This four-masted bark was built in Glasgow in 1903 under the name *Mneme* (Greek for memory) for the shipowners B. Wencke & Sons of Hamburg. For reasons of economy she was rigged as a 'baldheader' with no royals, and all her yards were interchangeable. The ship had no upper deck and consequently had a very large open deck space between the poop and forecastle as was common in nineteenth-century sailing freighters. The large deckhouse between the fore- and mainmasts housed the galley, the boiler room and the crew's quarters. A smaller deckhouse between the poop and the mizzen was connected to the poopdeck by a short cat-walk. She was helmed in traditional manner from the poop, with no protection for the helmsman. Her full-length figurehead represents a Greek muse. The Rhederei Actiengesellschaft of 1896 bought the vessel in 1906, but a year later she was

added her to his fleet of 'P-Liners' and renamed her *Pommern*. Until the First World War she was a nitrate trader and was in Valparaiso when war broke out. It was not until 1921 that she returned to Europe with other sailing ships, discharging her cargo at Delfzijl before being handed over to Greece as war reparations.

The Greeks were not able to make use of her, and in 1923 the *Pommern* was

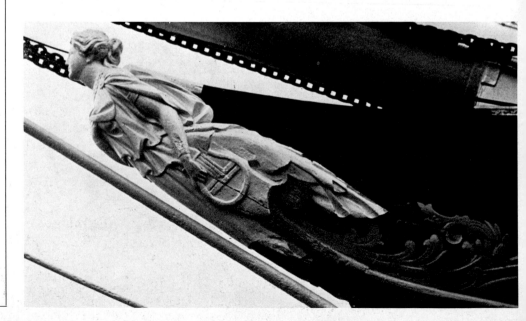

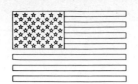

Champigny

bought by Gustaf Erikson of Mariehamn on the island of Aaland. From then until the Second World War she was engaged mostly in the Australian grain trade. During the war she was at first laid up in Mariehamn, but later was used in Stockholm as a grain-store. She returned to Mariehamn without setting sail again at the end of the war, and in 1952 Gustaf Eriskon gave the *Pommern* to the town of Mariehamn where she belongs to the Aalands Sjöfartsmuseum and is moored close by in Mariehamn harbour.

ex *Fennia*
ex *Champigny*

Type: 4-masted bark. Steel

Country: U.S.A.

Owner:
Mr. William Swigert Jr. (President of the Pacific Bridge Co.), San Francisco, California

Location:
San Francisco, California (after restoration)

Year of construction: 1902

Builders:
Forges et Chantiers de la Méditerranée, yard at Le Havre, France

Tonnage: 3230 tons gross

Dimensions:
Length between perpendiculars	311 ft
Breadth extreme	45 ft
Depth in hold	23 ft 7 in

Rig:
33 sails. 4 headsails, double topsails, double topgallants, royals

Use: museum ship

The four-masted bark *Champigny* was built purely as a merchantman for the Société Anonyme des Voiliers Long Courriers. After a long spell in the Martinière channel near Nantes where a lot of sailing ships were lying idle at the time, she was sold in 1923 to the Finnish Steamship Company of Helsinki for use as a cargo-carrying schoolship and was renamed *Fennia II*. (The *Fennia I*, ex *Goodrich*, was a four-masted bark of 2,262 gross tons which had been built in Belfast in 1892.)
The difficulty of competing with steam-driven vessels at the time is shown clearly by the fact that in January 1926 the *Fennia* reached Melbourne in company with the *Favell* which belonged to the same owners. Only the *Favell* succeeded in obtaining a cargo of grain, while the *Fennia* lay waiting fruitlessly for four months. She then sailed to the west coast of South America where eventually she was ordered to load a cargo of nitrate at Antofagasta.
On her next voyage from Cardiff to Valparaiso she was dismasted off Cape Horn in April 1927 and had to be towed into Port Stanley. Repairs were out of the question on account of cost, so she was stripped and moored as a hulk in Port Stanley. During the war captured German seamen were kept on board. In 1967 the *Fennia* was bought by Mr. W. Swigert who intends to turn her into a museum in San Francisco under her old name *Champigny*. In June 1968 she was moored in Montevideo in the course of her voyage in tow to San Francisco.

Moshulu

ex *Oplag*
ex *Moshulu*
ex *Dreadnaught*
ex *Kurt*

Type:
four-masted bark. Steel. At present a
mastless hulk

Country: Finland

Owner: Finnish State

Location:
Naantali (Nådendaal), nr Turku,
Finland

Year of construction:
1904. Launched April 20, 1904

Builders:
William Hamilton & Co Ltd., Port
Glasgow, Scotland

Tonnage: 3116 tons gross, 2911 tons net

Dimensions:

LOA	400 ft	4 in
Length hull	359 ft	10 in
Length between perpendiculars	334 ft	4 in
Breadth extreme	46 ft	7 in
Depth moulded	28 ft	
Depth in hold	26 ft	3 in

Sail area: 45,000 sq ft

Rig:
originally 34 sails. 4 headsails, double
topsails, double topgallants, royals.
Jigger mast: double spanker, gaff
topsail

Masts and spars:

height of mainmast over deck	164 ft	5 in
Length of main yard	96 ft	6 in
Length of main royal yard	48 ft	7 in

Engine: diesel engine

Complement:
on a voyage in 1937, 19 crew,
6 apprentices, 8 deckboys

Use: grain storage hulk

At the turn of the century a large number of four-masted barks were built as 'three-island' vessels with a raised forecastle, poopdeck and a midships bridge-deck lying somewhere between the two. This midships bridge-deck and the cat-walks which linked it with the forecastle and poop served to increase the safety of the crew, particularly in rough weather. The whole midships structure, which housed the crew quarters, galley etc., divided the otherwise large area of open deck with the result that, when the ship heeled, no dangerous amount of water was taken aboard. The *Moshulu*, ex *Kurt*, was built in this style for the German firm of G. H. J. Siemers of Hamburg, and she was named after Dr. Kurt Siemers who ran the firm up to the Second World War. Under the German flag the *Kurt* was engaged only in the nitrate trade, carrying coal to South America and Mexico and returning to Germany laden with nitrate on each of her nine voyages. Her tenth trip was to Santa Rosalia, Mexico, where she discharged her coal and then sailed in ballast for Portland, Oregon to load grain. During this passage the First World War broke out and the *Kurt* ran to Astoria, Oregon for safety where she was taken as a prize and handed over to the U.S. Shipping Board Emergency Fleet Corporation.

All ships taken as booty were kept in commission and renamed after famous American clippers. *Kurt* was renamed *Dreadnaught* and spent some time in the Pacific sailing between the Philippines, Australia and the U.S.A. It then transpired that many of these clipper names were already in use. Mrs. Woodrow Wilson, wife of the President, who was herself of Indian extraction, chose various Indian names for the ships and

since September 18, 1917 *Dreadnaught* has been called *Moshulu*, which in fact means exactly the same: Fear Nothing. In 1922 *Moshulu* was bought by the shipowners Charles Nelson & Co. of San Francisco for $ 40,000 and used in the timber trade with Australia and Africa, her last voyage being in 1927—8 with sawn timber for Melbourne and Geelong, Australia. She then lay idle for seven years in Union Lake, Seattle and later in Winslow, Washington. She was bought for $ 20,000 in February 1935 by the Finnish shipowner Gustaf Erikson of Mariehamn, Aaland. Captain Gunnar Boman, the present head of the Mariehamn Maritime Museum, travelled to Winslow, took over *Moshulu*, sailed her to Port Victoria, Australia and returned to Europe in July 1936 with a cargo of grain.

At that time Erikson owned the largest fleet of merchant sailing ships in the world. Including his newly-acquired *Moshulu* he had 25 vessels: 3 schooners of which two were four-masted, 3 barentines, two of them four-masted, 8 barks and 11 four-masted barks—a total of 44,728 gross tons. Most of them, including *Moshulu*, carried grain from Australia. On May 22, 1940 she made her last grain run under Erikson's flag, discharging her cargo at Kristiansand, Norway.

From March to July 1942 she was confiscated by German troops and in November of the same year was towed to Horten, Oslo Fjord and stripped. She then went to Kirkenes where she stranded, capsized and was raised in September 1947. She was bought for about $ 20,000 by Miss Disken Jacobsen whose plans to convert the one-time sailing-ship into a motor-vessel were frustrated. In 1948 Trygve Sommerfeldt of Oslo bought her and took her to

Bergen. She then spent four years as a grain-store in Stockholm earning Kr 12 per ton per annum.

In the summer of 1952 T. Sommerfeldt sold *Moshulu* to Heinz Schliewen of Lübeck and she went to Germany. She was to have joined the *Pamir* and *Passat* under the name of *Oplag* as the third sailing merchantman in the Schliewen fleet, but Schliewen had to suspend payment, and plans to re-rig *Moshulu* came to naught. She was returned to Stockholm and in 1961 was sold to the Finnish Government who are again using her as a grain-store in Naantali near Abo.

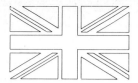

Duenna

ex *Sid, Will and Harry*

Type: brigantine. Wood

Country: Great Britain

Owner:
Mr. Lawrie D. Johns, Emsworth, Hants

Home port: Emsworth, Hants

Year of construction: 1903

Builders:
Aldous Bros., Brightlingsea, Essex

Tonnage:
25 tons displacement, 18.53 tons gross, 13.97 tons net

Dimensions:

LOA	61 ft 8 in
Length hull	48 ft
Length between perpendiculars	41 ft
Breadth extreme	11 ft 6 in
Depth in hold	6 ft 3 in
Draft	5 ft 7 in

Sail area:
1615 sq ft (total), 1248 sq ft (working rig)

Rig:
9 sails. 2 headsails (working rig); foremast: fore course, topsail; mainmast: main staysail, main course (gaff sail)

Masts:
height of mainmast over deck 44 ft

Engine:
48 hp Perkins P-4 diesel engine

Complement: 2 to 5

Use:
private yacht and home of the owner

It is hard to believe now that *Duenna* was once a single-masted fishing vessel. She was built originally as an oyster smack and named *Sid, Will and Harry* (S.W.H.) after her joint owners the brothers Sid, Will and Harry Myall of Tollesbury. Ships of this type had pleasant lines, they were fast, easy to work and exceptionally seaworthy. Decades of experience went into their construction.

At the beginning of the twenties an engine was installed for the first time, which was several times replaced by more powerful engines allowing a reduction in sail area. In 1960 *Sid, Will and Harry* was sold to a man who preferred sail to motor. He re-rigged her as a ketch, installed a smaller engine and gave her the name *Duenna*, a Spanish word meaning lady companion or governess. This name was chosen because for the most part his family sailed with him and the ship was their duenna.

In the spring of 1964 her present owner, Mr. Johns, bought the ship but did not change her name. She was completely converted by Frost & Drake Ltd. of Tollesbury, Essex and re-rigged as a brigantine. In particular the replacement of the old straight stem by a clipper bow gives her a most attractive appearance.

The rig has proved itself, for in spite of her yards the brigantine can sail within five points of the wind and her best logged sped is 9 knots in a Force 6 wind. To simplify sail handling only the topsail is furled to the yard, while the large forecourse is gathered to the centre of the yard like a curtain and made fast to the lower mast. *Duenna* is used not only as a yacht, but as the family's houseboat.

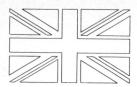

Worcester

ex *Exmouth*

Type:
built in steel to the design of a ship-of-the-line (First Rate)

Country: Great Britain

Owners:
The Incorporated Thames Nautical College, Ingress Abbey, Greenhithe. Merchant Navy

Location: Greenhithe

Year of construction: 1904

Builders:
Vickers Armstrong, Sons & Maxim, Barrow-in-Furness

Tonnage: 5480 tons gross

Dimensions:

Length hull	345 ft	3 in
Length waterline	313 ft	5 in
Breadth extreme	52 ft	10 in
Depth moulded	approx 47 ft	7 in
Draft	18 ft	4 in

Complement:
24 instructors and administration, 250 cadets

Use: stationary schoolship

The Metropolitan Asylums Board, later the London County Council, had this ship built in 1904 with the name of *Exmouth II* as a replacement for the 90-gun ship *Exmouth,* which until then had served as a stationary training ship.

The *Exmouth II,* which was never intended to put to sea, was built like a traditional three-deck ship of the line. Anchored in the river she was intended to give the boys the feel of being on a sea-going ship during their training days. By building a new vessel the inconveniences of a converted fighting ship could be avoided—particularly in so far as the height between decks was concerned: in the *Worcester,* ex *Exmouth* this is ten feet. Regular courses were run on this well-equipped ship until the outbreak of the Second World War when the *Exmouth* was at first evacuated and then commandeered by the Admiralty in 1942 and converted at Tilbury into a parent ship for minesweepers. She was towed round to Scapa Flow where she lay until June 1945. On her return to London she was taken over by the Thames Nautical Training College and her name changed to *Worcester.* The first *Worcester* had been a 50-gun frigate from 1862—1876, and the *Worcester II,* ex *Frederik William* had been an 86-gun ship from 1876—1946. The name *Frederik William* was in honour of Frederik William III of Prussia, and his bust is now the figurehead of the present *Worcester.* Four continuous decks give space for many instruction rooms, wash-rooms etc., officers' and instructors' cabins, together with a library, a small sickbay and a chapel. The open topdeck is 160 feet long and is used for drill and as a parade-ground. The boys are between 13 and 16 years of age and are training to be merchant navy officers. There is a strict timetable, and the boys sleep aboard in berths. All modern navigation aids are fitted for instructional purposes. The yards of the *Worcester* came from the *Arethusa,* ex *Peking* in Lower Upnor.

Viking

Type: four-masted bark. Steel

Country: Sweden

Owners:
City of Gothenburg, "Förening Viking". Merchant Navy

Year of construction:
1906. Launched December 1, 1906. Fitted out March 1907

Builders:
Burmeister & Wain, Copenhagen

Tonnage:
2959 tons gross, 2665 tons net

Dimensions:

LOA	approx 340 ft	5 in
Length hull	319 ft	3 in
Length between perpendiculars	292 ft	8 in
Breadth extreme	45 ft	7 in
Draft (loaded)	23 ft	2 in

Sail area: 30,680 sq ft

Rig:
31 sails. 4 headsails, double topsails, double topgallants, royals. Jigger mast: spanker, gaff topsail

Masts:
fore, main and mizzen with one topmast. Jigger mast in one piece. Height of mainmast over deck 154 ft

Engine: no auxiliary

Complement:
on her last voyage 32. As a training ship up to 150, of whom some 80 are apprentices

Use: stationary schoolship

This four-masted bark was built as a cargo-carrying training ship for the Danish merchant navy and was owned by the A/S Den Danske Handelsflades for Befalingsmænd. On March 18, 1907, while alongside the wharf prior to being delivered, she was struck by a heavy squall and capsized, due to the fact that at the time there was too little water in her ballast tanks. Her total water ballast was 1390 tons, of which 456 tons were carried in the double bottoms, 864 tons in the midships deep-tank, 44 tons in the forepeak and 26 tons in the afterpeak tanks. Fortunately she capsized towards the quay and did not sink, but her delivery was delayed by several months. The total cost of building was Kr 591,000. *Viking* was built to accommodate a large number of boys. By combining the poop with the midships bridge-deck a 200-ft long deckhouse was formed which provided ample accommodation above the main deck for all her crew. The main deck was made of steel plate, covered with teak. A continuous tween-deck originally divided the hold.

On July 16, 1907 the *Viking* made a short trial sail, and three days later left in ballast under tow for Hamburg to load coke for Peru. Her maiden voyage finally began on August 29, 1907. She made several voyages carrying nitrates until the First World War when she was laid up in Copenhagen. In 1916 the shipping line Det Forenede Dampskibsselskab bought the ship for Kr 320,000 intending to use her as a training ship again, but after the war freights proved hard to come by and a training vessel of this size had to earn her keep. This could only be done with great difficulty, so the *Viking* was laid up again in 1925, having made only short trips in the meanwhile.

In 1929 she was bought by Gustaf Erikson for his fleet at Mariehamn. Under his flag she always had many youngsters among her crew on her grain-carrying voyages from Australia. The outbreak of the Second World War brought an end to this trade, and like other vessels the *Viking* was used as a grain-store in Stockholm.

At the end of the war Erikson's ship was returned to him and in 1946 made a noteworthy voyage to Australia with a crew of thirty-two, carrying timber to South Africa and returning to Europe with 4,000 tons of grain in bags. She was then overhauled in Antwerp in preparation for future voyages, but the death of G. Erikson put an end to these plans. In 1949 the town of Göteborg decided to buy the *Viking* for use as a stationary training ship for the seamen's school there. She was also to be the much-prized 'Town Ship' as is found in many Scandinavian cities.

On May 28, 1951 *Viking* was towed to Göteborg with 2,000 tons of coke aboard, and her entry into harbour was a triumphal procession. At once large scale conversion of the whole hull began. Instruction rooms and workshops were built so that boys today can be instructed in all nautical subjects including marine engineering. There is accommodation for 120 boys in the tween-decks.

Arken

ex *Roscovite*

Type: 2-masted topsail schooner. Wood

Country: Denmark

Owner:
Sømanshøjskolen i Svendborg

Location: Svendborg, Fyn, Denmark

Year of construction: 1908

Builders:
E. Bonne, Keritz, Brittany, France

Tonnage: 112 tons gross, 99 tons net

Dimensions:
LOA	105 ft	4 in
Length hull	85 ft	4 in
Breadth extreme	23 ft	4 in
Depth moulded	16 ft	
Depth in hold	9 ft	2 in
Draft	7 ft	

Rig: 10 sails

Masts:
height of main mast over deck
72 ft 2 in

Engine: two-stroke diesel engine

Use: stationary schoolship

The *Arken* was built originally as the *Roskovite* and used as a fishing schooner in the North Sea. Later she traded as a merchantman in North Sea Ports. An auxiliary motor was installed in 1930. Before being sold to Denmark, she belonged to the French firm of F. Meudal & Le Foricher and was based on Treguier until 1939 when she was bought by the Sømandshøjskolen in Svendborg as a replacement for their 136-year old stationary training ship *Hvalfisken.* Her topsail yards were rigged at that time for training purposes.

Unyo Maru

Type: bark. Steel

Country: Japan

Owner:
Institute for Fishery Research, Tokyo

Year of construction:
1909, Launched February 2, 1909

Builders:
Osaka Iron Foundry Co Ltd., Osaka

Tonnage:
448.25 tons gross, 197.46 tons net

Dimensions:

Length hull	150 ft 7 in
Length between	
perpendiculars	134 ft 6 in
Breadth extreme	26 ft 6 in
Depth moulded	16 ft 5 in
Depth in hold	14 ft 9 in
Draft	11 ft 10 in

Sail area: 5,812 sq ft

Rig:
21 sails. Double topsails, single top-gallants, royals

Masts:
height of mainmast over deck
98 ft 6 in

Engine: 303 hp piston steam engine

Complement:
25 permanent crew, 15 to 30 boys

Use: museum ship

This small steam-powered bark was built as a sail training ship and run by the Ministry of Agriculture and Forests. After her days as a sailing schoolship were over she spent many years before the Second World War in Tokyo harbour as a stationary training ship with the *Meiji Maru*.

"Unyo" means large cloud or hawk, and "Maru" is word difficult to translate which is added to the names of almost all Japanese merchant ships*. Today the ship is used as a museum near the university grounds.

* According to Basil Hall Chamberlin, *Things Japanese* (London: Kelly & Walsh, 1905), pp. 314—15, the Japanese word "maru" means round, but at some time it became confused with the word "maru," an archaic term of endearment, and when the older word was abandoned, "maru" was applied, endearingly, to all sorts of other words—swords, musical instruments, birds, etc., but most especially to merchant vessels.

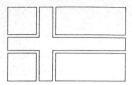

Regina Maris

ex *Regina*

Type: barkentine. Wood

Country: Norway

Owners:
Siegfried & John Aage Wilson,
Shipowners, Arendal. Registered by
the Oceanwide Sailing Company,
Valletta, Malta

Home port: Arendal

Year of construction: 1908

Builders: J. Ring Andersen, Svendborg

Tonnage: 186 tons gross

Dimensions:

LOA	139 ft 5 in
Length hull	114 ft 10 in
Length between perpendiculars	100 ft
Breadth extreme	25 ft
Draft	10 ft 10 in

Sail area: 5,920 sq ft

Rig:
16 sails (plus 6 studding sails). 4 headsails; foremast: double topsails, single
topgallant, royal; main and mizzen
masts: gaff courses, gaff topsails

Masts and spars:
foremast with top and topgallant
masts, main and mizzen masts with
topmasts. All masts of pitchpine.
Bowsprit with jib-boom. Height of
mainmast over deck 108 ft 3 in

Engine: 242 hp diesel engine

Complement: 16

Use: private yacht

In 1908 P. Reinhold of Raa in Sweden
built the *Regina* as a three-masted
schooner with a running square-sail. As
she was to be used in icy waters she was
particularly strongly constructed. Later
she was employed in the nitrate trade,
and in 1931 she belonged to the shipowner O. B. Bengtson of Raa. She has
had an auxiliary engine since about
1932/33.

In 1962 she was considerably damaged
by a fire in the engine room. The two
Norwegian brothers Siegfried and John
Aage Wilson (Ocean Transport Lines)
of Arendal bought *Regina,* which was
laid up at the time in Ystadt, and had
her converted by Hoivolds Mek. Verk-
sted A/S in Kristiansand at a cost of
$ 299,000. The former schooner became
a highly successful barkentine. Due to
her age no North European country
wanted her on their Register of Shipping, but Malta agreed to take her,
which is why although she is a Norwegian ship she is registered in Valetta.
It is exceptional for a sailing vessel of
this size to have all her running rigging
made of terylene. The standing rigging
is set up to outside chain plates with
turnbuckles. The bow carries a crowned
figure of a woman. She has two stocked
anchors. The exhaust is led up through
the lower mizzen mast, the only mast
made of steel. Conversion work was
finished in the summer of 1966, and in
August the ship set out on a one-year
trip round the world.

Dar Pomorza

ex *Pomorze*
ex *Colbert*
ex *Prinzess Eitel Friedrich*

Type: full-rigged ship. Steel

Country: Poland

Owner:
Polish State Sea School (Merchant Navy), Gdynia

Home port: Gdynia

Year of construction:
1909. Commissioned April 6, 1910

Builders: Blohm & Voss, Hamburg

Tonnage: 1561 tons gross

Dimensions:

LOA	293 ft 7 in
Length between perpendiculars	238 ft 3 in
Breadth extreme	41 ft 4 in
Depth in hold	20 ft 8 in
Draft	18 ft 9 in

Sail area: 20,450 sq ft

Rig:
25 sails. 4 headsails, double topsails, single topgallants, royals.

Masts: top and topgallant masts

Engine:
430 hp six-cylinder M.A.N. diesel engine

Complement:
30 crew, 150 apprentices

Use: sail training ship

The German Schoolship Asscociation put their second sail training ship, the *Prinzess Eitel Friedrich,* into service in 1909. In most ways her plans were very similar to the first ship that had been built for the Association in 1901 (the *Grossherzogin Elisabeth,* now the *Duchesse Anne*). Typical of training ships is her long poop which extends to the mainmast. She was used to train both apprentices and officer cadets. After the First World War she had to be handed over to the French, although they had no use for her and she was laid up in St. Nazaire until 1921. The Société Anonyme de Navigation 'Les Navires Ecoles Français' were at this time using the four-masted bark *Richelieu* for training, and it was planned to use the *Prinzess Eitel Friedrich* for this purpose as well under the name *Colbert.* But even after the loss of the *Richelieu* by fire these plans were never put into effect and the ship lay on at St. Nazaire. In 1926 she was sold to Baron de Forrest who intended to convert her into a yacht, but this plan never came off, either.

The Polish State Sea Training School were using the bark *Lwow* for training at the time, but because of her age she was due to be taken out of commission. A replacement was needed, and the *Colbert* seemed to be ideal. With money raised by voluntary contribution from the people of Pomorze (a Polish province) the ship was bought in 1929 and renamed *Pomorze.* She used this name only during her journey from St. Nazaire to Nakskov and on her arrival in Poland was renamed *Dar Pomorza* (Gift of Pomorze).

On December 26, 1929 the tug *Poolzee* towed her out of St. Nazaire, but three days later *Pomorze* had to anchor during a heavy storm and the crew took to the boats fearing total loss. She could only be got under control again with the help of a second tug. On January 9, 1930 *Pomorze* finally reached Poland, where an auxiliary engine was installed and she was handed over to the Sea Training School. Until 1939 she made regular training voyages which many times took her across the Atlantic. On the outbreak of the Second World War *Dar Pomorza* took refuge in Swedish waters and lay interned in Stockholm for the duration. When peace was declared she was returned to Poland and since then she has sailed regularly on training service. In June 1968 she was on a voyage to Odessa.

Passat

Type: four-masted bark. Steel

Country: Federal Republic of Germany

Owner: City of Lübeck

Location: Am Priwall, Travemünde

Year of construction:
1911; keel laid March 2, 1911, launched September 20, 1911, ready for sea November 25, 1911

Builders:
Blohm & Voss, Hamburg (Slipway 1 of the Alten Werft on the north bank of the Elbe)

Tonnage:
3180.61 tons gross; as a sailing vessel without engine, 2870 tons net, 4750 tons burden; as a training ship with engine, 2593 tons net, 4223 tons burden

Dimensions:
LOA	377 ft 4 in
Length hull	349 ft
Draft (loaded with nitrates)	22 ft

Sail area: 44,132 sq ft

Rig:
34 sails. 4 (5) headsails, double topsails, Jigger mast: double spanker, gaff topsail

Masts:
height of mainmast over deck 170 ft 7 in. Fore, main and mizzen masts with one topmast. Jigger mast in one piece

Engine:
900 hp 6-cylinder Krupp diesel engine (since refit in 1951). Speed under power 6.5 knots. The highest speed logged under sail was 16.4 knots

Complement:
after the 1951 refit, a total of 80 to 90, of which 50 to 55 are apprentices and deckboys

Use: museum ship and stationary schoolship

The *Passat* was built at a cost of RM 680,000 for the shipowner F. Laeisz of Hamburg, by Blohm & Voss, Builder's No. 206, together with her sister ship *Peking*, Builder's No. 205. In January 1912 the *Passat* made her first voyage to Chile, and up to the First World War she made five more as a nitrate trader. At the beginning of the war she was lying in Iquique with several other sailing vessels, and her return passage carrying a cargo of 4,700 tons of nitrate could not start until May 27, 1921 when she sailed to Marseille and was handed over to the French.

At that time France had no use for the large four-masted bark so Laeisz bought back his ship in December 1921 for £13,000—the German crew embarking on January 3, 1922. After being fitted out in Hamburg she was engaged in the nitrate trade until 1927 when she was converted to a cargo-carrying training ship. She was in collision in the English Channel with the French steamer *Daphne* in August 1928 as a result of which the steamer sank in a few minutes. A further collision in the Channel with the British tanker *British Governor* in June 1929 damaged the *Passat* considerably. On both occasions she put in to Rotterdam for repairs. In 1932 she was sold to the Finnish shipowner Gustaf Erikson of Mariehamn for £6,500 and until the Second World War sailed under the Finnish flag on the Australia run. During the war she was laid up in Mariehamn until July 6, 1944 when she was towed to Stockholm and used as a grain store for two years.

Her first voyage after the war was to South Africa and Australia and she carried 56,000 bags of grain on her return voyage to England. Both *Passat*

Above: signal cannon on the chart room; extreme right, from top to bottom: the port anchor on the forecastle, the capstan on the forecastle and a brace winch

and *Pamir* then lay idle for some time in Penarth near Cardiff. In January 1951 it was announced that both ships were to be broken up by a Belgian ship-breaking firm and they were towed to Antwerp soon afterwards. Captain Helmut Grubbe and the shipowner, Heinz Schliewen, stepped in just in time and decided to buy both the sailing ships. The new owner was Schliewen, home port Lübeck. On June 20 the *Passat* arrived in Travemünde for a thorough overhaul and modernisation by the Kiel Howaldt Works, at a cost of DM 2,700,000. An engine, watertight bulkheads, two deckhouses, cat-walks, brace- and halyard winches on the upper deck were installed, and much else besides. German Lloyd classified her + 100 A 4, the highest. On February 12, 1952 the *Passat* sailed for Brazil and the Argentine with a cargo of cement, returning at the end of June laden with grain. Her second voyage followed soon after in July the same year, again to South America. From February 1953 to June

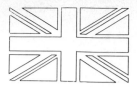

Arethusa

1955 she was laid up in Travemünde because Schliewen became insolvent. The National Bank of Schleswig-Holstein appointed Captain Grubbe trustee for both the *Pamir* and the *Passat*. During the second half of 1954 some 40 German shipowners got together to form the Pamir and Passat Foundation. Both ships now flew the house flag of Zerssen & Co., the firm of the shipowner Consul Thomas Entz of Rendsburg. Up to 1957 *Passat* made a further five voyages under the command of Captain Grubbe, on the last of which her cargo of grain shifted and she took on a dangerous angle of heel. The deep ballast tanks which were full of grain had to be flooded and she put in to Lisbon, where she was completely unloaded in order to clear out the tanks. On December 8, 1957 the *Passat* returned to Hamburg with a full cargo. Her last long voyage was from July 18 to December 8, 1957, since when she has not sailed again due to the loss of the *Pamir* on September 21, 1957. After two years in Hamburg Parkhafen *Passat* was sold to the town of Lübeck and on January 5, 1960 she was towed through the Kiel Canal to Travemünde, where she was used for instruction and accommodation by the Landesausbildungsstätte für seemännischen Nachwuchs—the boys living aboard during their three-month courses. In 1965 she was drydocked at the Flender yard in Lübeck. In the same year the school returned the vessel to the town of Lübeck. The *Passat* is now in the charge of the Lübeck Youth Council acting for the Government, and is at the disposal of various sailing and sporting organizations.

ex *Peking*

Type: four masted bark. Steel

Country: Great Britain

Owners:
The Shaftesbury Homes and Arethusa Training Ship. Merchant Navy

Location: Lower Upnor, River Medway

Year of construction: 1911

Builders: Blohm & Voss, Hamburg

Tonnage: 3100 tons gross, 2883 tons net

Dimensions:

LOA	377 ft 5 in
Length hull	347 ft
Length between perpendiculars	321 ft
Breadth extreme	47 ft
Depth in hold	26 ft 3 in

Sail area: 44,132 sq ft

Rig:
32 sails. 4 headsails, double topsails, double topgallants, royals
Jigger mast: double spanker, gaff topsail

Masts:
fore, main and mizzen masts with one topmast

Use: stationary schoolship

The *Peking* was built for the shipowner F. Laeisz of Hamburg and was the sister ship af the *Passat* although she was originally 85 gross tons smaller. She too was of the 'three-island' type (fo'csle, midship structure and poop) but she was steered from the main deck, the helmsman standing at the wheel forward of the poop. Characteristic of Laeisz ships, and indeed of many German sailing vessels, were the double spankers.

The *Peking* was engaged in the nitrate trade under the Laeisz flag from 1911 to 1921. After the First World War she had to be handed over to the Italians on May 10, 1921 as war reparations, but they had no use for the ship and in 1923 Laeisz bought his ship back for £ 8,500. She continued as a nitrate trader until 1932, although after conversion in 1926 she became a cargo-carrying school ship for the company. After 1932 the nitrate trade was no longer profitable, so Laeisz sold the *Peking* to the Shaftesbury Homes and Training Ship. She was named the *Arethusa II* and replaced the old wooden fighting ship *Arethusa* which had been built in 1849. A Rochester shipyard converted her for about £ 40,000, and since then she has served as a stationary training ship in Lower Upnor on the Medway near Rochester. The berth used by the *Arethusa I* at Greenhithe on the Thames was deemed unsuitable on account of the increasing river traffic.

The official opening was on July 25, 1933 by the future King George VI. The *Arethusa* has places for between 200 and 300 young boys of 13—15 years of age who are educated along semi-military lines.

Due to the considerable motion at the turn of the tide, almost all her yards

were removed. She only carries the forecourse-, lower topsail- and lower topgallant-yards on her foremast. A number of the other yards are to be found aboard the training ship *Worcester* which is anchored at Greenhithe on the Thames.
No major additional deckhouses were erected when she was converted. The former deckhouse between No. 1 and No. 2 hatches was extended over No. 2 hatch as far as the upper deck. The deckhouse between No. 3 and No. 4 hatches was removed and No. 4 hatch was decked over, thus providing a large parade area. In accordance with tradition the *Arethusa* has gunports painted on a white band. 'Arethusa' was the name of several springs in antiquity, the best known of which rose in the island of Ortigia off Syracuse. In mythology the nymph Arethusa was the daughter of Nereus and Doris. She was chased by Alpheus the river-god, fled through the sea and reappeared on Sicily as a spring.

Alve

ex *Erik-Hans*

Type: 3-masted schooner. Wood

Country: Federal Republic of Germany

Owner:
Zerssen & Co., Shipowners,
Rendsburg

Location:
Rendsburg, alongside a quay in the
Lower Eider

Year of construction: 1914

Builders: at Strömstad, Sweden

Tonnage:
approx 500 tons displacement;
181.47 tons gross; 133.49 tons net

Dimensions:
LOA	126 ft	4 in
Length hull	91 ft	3 in
Breadth extreme	26 ft	
Draft	10 ft	2 in

Rig:
8 sails. 3 headsails; fore- and mainmasts: gaff courses, gaff topsails;
mizzen mast: spanker

Masts and spars:
fore-and mainmasts with one topmast;
mizzen mast in one piece.
Bowsprit with jib-boom

Engine:
at one time a motor was installed

Use: stationary club ship

The schooner *Alve* is a typical sturdy
North Sea and Baltic merchantman,
reinforced against ice damage by
0.06 in steel sheathing along her sides.
A dinghy was usually carried across
her transom stern. The lower shrouds
were made fast with deadeyes and
lanyards. Below decks was used only
for cargo and stores, while the crew
lived in the two deckhouses. Until 1955
the *Alve* was used as a merchant sailer
by the Swedes, after which she lay in
the bay of Stokevik near Skärhamn. She
was towed from there to Rendsburg in
1956 when the shipowner, Consul
Thomas Entz, bought the schooner to
use as the Club ship for Zerssen & Co.
of Rendsburg. A thorough survey had
established that, in spite of her considerable age and the materials used in
her construction as well as her long
service, she was still in very good
condition. Her engine had been removed
before she was sold because it had
proved too powerful and was straining
the structural members of the ship.
Alve was then fitted out at a Rendsburg yard, converted to her new purpose
and then made fast to the Eider Quay.
Today she is used by employees of
Zerssen & Co. as a recreation centre.

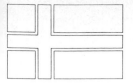

Statsraad Lehmkuhl

ex *Westwärts*
ex *Statsraad Lehmkuhl*
ex *Grossherzog Friedrich August*

Type: bark. Steel

Country: Norway

Owners:
Hilmar Reksten, Shipowners,
Fjøsanger, Bergen

Location: Bergen

Year of construction: 1914

Builders: J. C. Tecklenborg, Bremerhaven

Tonnage: 1701 tons gross

Dimensions:

LOA	321 ft	7 in
Length hull	287 ft	
Length between perpendiculars	247 ft	9 in
Breadth extreme	41 ft	4 in
Depth in hold	23 ft	4 in
Draft	16 ft	9 in

Sail area: 21,528 sq ft

Rig:
21 sails. 4 headsails, double topsails,
single topgallants, royals; mizzen
mast with spanker only

Masts:
height of mainmast over waterline
164 ft; fore- and mainmasts with
top and topgallant masts,
mizzen mast with one topmast

Engine: 450 hp diesel engine

Complement:
24 permanent crew, 180 boys

Use: sail training ship,
at present laid up

In 1914 the German Training Association added a new bark, the *Grossherzog Friedrich August* (of Oldenburg) to their existing ships, the *Grossherzogin Elisabeth* and the *Prinzess Eitel Friedrich*. Due to the outbreak of World War I no long voyages could be untertaken, and after the war she was handed over to England as war reparations. She was formally registered with the shipowners, J. Couil & Sons of Newcastle on Tyne, but they had no use for her as she had been designed purely as a training ship and not to carry cargo. In 1922 the Bergen Steamship Company bought her, changed her name to the *Statsraad Lehmkuhl* and gave her to the Bergens Skoleskib Association as a replacement for the corvette *Alfen* which had been paid off.
Up to 1939 the bark made regular training voyages, which usually lasted from April to September. In 1940 she was confiscated by the German troops in Bergen and under the name of *Westwärts* was used as a naval depot ship until she was handed back to her owners in 1945. They gave her back the name *Statsraad Lehmkuhl* and she was thoroughly repaired and overhauled until 1946, after which she spent a further three years making training voyages.

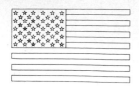

Tabor Boy

In 1949 her maintenance costs had become so high that the association decided she was not to set sail that year. For a year she was the stationary training ship of the Norwegian Fishing School and later that of the Bergens Skoleskib. In 1952 she put to sea again and sailed actively until the end of 1967. At that time the Norwegian Government decided to withdraw financial support because maintenance costs were too high and because there were sufficient alternative means of training. After it became known that there were plans to sell her abroad the shipowner, Hilmar Reksten of Sjøsanger near Bergen, bought her as patron so as to keep her in Bergen. Reksten decided to modernise the *Statsraad Lehmkuhl* at considerable expense in order to persuade the Government to pay the running costs. Bergens Skoleskib are hoping to be able to start training voyages again in the near future.
As is common in many sail training ships, the poop extends to the mainmast, while a large deckhouse stands aft of the forward mast. The bark carries nine boats and a stocked anchor on either side. The main wheel stands on the poop forward of the charthouse, with the emergency wheel aft of it, close to the stern: both of them are twin wheels. When she was the *Grossherzog Friedrich August* she sported a full-lenght figurehead: now she has tastefully painted scrollwork with the coat-of-arms of Norway and Bergen on her bow and stern. She took part in the Tall Ships Race in 1960, 1964 and 1966.

ex *Bestevaer*

Type: 2-masted topsail schooner
Country: U.S.A.
Owner:
Tabor Academy, Marion, Massachusetts
Year of construction: 1914
Builders: in Amsterdam, Netherlands
Tonnage:
265 tons displacement, 99 tons gross, 82 tons net
Dimensions:

LOA	118 ft
Length hull	93 ft
Length between perpendiculars	88 ft
Breadth extreme	21 ft 9 in
Depth in hold	10 ft 10 in
Depth moulded	16 ft
Draft	10 ft 8 in

Sail area: 10,420 sq ft
Rig:
7 sails. 3 headsails (staysail with boom); foremast: fore course, topsail, gaff sail; mainmast: bermudan sail
Masts and spars:
height of mainmast over deck: 88 ft. Single piece masts, bowsprit with jib-boom
Engine: 175 hp General Motors diesel
Complement: 28
Use: sail training ship

This sailing vessel was built in Amsterdam for the Dutch pilotage authorities as *Lotsenschoner II*. In 1923 she was taken over by the Dutch merchant navy for the training of their officer cadets and her name was changed to *Bestevaer*. The German navy commandeered her in 1939 and used her for their own purposes throughout the war. The schooner was in Russian hands for a short time and then was finally returned to Holland where she passed into private ownership.
In 1950 the *Bestevaer* was fitted out as a yacht never but was never much sailed as such because soon after she was bought by R. C. Allen of R. C. Allen Business Machines in Holland, Michigan, who gave her to the Tabor Academy in Marion, Massachusetts. Renamed *Tabor Boy* she is the fourth ship belonging to the Academy to bear the name.
The Tabor Academy is a college preparatory boarding school for boys and was founded in 1876. It is called after Mount Tabor in Israel, once a famous place of Christian worship, which is believed to be the mountain where the transfiguration of Christ took place. Rowing and sailing have a particular place in the Academy curriculum. During school terms the *Tabor Boy* makes weekend trips along the New England coast in which any of the boys can take part. During the spring and summer holidays the schooner cruises to South Carolina, Florida, the Bermudas or Nassau in the Bahamas.

Lucy Evelyn

Type: 3-masted gaff schooner. Wood

Country: U.S.A.

Owner:
Mr. Nathaniel T. Ewer,
Beach Haven, New Jersey

Location: Beach Haven, New Jersey

Year of construction: 1917

Builders:
Frye, Flynn & Co, Harrington, Maine

Tonnage:
800 tons displacement, 374 tons gross,
307 tons net

Dimensions:
Length hull	140 ft
Breadth extreme	33 ft
Moulded depth	11 ft
Depth in hold	7 ft
Draft	11 ft

Rig:
10 sails. 4 headsails; all masts with
gaff courses and gaff topsails

Masts and spars:
height of mainmast over deck 115 ft
(the topmasts have been taken
down); bowsprit with jib-boom

Engine: no auxiliary

Complement: 5

Use: museum ship

Merchant sailing vessels like the *Lucy Evelyn* were no speedy clippers but were extremely strongly built with a lot of stowage space, which made them very versatile.

In 1917 E. C. Lindsay of Machias, Maine had the schooner built at a cost of $ 60,000 and he remained her owner until 1942. Although the *Lucy Evelyn* later changed hands several times her name was never altered. During her long years of service at sea she was often in distress and almost every disaster than can befall a sailing ship was her lot. One of her main cargoes was sawn timber, which she was carrying when she narrowly escaped total loss during a storm in 1925. Heavy seas caused a seam to leak so severely that she filled and only her cargo kept her afloat. The American coastguard cutter *Tampa* took the damaged vessel in tow to Boston where she was pumped dry and continued her voyage a week later. At that time Machias in Maine was the main departure port for merchant voyages. On the outbreak of the Second World War the demand for shipping space became very pressing, so there were many opportunities even for sailing merchantmen like the *Lucy Evelyn*.

In August 1942 the Lucy Evelyn Shipping Company bought the schooner to trade with the West Indian islands, but after only one trip she was chartered by the U. S. Government. In October 1943 she carried a cargo of sawn timber which was destined for Iceland, but during a storm Captain Barnes had to run for shelter. Sailing into Vineyard Haven she ran onto the breakwater and tore her bottom out on the rocks. That cargo did not reach its destination.

A few months later Dr. Glenn of Oak Bluffs bought the ship in order to resell her to a firm in New Bedford which had trade relations with the Cape Verde Islands. They needed a suitable vessel to carry goods and passengers. The *Lucy Evelyn* was fitted out for this purpose and a deckhouse erected amidships for passengers. Even on her first homeward voyage she was in severe distress when the whole of her steering was carried away by breaking seas. The crew rigged jury lines and continued on their extremely arduous voyage until a coastguard vessel took her in tow and brought her to Norfolk, 63 days out from Dakar.

After repairs had been effected the *Lucy Evelyn* set sail from Norfolk for New Bedford on February 15, 1947, but she ran into a blizzard and again suffered damage. After lengthy attempts at salvage during which numerous warps broke, she was finally towed into New Bedford. She then made a further voyage to the Cape Verde Islands and for some time carried goods between the islands. On her homeward voyage she was yet again surprised by a storm and sprang a leak. As there was no petrol on board to work the mechanical pumps her crew had to pump her by hand all the way back across the Atlantic.

In the meanwhile her owner had run into financial difficulties and the *Lucy Evelyn* was put up for auction in order to provide the money for the crew's wages. The highest bid was $ 500 and she was withdrawn. At the beginning of June 1948 she was bought by Mr. Nathaniel T. Ewer of Beach Haven, New Jersey for $ 1,550. Today the ship is a souvenir shop and tourist attraction in a dry berth at Beach Haven.

Iskra

ex *St Blane*
ex *Vlissingen*

Type: 3-masted gaff schooner

Country: Poland

Owner: Polish Navy

Home port: Gdynia

Year of construction: 1917

Builders: G. Muller, Foxhol, Holland

Tonnage: 500 tons displacement

Dimensions:

LOA	170 ft 8 in
Length hull	135 ft 10 in
Breadth extreme	25 ft 7 in
Draft	11 ft 10 in

Sail area: 7,320 sq ft

Rig:
11 sails. 4 headsails, running squaresail (little used), gaff courses, gaff topsails

Masts and spars:
height of mainmast over deck approx 82 ft. All masts of the same height, each with one topmast. Fore staysail with boom. Hoisting gaffs

Engine:
260 hp Ursus-Nohab diesel engine

Complement: 55 to 60

Use: sail training vessel

The schooner *Vlissingen* belonged originally to the Dutch firm Zeevarts Maatschappij and was registered in Groningen. She carried cargo, mostly in the coastal waters of the Netherlands. After the 1914-18 war she often sailed with cargo to and from London and the south coast of England. In 1925 she was sold to the shipowners A. Kennedy & Son Ltd. of Glasgow and renamed *St. Blane*, still as a sailing merchant-man. In 1927 she was sold to the Polish Government and after a major conversion was used by the Polish Navy as a sail training ship with the new name of *Iskra*, meaning Flash. Two large deck-houses were erected to house part of the crew and for a variety of other purposes.

On the outbreak of war the *Iskra* was in harbour in French North Africa. When the French capitulated she was transferred to Gibraltar and as H.M.S. *Iskra* was supply ship to the British Coastal Forces. She was large-ly unrigged for the purpose, while the major part of her crew returned to Poland to continue to serve under arms. After the war the *Iskra* was given back to Poland and she continued to be used as a school ship.

Seute Deern

ex *Pieter Albrecht Koerts*
ex *Seute Deern*
ex *Bandi* (four-masted schooner)
ex *Elizabeth Bandi*
(four-masted schooner)

Type: bark. Wood

Country: Federal Republic of Germany

Owner:
Hans Richartz, hotel proprietor,
(Heligoland)

Location: Alter Hafen, Bremerhaven

Year of construction: 1919

Builders:
Gulfport Shipbuilding Company,
Gulfport, Mississippi

Tonnage (as a schooner):
767 tons gross, 648 tons net

Dimensions:

Length between perpendiculars	178 ft	6 in
Breadth extreme	36 ft	2 in
Depth in hold	15 ft	

Tonnage (as a bark):
1025 tons displacement, 814 tons
gross, 690 tons net

Dimensions:

LOA	248 ft	5 in
Length between perpendiculars	180 ft	9 in
Breadth extreme	36 ft	5 in
Depth in hold	15 ft	

Sail area: as bark 15,995 sq ft

Rig:
23 sails. 4 headsails, double topsails,
single topgallants, royals. Mizzenmast: double spanker, gaff topsail

Masts and spars:
bowsprit, jib boom, spanker boom
of wood. All others of steel. Fore-
and mainmasts with topmasts

Engine: no auxiliary

Complement:
as a training vessel, approx 30

Use: museum ship and restaurant

This ship was built in 1919 for the Marine Coal Co. of New Orleans as the four-masted schooner *Elisabeth Bandi,* and was mostly used in the timber trade. She was not copper-sheathed and even on her first voyage she sprang a bad leak due to the depredations of teredo. Nor was this her only trouble on that first voyage, for she lost her captain without trace and her crew deserted.

On her return she went into dry-dock but the leaks persisted on later voyages. By 1925 repair costs had become too high and the ship was sold to the firm of Walter E. Reid of Bath, Maine. They resold her in 1931 to the Finnish owner W. Uskanen of Sotkoma who shortened her name to *Bandi* and used her almost exclusively to carry timber to England, the cold Baltic waters soon killing off the teredo. In 1935/6 the *Bandi* was sold to the Finnish shipping company of Yrjänen & Kumpp of Raumo and she continued in the timber trade.

She changed hands again in November 1938 and her new owner J. T. Essberger of Hamburg renamed her *Seute Deern.* She was converted for him into a bark by the Hamburg firm of Blohm & Voss, the job being finished on May 15, 1939, and thereafter was used as a cargo-carrying schoolship. Many alterations were made: a white-painted strake, a figurehead of a girl and 70 tons of fixed ballast were added, shrouds and stays led to the bulwarks and fastened by bottlescrews to chainplates outboard, fo'csle and deckhouse united, the hull sheathed below the waterline. She was equipped with patent anchors that stowed in hawse pipes. A little later on the sail area was increased by lengthening the four topsail yards as well as the two topgallant yards. After a short Baltic trip the *Seute Deern* took her first cargo under the German flag to Finland, but during her return with a load of timber war was declared. The bark took refuge in a Danish harbour and remained there until the end of the war against Poland. During the early years of the Second World War she made short trips in the Baltic carrying salt, timber etc. and was laid up in Stolpmünde or Lübeck during the winters. But the risks attending these voyages became increasingly great and it was decided to operate only in Greifswald Bay.

During these trips Essberger trained cadets for his fleet, the crew consisting always of 10—12 ordinary seamen and 10—12 boys. At the end of September 1944 *Seute Deern* was transferred to Lübeck where she was laying when peace was declared. Her spars and yards were removed then. During the occupation she was used as a temporary guard-house.

In 1946 she was towed to Travemünde where she was rerigged by the Schlichting yard. From 1947—54 she was moored in Hamburg at Ferry No. 7 as a hotel-restaurant. At the beginning of 1954 she was bought by an American of Dutch origin, A. J. Koerts, who gave the ship to Delfzijl, his home town, for use as a youth hostel, renaming her *Pieter Albrecht Koerts.* She was towed there from Hamburg on April 19, 1954. Ten year later, the Emden *restaurateur* E. Hardisty bought the bark to reconvert her to a floating restaurant, and she was towed from Delfzijl to Emden on December 3, 1964. But the plan came to nothing, and the Helgoland hotel owner H. Richartz bought the ship to use her for the same purpose in Bremerhaven. The bark was thoroughly refitted at the Schröder yard in Emden

Sedov

and since June 1966 has lain as a floating restaurant in Bremerhaven under her old name of *Seute Deern*.

ex *Kommodore Johnsen*
ex *Magdalene Vinnen*

Type: four-masted bark. Steel

Country: U.S.S.R.

Owners: probably the Black Sea Fleet

Year of construction: 1921

Builders:
Germania Werft (Friedrich Krupp), Kiel

Tonnage:
5300 tons displacement, 3476 tons gross, 3017 tons net (under the German flag)

Dimensions:
LOA	385 ft	7 in
Length hull	357 ft	8 in
Length between perpendiculars	328 ft	10 in
Breadth extreme	48 ft	
Depth in hold	26 ft	7 in

Rig:
34 sails. 4 headsails, double topsails, double topgallants, royals. Jigger mast: double spanker, gaff topsail

Masts and spars:
height of mainmast over deck	178 ft	10 in
Mainyard	99 ft	9 in
Main royal yard	47 ft	6 in

Fore, main and mizzen masts with topmast. Jigger mast with topmast. Yards interchangeable with each other

Engine: diesel

Complement:
under the German flag, 33 permanent crew plus cadets

Use: sail training ship

Before the First World War the Bremen shipowners F. A. Vinnen owned a fleet of twelve large merchant sailing ships, one of which was the four-masted bark *Magdalene Vinnen I*, ex *Dunstaffnage*, which after the war had to be handed over to Italy as war reparations. The second *Magdalene Vinnen* was ordered soon after the end of the war and built in Kiel as a cargo-carrying schoolship with auxiliary engine. Like most of the four-masted barks of the time she spent the twenties for the most part in the South American nitrate trade. Haber-Bosch's process by which nitrogen was isolated chemically made Europe independent of deliveries of saltpetre from Chile. The large nitrate traders therefore sailed ever more frequently on the Australian grain run.

The *Magdalene Vinnen* was built on the 'three-islands' principle with poop, upper deck and fo'csle. The main wheel is amidships on the upper deck forward of the charthouse, while the emergency steering is under the poop deck with a skylight over it to enable the helmsman to watch the sails. The main deck is steel plate. Hatch No. 3 opens on the upper deck forward of the main wheel, an unusual feature in a three-island type ship, for usually all hatches open on the main deck. The ship has no special ballast-tanks, but the double bottoms can take a total of 345 tons of ballast water in three separate sections. It is possible that there is a different arrangement today now that the ship no longer carries cargo.

In 1936 the *Magdalene Vinnen* was sold to the Norddeutsche Lloyd in Bremen and renamed *Kommodore Johnsen*. From then until the Second World War she sailed only on the grain run from Australia. During a storm in 1937 the ship threatened to sink when her cargo of grain shifted, but the crew succeeded in restoring her to an even keel by shifting the grain before the ships answering her S.O.S. arrived on the scene. Her last long voyage was in 1939 when she left Port Lincoln, Australia on March 26 and reached Queenstown on July 11 after a 107-day passage. During the war the *Kommodore Johnsen* sailed in the Baltic during the summer month and was laid up in the winter in the Flensburger Förde. She was lying there when peace was declared and on allied instructions was taken to Hamburg. In 1949 she was handed over to the British authorities. Later a German and English crew took her to Kiel where she was taken over by the Russians. After lying some time in Swinemünde she was towed away, probably to Odessa, in 1950.

Her present name *Sedov* is that of the Russian polar explorer Georgij J. Sedov (February 20, 1877—March 5, 1914) who attempted to reach the North Pole in 1911 and who died in the ice after wintering there two years.

The *Sedov* and the Russian four-masted bark *Krusenstern* were seen lying in Kronstadt harbour, near Leningrad, in 1964, and at the end of that year the *Sedov* was photographed sailing off the West African coast. Both ships sailed through the English Channel on March 4, 1965. Under the Russian flag the *Sedov* is used purely as a training ship.

125

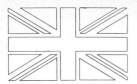

Norlandia

ex *Harald*

Type: 3-masted topsail schooner. Wood

Country: Great Britain

Owner:
Capt. J. S. Gibb, N. Ferriby,
Yorkshire

Home port: Jersey, Channel Islands

Year of construction: 1918

Builders:
C. Tommerup, Hobro, Denmark

Tonnage:
145 tons deadweight, 94.82 tons
gross, 72.22 tons net

Dimensions:

LOA	112 ft	
Length hull	92 ft	
Length between		
perpendiculars	82 ft	9 in
Breadth extreme	21 ft	8 in
Depth in hold	8 ft	5 in
Draft	8 ft	5 in

Rig:
12 sails. 4 headsails; foremast:
double topsails, gaff course; mainmast: gaff course, gaff topsail,
fisherman; mizzen mast: gaff course,
gaff topsail

Masts and spars:
height of mainmast over deck 59 ft;
all masts with topmasts. Bowsprit
with jib-boom

Engine:
228 hp Volvo Penta diesel engine

Complement: 8 (passengers additional)

Use: private charter vessel

This schooner carried cement until 1964
under the name *Harald* for the Danish
Cement Marketing Board of Copenhagen. She was then converted and
fitted out as a charter vessel by her
owner, Captain J. S. Gibb. She voyages
mostly to the Caribbean, and on
one 14-day Atlantic crossing this fast
schooner logged 12 knots.

Vema

ex *Hussar*

Type: 3-masted schooner. Steel

Country: U.S.A.

Owner:
Columbia University, New York.
New York
Lamont Geological Observatory,
Palisades, New York

Home port: New York, New York

Year of construction: 1923

Builders:
Burmeister & Wain, Copenhagen,
Denmark

Tonnage:
743 tons displacement, 533 tons
gross, 234 tons net

Dimensions:
Length hull	202 ft
Length between perpendiculars	185 ft
Breadth extreme	33 ft
Draft (with instrument box in the keel)	18 ft

Sail area:
originally 12,916 sq ft. Sails no
longer set today

Masts:
height of mainmast over deck
originally 131 ft. Now there is only
a bowsprit

Engine: 1000 hp diesel

Use: oceanographic research vessel

The *Vema* was built as the private yacht *Hussar* for Edward F. Hutton. Later Unger Vetlesen bought the ship and renamed her *Vema*. As a yacht she was remarkable for her speed. In 1941 the schooner was commandeered by the U. S. Maritime Commission and converted into a training ship.

At the end of the war the U. S. Government sold the sailing vessel to Captain Louis Kennedy of Nova Scotia who used her for charter work. In 1953 Columbia University acquired her. *Vema* is now the oceanographic research ship of the Lamont Geographical Observatory's students. She no longer goes under sail — only her lower masts and her fine lines are reminders of the former fast sailing vessel. Unfortunately both the eagle figurehead and the bowsprit were removed.

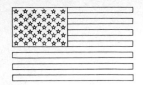

Bowdoin

Type: 2-masted gaff schooner. Wood

Country: U.S.A.

Owner:
Marine Historical Association Inc.,
Mystic, Connecticut

Location:
Camden, Maine

Year of construction:
1921. Launched September 9, 1921

Builders:
Hodgdon Bros., East Boothbay,
Maine. Designed by Admiral
MacMillan

Tonnage: 66 tons gross, 15 tons net

Dimensions:

LOA	91 ft	
Length hull	87 ft	
Length between perpendiculars	75 ft	7 in
Breadth extreme	20 ft	3 in
Depth moulded	9 ft	4 in
Depth in hold	6 ft	6 in
Draft	9 ft	6 in

Sail area: 2,566 sq ft

Rig:
4 sails. 2 headsails (fore staysail with
boom); fore- and mainmasts:
gaff courses

Masts and spars:
height of mainmast over deck 65 ft.
One-piece masts. No bowsprit

Engine:
100 hp Cummins diesel engine
(now removed)

Complement: 13, including instructors

Use: museum ship

Admiral MacMillan planned this schooner when he was stuck fast in the ice 700 miles from the North Pole. She was to be built so strongly that she would be able to withstand the most extreme ice pressures, and, indeed, MacMillan's construction has proved itself in many dangerous situations.

The name *Bowdoin* came from the Bowdoin College in Brunswick, Maine, where MacMillan had taken a degree.

The *Bowdoin* was sailed in Arctic waters every year until the Second World War, always under MacMillan's command. On these voyages there were always scientists aboard working on geographical, geological and mineralogical research. In 1923—4 the *Bowdoin* was trapped in the ice for 320 days in Refuge Harbor, North Greenland. She ran into difficulties on other voyages, too, but thanks to the soundness of her construction she always won through. Usually she wintered in Boothbay Harbor.

During the Second World War the schooner patrolled in Greenland waters with the U.S. Navy, her base then being South Strom Fjord in Greenland. After the war MacMillan was able to resume his expeditions, and in 1947 he made a voyage north with the backing of the Chicago Geographic Society. He reached 79° North, but was stopped by a barrier of ice. Again in 1948 MacMillan, by then 72 years old, led an expedition in which scientists from Bowdoin College and the Cleveland Museum of Natural History took part. Today the *Bowdoin* lies in Mystic Seaport, the most famous maritime museum in Connecticut, as a floating museum. The barrel in the foretop shows her from afar to be a polar explorer.

Carthaginian

ex *Wandia*

Type: bark. Wood

Country: U.S.A.

Owner:
Lahaina Restoration Foundation,
Lahaina (Maui/Hawaii)

Location: Lahaina, Maui, Hawaii

Year of construction: 1921

Builders:
J. Ring-Andersen, Svendborg,
Denmark

Tonnage: 135 tons gross

Dimensions:
LOA	135 ft	
Length hull	105 ft	
Length between		
perpendiculars	92 ft	4 in
Breadth extreme	22 ft	5 in
Depth in hold	12 ft	
Draft (with 50 tons ballast)	9 ft	

Sail area: 7,000 sq ft

Rig:
17 sails. 3 headsails; fore- and
mainmasts: single topsails, single
topgallants, royals; mizzen mast:
spanker, gaff topsail

Masts and spars:
height of mainmast over deck 83 ft;
bowsprit with jib-boom

Engine: 6-cylinder Albin diesel

Complement:
12 to 15 for present sail operation.
Whalers had much bigger crews

Use: museum ship

Her rig, whaling boats and painted ports on a white band give the *Carthaginian* the appearance of a genuine whaler of the 1850's. In fact she was built by J. Ring-Andersen of Svendborg as the three-masted gaff schooner *Wandia* in 1921 for use in the Baltic. She was later sold to Panama without a change of name and in 1964 was still sailing under the Panamanian flag and belonged to Mr. Walter Gillis.

The Mirish Corporation of Hollywood began to shoot the film 'Hawaii' in 1965. They had to convert two ships: the Danish galeas *Grethe* became the brigantine *Thetis* (now *Romance*) and *Wandia* became the whaler *Carthaginian*. While *Thetis* was converted in Holbaek, Denmark, *Wandia* went to San Pedro, California. Under the supervision of Alan Villiers an exact replica of a whaler took shape which sailed perfectly. Shrouds and stays are fastened to chain plates with deadeyes and lanyards, and six whaling boats hang in davits over the bulwarks. Exceptional in the present day and not easy to handle are the deep-cut, single topsails and topgallants.

A Carthaginian warrior was added as figurehead. After filming was over the Lahaina Restoration Foundation bought the ship and since 1966 the *Carthaginian* has been a floating whaling museum in Lahaina.

The whalers from New Bedford and Mystic Seaport had to round Cape Horn in the old days in order to get to their whaling grounds in the Arctic Ocean. Lahaina on Maui was their main station for replenishing fresh water and provisions before continuing further north. In the winter when weather conditions brought whaling to a halt, many ships returned to Lahaina to winter, sailing north again the following year. Some of the whales, too, moved south to their tropical breeding grounds. Now the *Carthaginian* houses a whaling museum in which many of the original tools and fittings are on view, as well as a picture documentary of whaling and parts of the skeletons of whales. Particularly interesting is the complete lower jaw of a sperm whale with no less than 50 mighty teeth.

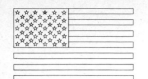

L.A.Dunton

Type: 2-masted gaff schooner. Wood

Country: U.S.A.

Owner:
Marine Historical Association Inc.,
Mystic, Connecticut

Location:
Mystic Seaport, Connecticut

Year of construction:
1921. Launched March 23, 1921

Builders:
Arthur Story, Essex, Massachusetts
Designed by Thomas F. McManus

Tonnage:
approx 175 tons gross (uncertain)

Dimensions:

LOA	158 ft	6 in
Length hull	123 ft	9 in
Length waterline	103 ft	5 in
Breadth extreme	25 ft	
Depth in hold	11 ft	6 in
Draft	14 ft	

Sail area: 8,610 sq ft

Rig:
8 sails. 3 headsails; foremast: gaff
course, gaff topsail; mainmast:
gaff course, gaff topsail, fisherman

Masts:
height of mainmast over deck
121 ft 5 in. Diameter of mainmast
at deck level 18 in. Both masts
with one stay

Engine:
160 hp Fairbanks-Morse diesel

Complement:
22 men as a fishing schooner

Use: museum ship

The fishing schooners of New England are among the most famous sailing vessels of America. Their voyages to the Grand Banks and the extremely tough races home make theirs the most thrilling of the stories of fishing under sail. One of the few survivors of this era is the schooner *L. A. Dunton,* a Gloucester fisherman. The boldness with which these ships were sailed brought ships and men alike the name of Gloucestermen, a title that commanded the highest respect and recognition. The *L. A. Dunton* was named after a famous sailmaker of Boothbay, Maine — Louis A. Dunton. To start with the schooner sailed without an engine, as was common at the time, from her home port of Gloucester, Massachusetts. Ten 13 ft two-man dories were used for fishing and these were nested on deck when not in use. The fishing lines were over 1600 ft long and had 300 baited cod hooks on them. While the dories were out working, only the captain and the cook remained on board. The fish were salted or, more rarely, frozen and stored.

At the end of the twenties the *L. A. Dunton's* spars were removed and a petrol engine installed. She sailed to the Grand Banks under the American flag until 1935 when she was sold to Canada. The number of 'Bankers' gradually dwindled. After a further change in ownership J. B. Foote & Sons bought the ship in 1960 to carry bulk goods in U. S. and Canadian coastal waters. The bowsprit was removed and the mainmast considerably shortened while the petrol engine was replaced by a 160 h. p. diesel. The former schooner was now a motor vessel with auxiliary sails. On October 8, 1963 she was taken over by the Marine Historical Association. She has been restored to her original condition and today belongs to the famous Maritime Museum in Mystic Seaport.

In spite of their purely commercial use, these schooners were constantly improved in design. The speed with which the catch could be sailed home was the main consideration of the builders, some of whom were pure yacht designers. Towards the end the races took on more and more of a sporting character.

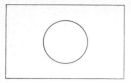

Shintoku Maru

Type:
originally a four-masted barkentine. Today an un-rigged motor vessel. Steel

Country: Japan

Owners:
Nautical College, Kobe. Mercantile Marine

Location: Kobe, island of Hondo

Year of construction:
1923/24. Launched December 9, 1923

Builders: Mitsubishi Shosen Kaisha, Kobe

Tonnage:
as a sailing vessel: 5113 tons displacement (max), 2518.42 tons gross, 1173.18 tons net; as a motor vessel; 5194.81 tons displacement (max), 2792.43 tons gross, 1316.74 tons net

Dimensions: as a sailing vessel

LOA	358 ft
Length hull	298 ft 7 in
Length between perpendiculars	280 ft
Breadth extreme	44 ft
Depth moulded	26 ft 6 in
Draft (max)	22 ft 10 in
LOA (as a motor vessel)	298 ft 7 in

(All other dimensions remain unaltered)

Sail area: originally 29,200 sq ft

Rig:
23 sails. 4 headsails; foremast: double topsails, double topgallants, royal; main, mizzen and jigger sails were, from 1929, subdivided by two standing gaffs; gaff topsails

Masts and spars:
height of mainmast over deck, originally, 167 ft 2 in. All masts in one piece. Fore yard 89 ft 5 in, fore royal yard 48 ft 6 in

Engines:
2625 hp Mitsubishi piston steam engines. Twin screw. Speed under power 10.5 knots

Complement:
as a sailing vessel, 16 officers, 56 crew, 120 cadets
as a motor vessel, 22 officers, 56 crew, 128 cadets

Use: at present laid up

The *Shintoku Maru* joined the four-masted barque *Taisei Maru* as a second sail training ship for the Japanese Government. She should not be confused with the 3,462-ton *Shintoku Maru II*, the motor schoolship belonging to the Kokai Kunrensho (Institute for Seamen's Education) which lies in Tokyo harbour. The motor vessel was built with diesel engines in 1962 and in 1964 took part in 'Operation Sail' in New York as an observer ship.

Strange to say the *Shintoku Maru I* was rigged as a barkentine which rather limited the training of cadets in sail handling, particularly as the giant gaff sails with their massive spars could only be handled with mechanical assistance. For this reason the sails were divided in 1929 and a second standing gaff added.

Shintoku means 'Virtue of knowledge' and symbolises the fact that the cadets can develop and improve their knowledge of many subjects while they are aboard. 'Maru' ist added to almost all Japanese merchant ships' names.

The 106 ft long poop was needed on account of the large number of cadets carried. When under power the ship was steered from the bridge forward of the mainmast, but while under sail the helmsman stood at the large twin wheel on the poop. A total of 507 tons of water ballast could be shipped, 292 in the double bottoms, 111 in the after deep-tank, 66 tons in the forepeak and 38 tons in the afterpeak.

On May 26, 1924 the *Shintoku Maru* sailed on her maiden voyage to San Pedro, California. When she visited Australia in February 1932 she could not get into the inner harbour at Sydney because her masts were too tall to allow her to pass under the giant Sydney Harbour bridge, a bridge which had been built far above the water with a view to allowing even the biggest of ships to enter. During a typhoon in the Pacific on October 24, 1935 she took on a measured angle of heel of 56°. That she was able to ride out this storm with no damage to speak of and only the loss of two of her boats shows that even such large sailing ships with a lot of superstructure could be very stable if the ballast was properly stowed. Training voyages were made to Hawaii, New Zealand, Australia and the U.S.A. During the Second World War the training of young officers continued in Japanese waters, but only under power. In August 1944 the *Shintoku Maru* was unrigged. American aircraft attacked her in May 1945 in a small harbour near Kobe where she caught fire and sank. After being raised she was repaired and converted, and resumed service in May 1947. The major alterations are a lengthened poopdeck which now reaches to a storm deck, and a very striking exposed bridge structure aft of the remaining lower foremast. On December 20, 1962 she was paid off as a schoolship and laid up in Kobe where, on March 16, 1965, she was transferred to the ownership of the Merchant Navy High School. There are plans afoot to preserve the *Shintoku Maru* in Kobe.

Two Shintoku Maru's — *left, as she looked in 1944; above after her conversion in 1947*

Krusenstern

ex *Padua*

Type: 4-masted bark. Steel

Country: U.S.S.R.

Owner:
Ministery of Fisheries, Moscow

Home port: Riga

Year of construction:
1926. Launched June 24, 1926

Builders: J. C. Tecklenborg, Wesermünde

Tonnage:
3545 tons gross, 1162 tons net,
1976 tons deadweight

Dimensions:

LOA	375 ft 6 in
Length between perpendiculars	319 ft 6 in
Breadth extreme	46 ft
Depth moulded	27 ft 10 in
Depth in hold	25 ft 7 in

Sail area: 36,597 sq ft

Rig:
34 sails. 4 headsails, double topsails,
double topgallants, royals.
Jigger mast: double spanker, gaff
topsail

Masts and spars:

height of mainmast over deck	174 ft 10 in
mainyard	95 ft 6 in
main royal yard	47 ft 7 in

fore-, main- and mizzen masts with
topgallant masts, jigger mast with
jigger topmast

Engine:
4-cylinder, 2-stroke diesel of
Russian manufacture

Use: sail training ship

The last cargo-carrying four-masted bark to be built was the *Padua,* which was constructed for the Hamburg ship-owner L. Laeisz in 1926. Although Laeisz had bought back a great number of his ships after the 1914—18 war it was decided to build this noteworthy new vessel. Four-masted barks of about 3,000 tons gross were at that time the most economic merchant sailers. Like most of the Laeisz sailing ships the *Padua* was engaged in the nitrate trade, and then later on the grain run from Australia. At that time she had no motor. The *Padua* was one of the 'three-island' vessels typical of the Laeisz fleet, with the three upper decks connected by catwalks. Special ballast tanks were not built in, but the cellular double bottoms carried 437 tons of water ballast in addition to 16 tons in the afterpeak tank. Laeisz had the ship built as a cargo-carrying schoolship from the start and under his flag the 40 places for boys were always filled. On her maiden voyage the *Padua* took 87 days for the passage from Hamburg to Talca-hualo in Chile, and 94 days for the return from Taltal to Delfzijl. Her record passage was from Hamburg to Port Lincoln, South Australia in 67 days in 1933/4. Although the ship had no auxiliary at the time, her passages between Europe and South America were noticeably consistent. In 1930 the *Padua* lost four men overboard during a severe storm off Cape Horn.

She was laid up in 1932 but with backing from the German Government she set sail again. Her last long voyage under the German flag was in 1938/9 under the command of Captain Boye Richard Petersen who, from 1902 to 1908, had been in command of the five-masted, full-rigged ship *Preussen.* The *Padua* left Bremen on October 15, 1938, reaching Port Lincoln, Australia via Valparaiso on March 8, 1939. She sailed again on April 3, 1939 with a full load of grain, reaching the Clyde on July 8 after a 93-day passage.

Until the end of the war the ship lay in Flensburg. In January 1946 the *Padua* went to Swinemünde and was handed over to Russia. She was renamed after the famous Russian seaman and explorer Adam Johann Ritter von Krusenstern (November 19, 1770—August 24, 1846). The *Krusenstern* was seen in Kronstadt near Leningrad in the summer of 1964 in company with the Russian four-masted bark *Sedov* ex *Kommodore Johnsen.* In February 1965 the two ships sailed through the English Channel together and they were seen in the North Sea the following March. Previously the *Krusenstern* had called at Gibraltar. She sails as a training ship, flying the signal letters EPNZ and is listed in the Leningrad register of ships under No. M-28609.

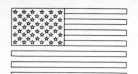

Adventure

Type: 2-masted gaff schooner. Wood

Country: U.S.A.

Owner:
Capt. Jim W. Sharp, Camden, Maine

Home port: Camden, Maine

Year of construction:
1926. Keel laid April, 1926
Launched September 16, 1926

Builders:
James Yard, Essex, Massachusetts
Designed by Thomas F. McManus

Tonnage: 134 tons gross, 62 tons net

Dimensions:

LOA	120 ft	
Length on deck	118 ft	9 in
Length between perpendiculars	106 ft	7 in
Breadth extreme	25 ft	
Depth in hold	11 ft	2 in
Draft	13 ft	6 in

Sail area: 5,166 sq ft

Rig:
4 sails. 2 foresails, gaff sail on each mast

Masts:
height of mainmast over deck 82 ft.
Today there are no longer any topmasts or bowsprit

Engine: no auxiliary

Complement:
5 permanent crew, 37 passengers

Use: private charter vessel

Adventure was one of the most successful bank fishing schooners ever to sail off Newfoundland, and the last to be built by an American yard. Her designer, Thomas F. McManus, put into her the accumulated experience of years in this type of vessel. The unmatched record of this 'Gloucesterman' proved that her design was right. The bank fishing schooners not only had to be strongly built to weather the heavy storms of the North Atlantic, they also had to be capable of getting their perishable cargoes to market at top speed. At the same time the holds had to be of a reasonable size to make the hazardous voyages pay. There are few branches of shipbuilding in which such widely divergent requirements have to be reconciled.

Adventure was initially rigged with topmasts on both masts, which increased the number of her sails by a gaff topsail on each of the fore and main masts to make six in all. The original auxiliary 120 hp diesel engine was later replaced by a 230 hp engine. This was removed in 1953, and today the vessel operates under sail alone.

She was taken on her first fishing voyage on October 16, 1926 by Captain Jeff Thomas. They fished for halibut in summer, haddock in winter, and sailed either from Boston or Gloucester. From the very first trip the schooner landed record catches. On October 3, 1927 she returned with 100,000 lbs of halibut which fetched a price of $ 11,770. She carried 14 dories manned by 28 dorymen. In a heavy gale in December 1933 she was badly damaged and was only kept afloat by great efforts. 40,000 lbs of fish had to be jettisoned.

On March 14, 1934 Captain Thomas died of a heart attack on board, while all the dories were at sea. He was succeeded by Captain Leo Hynes. On March 20, 1943 *Adventure* rammed the auxiliary schooner *Adventure II,* ex *Mary P. Goulart,* in Boston Harbour and sank her on the spot. The crew managed to get away in the dories. Both vessels belonged to the same owner. Captain Hynes usually carried 12 dories and a crew of 27. He had the sail area reduced and a 230 hp diesel engine installed. Under his command the schooner's catches broke all previous records. The best year was 1943 when *Adventure* landed fish to the value of $ 364,000. She was under the command of Captain Hynes for 19 years and earned about $ 3½ million during that time. No other fishing vessel on the whole of the Atlantic coast of America has ever matched that figure. When *Adventure* was awarded the coveted title of 'High Liner' she had deserved it. Her career as a fishing vessel came to an end in 1953. All her crew were then aged 70 or over and it was no longer possible to find younger men to venture on these hazardous fishing trips. Her retirement marked the end of one of the most glorious eras in deep-sea fishing. As though by a miracle *Adventure* survived her retirement. She was bought by Doland P. Hurd who converted her into a passenger-carrying sailing vessel without altering her outward appearance. The former hold was turned into a saloon and luxury cabins, the galley was enlarged, the engine had to come out, but the sail area was once again increased. All the schooner's old gear is still on board today.

Adventure is now owned by Captain Jim W. Sharp, who runs her for charter. Throughout the summer she cruises the waters off Maine. The guests may help with the working of the ship if they wish.

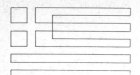

Creole

Type:
  3-masted staysail schooner.
  Composite construction

Country: Greece

Owner: Stavros Niarchos, Athens

Home port: Hamilton, Bermuda

Year of construction:
  1927. Launched October, 1927

Builders:
  Camper & Nicholson Ltd.,
  Southampton & Gosport. Designed
  by Charles E. Nicholson

Tonnage:
  697 tons displacement, 433 tons
  gross, 272 tons net

Dimensions:

LOA	214 ft	
Length hull	189 ft	7 in
Length between		
perpendiculars	166 ft	7 in
Breadth extreme	30 ft	9 in
Depth in hold	16 ft	5 in
Draft	18 ft	4 in

Sail area: 21,958 sq ft (total)

Rig:
  10 sails (total). 3 headsails (spinnaker
  additional); foremast: trysail;
  mainmast: staysail, trysail; mizzen
  mast: bermudan sail

Masts:
  height of mainmast over deck
  129 ft 7 in. All masts in one piece

Engines:
  2 diesels with a total of 3,000 hp

Complement: 25. Cabins for a further 10

Use: private yacht

Creole is one of the largest and most beautiful offshore yachts ever built. She was commissioned by Alex Smith Cochrane, but after completion belonged to Major Maurice Pope and Sir Connop Guthrie.

During the Second World War the schooner was confiscated by the British Admiralty and used as an auxiliary vessel in Scottish waters. After the war *Creole* was taken out of commission and returned to the yard that built her. She remained there until 1951, when the Greek shipowner, Stavros Niarchos, bought her.

Niarchos lent his ship to a British crew for the 1956 Tall Ships Race from Torbay to Lisbon, in which she took part under the British flag.

The hull is constructed of 4 inch (10 cm) teak on steel frames. Below the water-line she is copper sheathed.

Schulschiff Deutschland

Type: full-rigged ship. Steel

Country: Federal Republic of Germany

Owner:
Deutscher Schulschiff Verein (German Sail Training Association), Nautical College, Bremen

Location:
Stephaniebrücke, Kleine Weser, Bremen

Year of construction: 1927, launched June 1927

Builders:
J. C. Tecklenborg, Bremerhaven

Tonnage:
1257 tons gross, 770 tons net

Dimensions:

LOA	282 ft	9 in
Length hull	241 ft	1 in
Length between perpendiculars	221 ft	5 in
Breadth extreme	39 ft	
Depth moulded	20 ft	8 in
Draft	16 ft	5 in

Sail area: 20,450 sq ft

Rig:
25 sails. 3 headsails, double topsails, double topgallants, royals

Masts:
with topgallant masts only

Height of foremast	164 ft
Height of mainmast	170 ft 6 in
Height of mizzen mast	157 ft 6 in

Engine: no auxiliary

Complement:
as a training vessel at sea, 6 officers, doctor, purser, 12 petty officers, approx 120 boys

Use: stationary schoolship

After World War I the Deutsche Schulschiff-Verein, founded in 1900, had to give its sail training ship *Prinzess Eitel Friedrich* to France. To replace her, *Schulschiff Deutschland* was built in 1927. Traditionally, all ships belonging to the association were registered in Oldenburg. The former Grand Duke of Oldenburg had shown a special interest in the association and been one of its staunchest supporters and patrons.
S. S. Deutschland was designed purely as a non-cargo-carrying training vessel. The long poop is characteristic of a large crew and a correspondingly large number of instructors for the boys. The forecastle is joined to the deckhouse. Originally, the hull was painted white. The ship has two through decks and six watertight bulkheads and she carries 560 tons fixed ballast.
Her first long voyage to South America lasted from September 1927 to February 1928. Until 1939 she regularly sailed in the Baltic in summer, to North, Central or South America or to South Africa in the winter. Shortly before the outbreak of the Second World War she returned to the river Weser.
During the winter of 1939/40 she lay at Elsfleth. Training was continued in spite of the war. In April 1940 she moved to the Baltic and the following winter lay at Stettin. In the summer of 1941 short training trips were made in the Baltic, and during the winter of 1941/42 she lay at Lübeck. In 1942 she was fitted at Kiel with degaussing equipment to protect her from magnetic mines. She spent another winter in Lübeck and in 1943 sailed once again in the Baltic. Her last summer trip was in 1944 when she sailed off Bornholm. In the winter of 1944/45 she was once again in Lübeck. Shortly before the end of the war she was turned into a hospital ship, and this saved her from being seized when Germany was occupied. When the patients were finally taken off the ship in June 1945 *S. S. Deutschland* lay idle at Lübeck until August 1946. Then she was towed to Cuxhaven where she was permanently moored to accommodate the Deutsche Minensuchverband (German mine disposal authorities) until January 1, 1948. After that the ship was returned to the Deutsche Schulschiff-Verein. In the summer of 1948 she was moved to Bremen and moored in the Europa-Hafen to serve as a youth hostel. From April 1, 1952 she housed the association's school for apprentices and thus became its stationary schoolship. Since 1956 the ship has been part of the Seemannsschule (Nautical School) at Bremen. There are places for 114 apprentices on board. Training is provided by three officers (Master's Certificate A6), two boatswain instructors and a captain, who is head of the school. The permanent crews of *Gorch Fock II* and the Indonesian barkentine *Dewarutji* were trained on her.

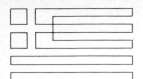

Fantome III

ex *Flying Cloud*

Type: 4-masted, gaff schooner. Steel
Country: Greece
Owners: Olympic Maritime S.A.
Year of construction: 1927
Builders: Ansaldo S.A., Livorno
Tonnage:
1722 tons displacement, 1260 tons gross, 688 tons net

Dimensions:

LOA	262 ft	6 in
Length hull	220 ft	
Length between perpendiculars	181 ft	2 in
Breadth extreme	38 ft	3 in
Draft, aft	17 ft	9 in
fore	13 ft	2 in

Sail area: 18,525 sq ft
Rig:
12 sails. 4 headsails; foremast: gaff sail; main- and mizzen mast: gaff sails and topmast staysails; jigger mast; spanker, gaff topsail, topmast staysail

Masts and spars:
all masts with one topmast. Height of mainmast over designed waterline 128 ft. Gaff sail on fore and mizzen masts, loose-footed

Engines:
2 787 hp Atlas-Polar diesels. Twin screws. Speed under power approx 12 knots

Complement:
34 crew. Cabins for 17 guests

Use: private yacht

From 1939 to 1949 the very large luxury yacht *Fantome III* was one of Seattle's principal sights as she lay in Portage Bay. Her owner at that time was A. E. Guinness, an Englishman, who had sailed her to Vancouver to be present at the opening of Lion's Gate Bridge by the British King and Queen. The outbreak of war prevented him from taking the ship back to Europe.

The yacht was built as *Flying Cloud* for the Duke of Westminster and she was cruised mainly in the Mediterranean. (The Italian barkentine, *Giorgio Cini*, too, was once owned by the Duke of Westminster. The Baroque poop balustrade is a common feature of both ships). In 1932 the new owner, Nelson B. Warden of Philadelphia, had the present more powerful diesel engine installed. In 1937 she sailed once again under British colours. Her home port was Southampton, her owner H. J. P. Bomford.

Late in 1937 A. E. Guinness bought the four-masted schooner and changed her name to *Fantome*. He had two previous ships with the same name. *Fantome II* had been the former bark *Giorgio Cini*, now rigged as a barkentine. He had a large amount of work done to *Fantome III*, especially to the accommodation. Where the Duke of Westminster used to keep a cow for fresh milk he had a saloon built. Her equipment was improved and extended. The furniture, in keeping with the fashion of the period, was made from decorative hard woods. Each of the eight double cabins for guests had its own bathroom installed.

When under power the ship is steered from the bridge aft of the foremast, when under sail by a large wheel from the poop. The bow is decorated by a large golden eagle. A compass is mounted in the ceiling above the owner's berth to enable him to follow the ship's movements and alterations in course.

A. E. Guinness died in Ireland in 1948. From his estate *Fantome III* passed into American hands. In 1956 she was bought by Omiros Maritima SA. She was then refitted by the Howaldt-Werke at Kiel. The major change to her outward appearance was the removal of the deckhouse with its chimney from aft of the mizzen mast.

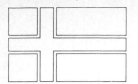

Sørlandet

Type: full-rigged ship. Steel

Country: Norway

Owner:
Sørlandets Seilende Skoleskibs
Institution, Kristiansand S

Home port: Kristiansand S

Year of construction: 1927

Builders: Høivolds Mek Verkstad A/S,
Kristiansand S

Tonnage: 568 tons

Dimensions:

LOA	198 ft	6 in
Length hull	186 ft	5 in
Length between		
perpendiculars	171 ft	7 in
Breadth extreme	31 ft	6 in
Depth in hold	15 ft	9 in

Sail area: 10,765 sq ft

Rig:
26 sails. 4 headsails, double topsails,
single topgallants, royals

Engine:
240 hp Peter MacLarsen diesel.
Until the winter of 1959/60 she
was the last sail training vessel
without an engine

Complement:
captain, 1st, 2nd and 3rd officers,
4 petty officers, doctor, steward,
cook, approx 85 boys

Use: sail training ship

The building of *Sørlandet* was made possible by a foundation by the Norwegian shipowner A. O. T. Skelbred, who made it a condition that she should be a pure sailing ship. In 1933 *Sørlandet* (meaning Southern Land) visited the Chicago World's Fair, via the St. Lawrence River and the Great Lakes. Until the Second World War she made regular training voyages. At the outbreak of the war she was taken over by the Norwegian Navy. At Hörten she was promptly seized by the German occupation forces, who, in 1942, towed her to Kirkenes, where she was used as a military prison.

Having been damaged just above the waterline by an allied bomb, she eventually sank. She was later raised by the Germans and towed to Kristiansand, where she served as submarine depot ship until the end of the war. All her masts were removed for this purpose and a large deckhouse added. At the end of the war the ship was returned to her owners in very poor condition. Repairs and modernisation were started at once. The work that had to be done was extensive and took until 1947. Since then, the ship has once again been used as a training vessel.

Sea-going courses for boys last eleven weeks. The trainees are divided into three groups, and each boy remains in his group throughout the course:

1. Work on deck and aloft, general seamanship
2. Catering
3. Marine engineering

These separate types of training are preceded by a basic course for all boys. Boys have to be 15 years of age to be admitted, except for the engineering course, for which the minimum age is 16. The ship is equipped with modern navigational aids and is electrically heated. Current is provided by a 65 hp and a 14 hp diesel engine. The school also has land-based facilities in a building near *Sørlandet's* winter berth. Training is free for all boys. Training voyages are usually to the North Sea and Baltic.

Participation in the Tall Ships Race: 1956, 1960, 1962, 1964, 1966, 1968.

Juan Sebastian De Elcano

Type: 4-masted topsail schooner. Steel

Country: Spain

Owners:
Spanish Navy. Buque Escuela de Guardias Marinas

Home port: San Fernando, Cadiz

Year of construction:
1927. Launched March, 1927

Builders:
Echevarrieta y Larrinaga, Cadiz. Designed by Camper & Nicholson Ltd., Southampton, England

Tonnage: 3750 tons displacement

Dimensions:
LOA	350 ft	6 in
Length hull	289 ft	2 in
Length between perpendiculars	259 ft	7 in
Breadth extreme	43 ft	
Depth moulded	29 ft	6 in
Draft	22 ft	7 in

Sail area: 26,555 sq ft

Rig:
20 sails. 5 headsails; foremast: foresail, double topsails, single topgallant, gaff sail, gaff topsail; the other masts; gaff sail, gaff topsail, topgallant

Masts and spars:
all masts equal height.
Height above deck 150 ft
Height over waterline 160 ft
Lower masts, bowsprit, foreyard all steel. Topmasts and all other spars of Oregon pine. Lower jigger mast serves as exhaust pipe for the engine. Bowsprit length 63 ft

Engine:
1500 hp Sulzer-Bazán (Cartagena) diesel. Speed under power approx 9 knots

Armament:
4 5.7 cm quick-firing guns

Complement:
243 officers, petty officers and crew, 89 cadets

Use: sail training ship

The schooner was built in 1927 for the then Royal Spanish Navy. She is named after the Spanish seafarer Juan Sebastian de Elcano, who completed the first circumnavigation of the globe in 1526, after Magellan's death. The ship carries the old 'original' schooner rig in which all gaffs are hoisted and lowered, and she uses mast-hoops on the luffs of her sails. Being a training vessel she has a very long poop. On top of the large deckhouse amidships there is a small navigation bridge. Below the boat skids, this deckhouse was later extended out to the ship's sides. This feature, the shorter forecastle and the fact that the square sails are gathered to the centre of the yards, are the things in which *Juan Sebastian De Elcano* differs from her sister-ship *Esmeralda*. The schooner is equipped with the most up-to-date navigation instruments. She carries twelve boats in all: 2 motor lifeboats, 4 rowing lifeboats, 1 captain's launch, 1 officers' launch, 1 cutter, 1 cadet gig, 2 dinghies. There are, furthermore, ten fully-equipped inflatable boats, eight of them lashed to the bulwarks, and several automatically inflatable life-rafts. The figurehead is a female figure bearing a crown.

Training voyages are made to many parts of the world. Participation in the Tall Ships Race: 1964.

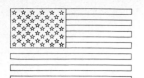

Polynesia

ex *Elk*

Type: 2-masted staysail schooner. Steel

Country: U.S.A.

Owner:
Windjammer Cruises Inc., Miami Beach, Forida. (Capt. Mike Burke)

Home port: Miami Beach, Florida

Year of construction: 1928

Builders: Scott Shipbuilding

Tonnage:
350 tons displacement, 180 tons gross, 108 tons net

Dimensions:

LOA	151 ft	
Length hull	130 ft	7 in
Breadth extreme	25 ft	
Headroom	10 ft	2 in
Draft	16 ft	

Sail area: 10,500 sq ft

Rig:
6 sails. 3 headsails; foremast: fore trysail; mainmast: main staysail, bermudan mainsail

Masts:
height of mainmast over deck 210 ft

Engines: 2 180 hp petrol (gasoline)

Complement:
12 permanent crew. Cabins and facilities for 46 people

Use: private charter vessel

Polynesia ist the former *Elk* built for Sir Oliver Simmonds. She is one of the largest staysail schooners in the world. Like *Yankee Clipper* and *Caribee* she belongs to Windjammer Cruises, an enterprise built up by Capt. Mike Burke after the Second World War. All the year round she sails on ten-day charter cruises from Miami Beach to the Bahamas.

Yankee Clipper

ex *Cressida*

Type: 2-masted staysail schooner. Steel

Country: U.S.A.

Owner:
Windjammer Cruises Inc.,
Miami Beach, Florida,
(Capt. Mike Burke)

Home port:
St. Martin, Leewards Islands, West
Indies

Year of construction: 1927

Builders:
Friedrich Krupp, Germaniawerft,
Kiel, Germany

Tonnage:
600 tons displacement, 350 tons
gross, 180 tons net

Dimensions:

LOA	197 ft
Lenght between perpendiculars	172 ft
Breadth extreme	30 ft
Headroom	10 ft 10 in
Draft	17 ft

Sail area: 10,220 sq ft

Rig:
7 sails. 3 (4) headsails; foremast:
fore-trysail; mainmast: main
staysail, bermudan mainsail

Masts:
height of mainmast over deck 110 ft

Engine: 2 180 hp petrol (gasoline)

Complement:
15 permanent crew. Cabins and
facilities for 70

Use: private charter vessel

For descriptive text of Yankee Clipper
see over

Urania

This large yacht was built as *Cressida* by the Vanderbilt family. She was used primarily as luxury cruiser on long voyages and for voyages of exploration. The idea of the Windjammer Cruises was thought up by Captain Mike Burke of Miami Beach, Florida. After the Second World War he bought three very large yachts, *Cressida, Elk* and *Caribee* (*Elk* has since been renamed *Polynesia*), had them converted to accommodate a large number of passengers and now runs them on charter cruises to the West Indies and the Bahamas all the year round. *Yankee Clipper* sails to the Caribbean (Leeward and Windward Islands) twice a month.

While in port the ship serves as hotel. The charterers may join in the working of the ship.

ex *Tromp*

Type: ketch. Steel

Country: Holland

Owners:
Royal Netherland Navy. Koninklijk Institut voor de Marine, Den Helder

Home port: Den Helder

Year of construction: 1928

Builders:
Haarlemse Scheepbouw Mij., Haarlem, Holland

Tonnage:
38 tons displacement, 50.96 tons gross, 38.36 tons net

Dimensions:

LOA	78 ft	
Length hull	62 ft	4 in
Length between perpendiculars	54 ft	2 in
Breadth extreme	18 ft	
Draft	10 ft	6 in
Freeboard	4 ft	7 in

Sail area:
2,524 sq ft (for windward work). In addition there is a 1,464 sq ft genoa, a 2,800 sq ft spinnaker and a 1,130 sq ft mizzen staysail

Rig:
4 sails (for windward work). 2 headsails, bermudan main and mizzen

Masts:

height of foremast over deck	77 ft
height of mizzen mast over deck	64 ft

Engine: 65 hp diesel

Complement:
17, consisting of 3 officers, 2 seamen, 12 cadets

Use: sail training ship

Hr. Ms. *Urania* was built in 1928 as the schooner yacht *Tromp* for the Dutchman, Nierstrasz. On April 23, 1938 the Koninklijk Instituut voor de Marine (Royal Naval Institute) took her over and renamed her *Urania*. Since then she has served as a training vessel for cadets. During the Second World War the schooner spent some time in Germany and when she was returned was re-rigged as a ketch. She regularly takes part in offshore races, rating as R.O.R.C. Class I. Her sail number in races is HB-31. She took part in Tall Ships Races in 1960, 1962 and 1966.

Dunay

ex *Cristofero Colombo*

Type:
full-rigged ship (frigate). Steel

Country: U.S.S.R.

Owner: believed to be the Russian Navy

Home port: probably Odessa

Year of construction:
1928. Launched April 4, 1928

Builders:
one-time Royal Shipyard at
Castellamare di Stabia

Tonnage: $\dfrac{2787}{3515}$ tons displacement

Dimensions:

LOA	approx 318 ft	4 in
Length hull	257 ft	
Length between perpendiculars	218 ft	3 in
Breadth extreme	48 ft	7 in
Depth moulded	35 ft	6 in
Depth in hold	21 ft	8 in
Draft	approx 21 ft	8 in

Sail area: 20,450 sq ft

Rig:
23 sails. 4 headsails, double topsails,
single topgallants, royals

Masts and spars:
height of mainmast over deck
approx 147 ft 8 in. All masts have
top- and topgallant masts. Bowsprit
with jib-boom and outer jib-boom,
spritsail yard

Engines:
while under the Italian flag,
2 6-cylinder Tosi diesels, plus
2 generators and 2 electric motors.
Twin screws. Speed under power
approx 10 knots

Complement:
while under the Italian flag,
24 officers, 30 petty officers,
210 crew, 150 cadets,
40 servants for the cadets

Use: sail training ship

Until the end of the Second World War the Italian Navy owned two large sail-training ships: *Cristoforo Colombo*, built in 1928, and her sister ship *Amerigo Vespucci*, built in 1930 and still sailing under the Italian flag today. Both ships are like the large 19th century frigates, with high freeboard, stern galleries and two white-painted strakes. These two remarkable ships were the brain-child of Francesco Rotundi, Lt. Colonel in the Naval Engineering Corps. At the end of the war *Cristoforo Colombo* was made part of war reparations to the Soviet Union. For some time afterwards she was known as Z. 18. Later she was re-named *Dunay* (Danube). According to official information from the Italian Navy it is thought that she is used as training ship by the Soviet Navy. On August 5, 1963 *Dunay* was seen at Odessa, and Odessa is likely to be her home port. In 1955 she featured in the Russian colour film 'Othello.'

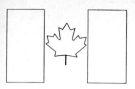

St. Roch

Type: 2-masted gaff schooner. Wood

Country: Canada

Owner:
Maritime Museum, Vancouver,
British Columbia

Location:
Vancouver, British Columbia

Year of construction:
1928. Launched April 1928

Builders:
Burrard Drydock Company Ltd.,
North Vancouver

Tonnage:
323 tons displacement, 193.43 tons
gross, 80.60 tons net

Dimensions:

Length between		
perpendiculars	104 ft	3 in
Breadth extreme	24 ft	9 in
Depth moulded	13 ft	
Depth in hold	10 ft	9 in
Draft (fully equipped)	13 ft	

Sail area: 2,435 sq ft

Rig:
3 sails. 1 headsail. Gaff sail on each
mast

Masts:
height of mainmast over deck
62 ft 3 in

Engine:
in 1928, 150 hp Union diesel;
since 1944, 300 hp

Complement: 9

Use: museum ship

Mention of the name of the Royal Canadian Mounted Police (R.C.M.P.) inevitably conjures up visions of men on horses in red uniforms, wearing wide-brimmed hats and having a world-wide reputation as crack shots and horsemen. Few people know that this police force has a waterborne division. Today it is mainly aircraft and motor vessels which run supply and patrol services to the remote provinces of the Canadian north. Up until a few years ago it used to be *St. Roch* who made headlines with her daring passages to the Arctic.

The schooner, which was built especially for Arctic conditions, was the second ship to negotiate the North-West Passage from west to east (and the third to sail through it at all). She was also the first ship to make the North-West Passage in both directions and the first ship to circumnavigate North America completely (using the Panama Canal). The first of these spectacular voyages started on June 23, 1940 in Vancouver and ended twenty-eight months later, on October 11, 1942, in Dartmouth, Nova Scotia. In 1944 *St. Roch* returned to Vancouver from east to west, equipped with a more powerful engine. On these Arctic trips she was under the command of Staff Sergeant Henry A. Larsen, R.C.M.P.

In 1954 *St. Roch* finally returned to Vancouver. She was presented by the Canadian government to the town of Vancouver to be incorporated in her Maritime Museum. The museum has had a tent-shaped building erected, 118 ft long, 49 ft wide and 59 ft high, to house the distinguished schooner. Her masts and rigging, which had been shortened and altered during the years she was in commission, have been restored to their original state.

St. Roch *in her special building (above), which looks from a distance like a gigantic tent (below)*

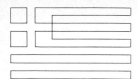

Eugene Eugenides

ex *Flying Clipper*
ex *Sunbeam II*
Type:
3-masted topsail schooner. Steel
Country: Greece
Owner:
National Merchantile Marine
Academy
Home port: Piraeus
Year of construction:
1929. Launched August, 1929
Builders:
W. Denny Bros., Dumbarton.
Designed by G. L. Watson & Co.,
Glasgow
Tonnage:
1300 tons displacement, 634.34 tons
gross, 225.11 tons net
Dimensions:

LOA	195 ft	
Length between perpendiculars	162 ft	9 in
Breadth extreme	30 ft	
Depth moulded	19 ft	8 in
Draft	17 ft	5 in

Sail area: 16,580 sq ft
Rig:
12 sails. 3 headsails; foremast: gaff
sail, single topsail, single topgallant;
mainmast: gaff sail, gaff topsail,
main topmast staysail; mizzen mast:
gaff sail, gaff topsail, mizzen
topmast staysail
Masts and spars:
height of mainmast over deck
131 ft. All masts with one topmast.
Lower masts, bowsprit; steel,
topmasts, yards, gaffs; wood
Engine: 400 hp Polar diesel
Complement:
22 permanent crew, 70 cadets
Use: sail training ship

In 1874 Lord Brassey had the famous yacht *Sunbeam* built for himself. In 1922 she was acquired by Sir Walter Runciman, later Lord Runciman of Shoreston. When she eventually succumbed to old age and had to be scrapped (she was of composite construction), Lord Runciman, in 1929, had his new *Sunbeam II* built in steel. Like her predecessor, she was originally rigged as a three-masted schooner, but before she had even completed her trials the foremast was rigged with a square topsail and topgallant. She remained her owner's private yacht up until the Second World War. At the beginning of the war *Sunbeam II* was taken over by the British Admiralty and used for a variety of purposes until the end of the war. In 1945 she was sold to the Abraham Rydberg Foundation in Stockholm. Contrary to its usual custom it did not rename the ship after its founder, but retained her old name. After having undergone the necessary refit for her new purpose, the former yacht became the foundation's new training vessel, replacing the four-masted bark *Abraham Rydberg,* which had been sold in 1942. Most of her training voyages were in European waters. During a long voyage to the West Indies in 1949 she suffered heavy gale damage aloft.

In 1955 Einar Hansen's Clipper Line in Malmö bought her as training vessel for its cadets and renamed her *Flying Clipper*. After a refit at Karlskrona she took part in the 1956 Tall Ships Race from Torbay to Lisbon. She competed again in 1958. From 1960 she sailed mainly in the Mediterranean. This is also where the film 'Flying Clipper' was shot in 1961/62. In the ten years during which the ship sailed under the flag of the Clipper Line over 200

apprentice deck officers, 60 apprentice engineer officers and 27 apprentices in the catering department were trained on her. On the June 4, 1965 the ship was sold to the Greek Ministry of Mercantile Marine. On the June 12 she sailed to Piraeus under her new name *Eugene Eugenides*. Eugene Eugenides was a Greek shipowner who died in 1954. In his memory his successors made a donation to the fund set up for the training of officer cadets in the Greek Merchant Navy. It was from this fund that the purchase of the training vessel was financed.

The various schools of the Greek Merchant Navy are scattered all over the country. Apprentices join the *Eugene Eugenides* from all these for further training. The syllabus provides courses for deck officers, engineers and wireless operators. Although the ship belongs to the Merchant Navy, training is along strictly military lines. The ship makes a three-months training trip every summer. In winter only short trips are made.

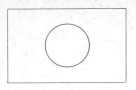

Nippon Maru
and Kaiwo Maru

Type: four-masted barks. Steel

Country: Japan

Owners:
Ministry of Transport. Run by
Kokai-Kunrensho, Tokyo
(Institute for Nautical Training)

Home port: Tokyo

Year of construction: 1930,
launched January 27, 1930

Builders: Kawasaki Yard, Kobe, Hondo

Tonnage:
4343 tons displacement, 2285.77 tons
gross, 743.53 tons net

Dimensions:
LOA	318 ft 4 in
Length hull	306 ft 10 in
Length between	
perpendiculars	260 ft
Breadth extreme	42 ft 6 in
Depth moulded	25 ft 9 in
Depth in hold	17 ft 8 in
Draft	22 ft 7 in

Sail area: 25,800 sq ft

Rig:
32 sails. 3 headsails, double topsails,
double topgallants, royals. Jigger
mast: spanker, gaff topsail

Masts:
height of mainmast over deck 145 ft.
Fore-, main- and mizzen masts each
with one topmast. Jigger mast in
one piece

Engines: 2 600 hp 6-cylinder diesels

Complement:
27 officers, 48 crew, 120 cadets

Use: sail training ship

On account of its geographical location and configuration Japan is largely dependent on sea trade. Inter-island trade, too, is carried on mainly by sea. In order to satisfy the growing demand for officers to man the ever increasing Japanese fleet, two sister-ships, *Nippon Maru* and *Kaiwo Maru*, were built in 1930. Future officers in the Merchant Navy are trained in them. The young men do three years' preliminary training at one of the country's nautical colleges, after which they go to sea for one year in one of the big sailing ships. After a further year on board a motor training vessel they can sit for their second mate's certificate.

Before the war the general training in seamanship, navigation and meteorology was supplemented by instruction in gunnery and torpedo drill. If need be, the young officers could then be taken into the Navy Reserve.

Nearly all ships of the Japanese Merchant Navy have the suffix Maru to their names, which is the general designation of merchant vessels. *Kaiwo* is the King of the Seas in Japanese mythology.

The ship was designed to accommodate a large number of cadets and to admit daylight to all common and lecture rooms. This is why she has a remarkably high freeboard. With a funnel between her main and mizzen masts she rather resembles a sleek passenger liner. Her awning deck is 213 ft long and extends from the stern to between the fore and main masts. Between this and the short forecastle deck, just big enough to handle the ground tackle, only a very short length of main deck is left exposed. The navigation bridge, with wings extending to the ship's sides, is situated on the awning deck between the foremast and the mainmast. There is one steering wheel on the bridge, in the open, and another in the wheelhouse below, where the cadet's sextants are kept. The large deckhouse aft of the mizzen mast contains another chart-room. The big double wheel used for hand steering is situated aft of the jigger mast.

Despite the large crew the ship carries, all cadets sleep in eight-berth cabins. There are no brace or halyard winches whatever on board. All the hard work involved in sail handling is done with the help of six capstans. A donkey boiler provides power for winches, anchor windlass and the steam-operated steering engine.

Besides the six lifeboats slung in davits the ship carries a motor-cutter and a gig, which are lashed down on the awning deck. All of the sails and rigging were supplied by Ramage & Ferguson of Leith. The rig is scaled to suit the smaller stature of the Japanese, which is why the sail area, to European eyes, appears rather small in relation to the hull. 640 tons of copper and 130 tons of reinforced concrete as fixed ballast provide the necessary stability for the high freeboard. Additional ballast is provided by five water-ballast tanks in the double bottom. Before the war both ships sailed regularly, mostly to the Pacific. At the beginning of the war all the yards were taken down and the barks turned into pure motor vessels. As such they continued to operate as training vessels in home waters. After the war they helped with the repatriation of Japanese troops and civilians. Eventually both ships were re-rigged and re-commissioned as training vessels, *Nippon Maru* in 1952, *Kaiwo Maru* in 1955. In 1954

Above right: Nippon Maru, *below:* Kaiwo Maru

Jadran

Nippon Maru visited the United States for the first time. In 1960 she represented her country in New York at the centenary celebrations of the first visit to this city of a Japanese mission. At present, training voyages usually start in May and take in Hawaii and the west coast of the United States. The two ships do not normally sail in company.

Nippon Maru and *Kaiwo Maru* were preceded by the four-masted bark *Taisei Maru,* built in 1904. In 1945, after the end of the war, she struck a mine in Kobe inner harbour and became a total loss. The motor vessel *Otaru Maru,* which is now run as a training vessel by the Kokai Kunrensho continues under her old name. Another former sail training vessel, the four-masted barkentine *Shintoku Maru,* was built in 1924 and in 1943 went aground in a small harbour near Kobe after catching fire during an air raid. After the war she was raised and put back into commission as a training vessel until 1962. The government plans to preserve her as a floating museum. Her name was passed on to one of the institute's motor training vessels which took part in 'Operation Sail' in New York in 1964. The Kokai Kunrensho owns six large training ships in all, two of them sailing vessels.

ex *Marco Polo*
ex *Jadran*

Type:
3-masted topsail schooner. Steel

Country: Yugoslavia

Owners:
Yugoslav Navy. Naval Academy at Bakar

Home port: Bakar

Year of construction:
1931/32. Launched June 25, 1931. Commissioned June 1933

Builders:
H. C. Stülcken Sohn, Hamburg

Tonnage: 700 tons displacement

Dimensions:

LOA	190 ft	4 in
Length hull	157 ft	6 in
Length between perpendiculars	134 ft	6 in
Breadth extreme	29 ft	3 in
Depth moulded	15 ft	
Draft	13 ft	2 in

Sail area: 8,600 sq ft

Rig:
12 sails. 4 headsails; foremast: square topsail (1,600 sq ft), single topsail, single upper topsail, gaff sail. Main- and mizzen masts: gaff sails, gaff topsails

Masts:
height of mainmast over deck 111 ft 6 in

Engine:
375 hp Linke-Hofmann-Buschwerke diesel. Speed under power 8 knots

Complement:
accomodation for commandant, 10 officers, doctor, 20 officer cadets, 8 warrant officers, 16 petty officers, 132 cadet petty officers

Use: sail training ship

Jadran, meaning 'Adriatic,' was built for the Yugoslav Naval Training Association Jadranska Straza. While she was on the stocks, work had to be suspended for 19 months because of the world depression. The ship's main dimensions are similar to those of the former German Navy's *Niobe* which sank in 1932. The main deck aft, where the officers' quarters are, is lowered by 20 inches. The tween-deck extends from the forward bulkhead of the engine room to the stem, while the shelter deck, also a through deck, links up the poop and forecastle, covering the midship-house. Because of the large complement the crew and cadets sleep in hammocks. To give the cadets the opportunity of training with different types of sails the ship was rigged as a topsail schooner. To extend the scope of work in the rigging, the topmasts have been made capable of being hoisted and lowered, and this is done by the cadets themselves. Jadran carries seven boats: 3 sailing cutters, 1 jolly boat, 2 dinghies and 1 gig. Five of these boats are swung out on davits so that they interfere very little with the deck space. The exhaust gases of the engine are led out through the mizzen mast. Because of the rocky bottom of the Adriatic the ground tackle has to be particularly strong.

During the Second World War the ship was confiscated by Italy and sailed under the Italian war flag as *Marco Polo,* but was returned to Yugoslavia at the end of the war. She now cruises mainly in the Mediterranean.

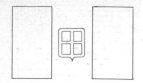

Amerigo Vespucci

Type:
full-rigged ship (frigate). Steel

Country: Italy

Owners:
Italian Navy. Accademia Navale, Livorno

Home port: La Spezia

Year of construction:
1930. Keel laid May 12, 1930.
Launched February 22, 1931

Builders:
one-time Royal Shipyard at
Castellamare di Stabia

Tonnage: $\frac{3550}{4100}$ tons displacement

Dimensions:

LOA	331 ft	6 in
Length hull	269 ft	2 in
Length between perpendiculars	229 ft	9 in
Breadth extreme	50 ft	10 in
Depth moulded	37 ft	
Depth in hold	22 ft	7 in
Draft (amidships)	21 ft	6 in

Sail area: 22,600 sq ft

Rig:
23 sails. 4 headsails, double topsails, single topgallants, royals

Masts and spars:
height of mainmast over deck 151 ft.
All masts with top and topgallant
yards. Bowsprit, jib-boom, outer
jib-boom, spritsail yard

Engines:
Fiat diesel-electric engine, two
diesels, two generators, two electric
motors, with a total hp of 1900.
Single screw. Speed under power
approx. 10.5 knots

Complement:
24 officers, 34 petty officers,
205 crew, 150 cadets, 40 servants for
the cadets

Use: sail training ship

Until the end of the Second World War the Italian Navy owned two large sail training ships, the *Cristoforo Colombo*, built in 1928, and her sister-ship, *Amerigo Vespucci*, built in 1930. *Cristoforo Colombo* was handed over to Russia at the end of the war and is now sailing under the name of *Dunay* (Danube). Both ships were built along the lines of the big 19th century frigates with a very high freeboard, a stern gallery and white-painted strakes. The idea for these two remarkable ships came from Francesco Rotundi, Lt. Colonel in the Naval Engineering Corps. *Amerigo Vespucci* belongs to the *Accademia Navale* in Livorno. In the yard of the academy two square-rigged masts complete with bowsprit and its essential fittings have been erected. They rise to almost their true height above the groundlevel 'main deck.' Guarded by safety nets, the boys practise here before actually going on board. Since she was first put into commission, *Amerigo Vespucci* has always served the training of officer cadets of the Naval Academy. By 1965, besides short cruises in the Mediterranean, she had completed 31 ocean voyages lasting from three to five months, among them four trans-Atlantic runs to North and South America. The ship was built on the lines of a frigate so as to accommodate the maximum number of crew in a given length. There are three through decks above the waterline. She has an unusually high superstructure. Her navigation instruments are of the most up-to-date type. All belaying pins and cleats are marked with small brass plaques bearing the name of each piece of running rigging, because the training programme does not require the cadets to learn these names by heart. The ship's

bow and stern are decorated with intricate gilt carvings, and the figure-head at the bow is a fullheight statue of Amerigo Vespucci. The stern gallery is accessible only from the captain's quarters. The decorations and furnishings of the ward rooms are so elegant that one tends to forget that one is on board a training ship.

Amerigo Vespucci was a Florentine navigator, who made four voyages of exploration to South America between 1497 and 1504. His detailed account of his travels, which were published all over Europe at the time, made him famous and led to the claim that he had discovered America. The German geographer Martin Waldseemüller suggested in 1507 that the newly-discovered land should be called 'America.'

Amerigo Vespucci was modernised in 1951 and again in 1958. Her last extensive refit was in 1964, when new engines were installed. The ship took part in the Tall Ships Race in 1962.

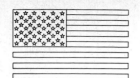

Patria

ex *Angelita*
ex *Sea Cloud*
ex *Hussar II*

Type: 4-masted bark. Steel
Country:
U.S.A. (operated under the Panamanian flag)
Owner:
John Blue, Coral Gable. Florida
Home port: Panama
Year of construction: 1931
Builders:
Friedrich Krupp, Germaniawerft, Kiel, Germany
Tonnage:
3530 tons displacement, 2323 tons gross, 1147 tons net
Dimensions:

LOA	316 ft
Length waterline	253 ft 4 in
Breadth extreme	48 ft 11 in
Depth in hold	24 ft 7 in
Draft	16 ft 5 in

Sail area: 34,000 sq ft
Rig:
31 sails. 4 headsails; fore-, mizzen masts: double topsails, single topgallants, royals; main mast: double topsail, single topgallant, royal, skysail
Jigger mast: double spanker
Masts:
height of mainmast over deck 191 ft 7 in
Engines:
4 8-cylinder Enterprise diesels with a total of 6,000 hp
Complement: crew and guests, 60
Use: private yacht

This remarkable ship is the last four-masted bark ever built and unique in that she was designed and built as a pure yacht. It is for this reason that *Patria,* apart from her rig, looks rather different from a cargo-carrying four-master or a sail training ship. An unusual feature of her rig is the skysail above the main royal. Everything about the ship is designed for elegance and speed, from the fine bow to the broad counter and the pronounced taper of the rig upwards. A large eagle decorates her bow. *Patria,* then *Hussar II,* was built for Edward F. Hutton of New York under the supervision of her first captain, Capt. C. W. Lawson. The luxury of her accommodation was typical of a five-star hotel rather than a sea-going vessel. She cost around $ 1 million to build. Unfortunately her rather clumsy superstructure and short, stumpy funnel are not quite in keeping with the elegant appearance of the rest of the vessel. Several years before the outbreak of the Second World War the ship became the property of the then U.S. Ambassador in Russia, Joseph E. Davies, and was renamed *Sea Cloud.* During his term of office she was moored in Leningrad harbour as a floating palace. When he became Ambassador to Belgium the ship went with him to Antwerp. Later she was moored at Jacksonville, partly unrigged, until, in 1942, J. E. Davies put her at the disposal of the U.S. Coast Guard for an annual fee of one dollar. With her sail area drastically reduced she was run as patrol vessel. At the end of the war Davies asked for her back only just in time to prevent all her sails being transferred to the Danish full-rigged ship *Danmark,* which was also serving in the Coast Guard at the time. Even then he spent close on another $ 1 million on her refit.

Sea Cloud's next owner was General Rafael Trujillo, President of the Dominican Republic. She never became a state vessel, but continued to be used as private yacht, even under Trujillo Jr. She was named *Angelita* after the President's daughter.
In 1963 she was offered for sale at $ 2 million. She was registered in Panama by the Corporation Sea Cruise Inc., a firm of solicitors in Panama, under the name of *Patria,* and an American, John Blue of Florida, became her new owner.
Patria was laid up for a refit with a yard in Naples from the end of 1967 until the middle of 1968, when she made sail again.

Mercator

Type: barkentine. Steel

Country: Belgium

Owner: Association Maritime Belge

Location: Mercator Dock, Ostend

Year of construction:
1932. Handed over April 7, 1932

Builders:
Ramage & Ferguson, Ltd., Leith.
Designed by G. L. Watson & Co.,
Glasgow

Tonnage:
770 tons gross, 159 tons net

Dimensions:

LOA	257 ft	8 in
Length hull	223 ft	2 in
Length between perpendiculars	190 ft	
Breadth extreme	34 ft	9 in
Depth in hold	16 ft	9 in

Sail area: 13,560 sq ft

Rig:
15 sails. 4 headsails; foremast:
double topsails, single topgallant;
main- and mizzen masts: gaff sails,
gaff topsails

Masts:
height of mainmast over keel 128 ft.
Foremast: topsail and topgallant
yards. Main- and mizzen masts
each have one topmast

Engine: 500 hp diesel

Complement:
earlier, when used at sea, approx.
100, of which some 45 were boys

Before *Mercator* was built the Association Maritime Belge, S.S., which was then a private enterprise but with a state-subsidy, ran the sail-training ship *L'Avenir,* a four-masted bark, and also owned a stationary schoolship, the *Comte de Smet Naeyer,* ex-*Linlithgowshire.* When the Belgian Government had the state-owned *Mercator* built, the association losts its subsidy and with it most of its financial backing. Both ships had to be sold. *L'Avenir* joined Gustaf Erikson's merchant fleet at Mariehamn. *Mercator* was originally rigged as topsail schooner with a topmast to the foremast, a square foresail, gaff foresail, single topsail and single topgallant. Her passage from Leith to Ostend was not a success. As a result of grounding she suffered damage aloft and was holed up forward. A Normandy yard subsequently re-rigged her as a barkentine.

During the seven years before the Second World War *Mercator* made voyages to all parts of the world. During one long voyage in 1934/35 she collected several of the famous monolith sculptures from the Easter Islands for Belgian and French museums. In 1936 she went up the Amazon as far as Manaos, which is 750 miles from the mouth of the river. In February 1940 she sailed to the West Indies and South America. On her return she was forced to cut the voyage short off the West African coast because of the war. The cadets returned home on other vessels. For some time afterwards the barkentine was used for hydrographic work. On the January 11, 1943 she was handed over to the British Navy at Boma in what was then the Belgian Congo. As a British Navy vessel she sailed to Freetown (Sierra Leone) where she served as submarine depot ship. She was returned to Belgium in 1948.

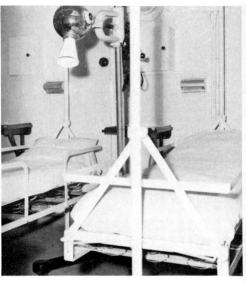

Above: the sickbary, top right, a glimpse of the crew accommodation on board Mercator

After an extensive refit and modernisation *Mercator* sailed on her first post-war voyage on the January 20, 1951. In recognition of the services rendered during the war the Royal Navy contributed to the cost of her refit. The ship was taken over and maintained by the Association Maritime Belge, which was now nationalised.

Since 1961 *Mercator* has been laid up. After a refit in Antwerp she was moored in Ostend as a museum in 1963. In 1967 she visited Rotterdam for three months, returning to Ostend on July 28, 1967. The inner basin of the old Commercial Dock in Ostend has been renamed Mercator Dock in her honour. *Mercator* took part in the Tall Ships Race in 1956, 1958 and 1960.

La Belle Poule and L'Etoile

Type:
2-masted topsail schooner. Wood

Country: France

Owners:
French Navy, Marine Nationale, Ecole Navale, Lanveoc-Poulmic/Brest

Home port: Brest

Year of construction:
1932. Launched January, 1932

Builders:
Chantiers Naval de Normandie, Fecamp

Tonnage: $\frac{227}{275}$ tons displacement

Dimensions:
LOA	123 ft
Length between perpendiculars	83 ft
Breadth extreme	23 ft 7 in
Draft	11 ft 10 in

Sail area: 4,560 sq ft

Rig:
9 sails. 3 foresails (plus flying jib); foremast: gaff sail, single topsail; mainmast: gaff sail, gaff topsail, topmast staysail

Masts:
height of mainmast over the waterline 106 ft 6 in. Both masts have topmasts

Engine:
100 hp Deutz diesel. Speed under power 6 knots

Complement:
3 officers, 5 petty officers, 12 crew, 30 cadets

Use: sail training ships

La Belle Poule is the fourth ship in the French Navy to carry that name. Her predecessors were 18th and 19th century frigates. One of them, the frigate *La Belle Poule*, carried Napoleon's exhumed body to France on the October 15, 1840, twenty years after the emperor's death. The name was originally handed down from a famous pirate ship which rendered valuable services to the Navy in Bordeaux. It was Louis XV in person who decreed that the name should be preserved.

Together with her sister-ship *L'Etoile*, the schooner was built especially as a sail training vessel. They were designed along the lines of the Paimpol schooners which fish off Iceland. The very deep square topsail is furled by roller reefing. The gaffs are lowered. In this way all sails can be handled from the deck. Both lower gaff sails as well as the gaff topsail are bent to the masts by hoops. There are two deckhouses, one aft of the foremast, another aft of the mainmast. The cadets' cap-band bears the inscription 'Ecole des Mousses.'

L'Etoile is the fifteenth ship of the French Navy to bear that name since 1622.

During the Second World War both ships were moored in Portsmouth Harbour. They make regular training voyages, most in European waters, and took part in the Tall Ships Race in 1958 and 1968.

Above La Belle Poule, right L'Etoile,
top right both ships alongside each other

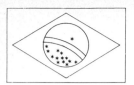

Almirante Saldanha

Type:
formerly 4-masted topsail schooner. Steel. Now unrigged motor vessel

Country: Brazil

Owners: Brazilian Navy

Home port: Rio de Janiero

Year of construction:
1933. Launched December 19, 1933

Builders:
Vickers Armstrong, Barrow-in-Furness

Tonnage:
2815 tons displacement, 3189.2 tons gross, 2079.1 tons net

Dimensions:
LOA (as sailing vessel)	351 ft	2 in
Length hull	304 ft	3 in
Length between perpendiculars	261 ft	6 in
Breadth extreme	51 ft	8 in
Draft	19 ft	9 in

Sail area: 23,500 sq ft

Rig:
19 sails. 4 headsails; foremast: square foresail, double topsails, single topgallant, no gaff sail; mainmast: gaff sail, gaff topsail, staysail, topmast staysail, topgallant staysail. Mizzen and jigger masts: gaff sails, gaff topsails, topgallants

Masts:
lower masts all the same height with one topmast. Height over waterline 183 ft 9 in

Engine: 2100 hp diesel

Complement:
as a training ship 380. Now 243

Use: oceanographic research vessel

Until 1964 the ship was the sail training vessel of the Brazilian Navy, visiting ports all over the world. Since then she has been completely unrigged and turned into a pure motor vessel with a high superstructure. She is now used by the Brazilian Navy as an oceanographic research vessel. *Almirante* (= Admiral) *Saldanha* was named after a Brazilian naval hero.

From the way the foremast was rigged the vessel ought to have been called a barkentine, but since all lower masts were of equal height, she was, strictly speaking, a topsail schooner.

Being the only large sail training ship of the Brazilian Navy, she had to accommodate a large number of cadets. (In fact, during her days as a training vessel she had hammocks slung from every available beam.) There were limits to how long a four-master could be built, so the extra space had to be obtained by giving her a broad beam. This gives the vessel a somewhat unconventional appearance. She cost £ 314,500 to build. There were a number of unusual features about her rig and deck layout. Her foremast carried standing yards, the braces of which were led to the foot of the mainmast (instead of down to the rail, as was normal). She had standing gaffs, the sails being furled to the gaffs and lower masts. Her topmasts were rigged with Jacob's ladders up to the mastheads. There were two tall funnels near the mainmast. The bulwarks were so high that they came level with the forecastle and poop. This gave her the appearance of a flush-decker when viewed from abeam. Narrow gangways along the bulwarks connected the forecastle to the poop as they used to do in the frigates.

Sixteen watertight bulkheads give the *Almirante Saldanha* a considerable safety margin. Even as a sailing ship she has always used stockless anchors. Her graceful bow still bears the old decorative shield with the Southern Cross on it. Her official name is now *Navio Oceanografico Almirante Saldanha.*

Danmark

Type: full-rigged ship. Steel

Country: Denmark

Owner:
Ministry for Trade, Shipping and Industry, Copenhagen

Home port: Copenhagen

Year of construction:
1933. Launched November 19, 1932

Builders:
Nakskov Skibs, Nakskov, Lolland, Denmark. Designed by Aage Larsen

Tonnage:
790 tons gross, 216 tons net, 150 tons deadweight

Dimensions:

LOA	252 ft	9 in
Length hull	210 ft	
Length between perpendiculars	178 ft	10 in
Breadth extreme	32 ft	10 in
Moulded depth	17 ft	
Draft	13 ft	9 in

Sail area: 17,610 sq ft

Rig:
26 sails. 4 headsails, double topsails, single topgallants, royals

Masts and spars:
all masts with top and topgallant masts. Bowsprit with jib-boom. Height of mainmast over waterline 130 ft. Length of mainyard 66 ft

Engine:
486 hp diesel engine. Speed under power 9½ knots

Complement:
80 boys in addition to permanent crew and instructors

Use: sail training ship

After the sale of *Viking* and the tragic loss of *København* the Danish Government, in December 1928, had the state-owned, full-rigged ship *Danmark* built. She was built as a training ship for cadet officers in the Merchant Navy. Originally she had places for 120 boys, but after her modernisation in 1959 the number was reduced to 80. Some of the boys who join her, between 15 and 18 years of age, have previously sailed in the *Georg Stage*. *Danmark* has the lines of a classical merchant sailing vessel. She has no high superstructures, and the two deckhouses are not very conspicuous. She carries stock anchors to port and starboard. Of the six lifeboats slung in davits two have motors. In addition, there are self-inflating lifeboats and life-rafts. The permanent crew members sleep in berths, the boys in hammocks. The ship is equipped with modern navigation instruments like radar, Decca and echo-sounder. She is steered with a double wheel forward of the poop charthouse, while the emergency steering gear is situated aft of the charthouse. Until the Second World War *Danmark* made regular training voyages. In 1939 she sailed to New York to represent her country at the World's Fair. During her stay there the war broke out, and her captain was instructed not to take the risk of sailing her back to Europe. She was moored in Jacksonville, Florida, until America entered the war, when she was put at the disposal of the U.S. Government.
She served as training vessel of the U.S. Coast Guard at New London, Connecticut, until the end of the war, and 5,000 cadets were trained in her during that time.
The experience gained from the use of *Danmark* as a training ship prompted

the U.S.C.G. after the war to commission the ship *Eagle*, ex *Horst Wessel*. There is a commemorative plaque on board the *Danmark* expressing the U.S.C.G.'s appreciation for her services rendered in the war.
On November 13, 1945 the ship returned home to Denmark. The following year she once again had Danish cadets on board. In 1959 she was extensively refitted and modernised and has been sailing regularly since then.
She took part in the Tall Ships Race in 1960, 1964 and 1966.

Tovaristsch

ex *Gorch Fock I*

Type: bark. Steel
Country: U.S.S.R.
Owner: Ministry of Shipping, Moscow
Home port: Odessa
Year of construction:
1933. Launched May 3, 1933
Builders: Blohm & Voss, Hamburg
Tonnage:
1392 tons gross, 230 tons net,
292 tons deadweight, $\frac{1760}{1350}$ tons
displacement
Dimensions:

LOA	269 ft	6 in
Length hull	241 ft	10 in
Length between perpendiculars	203 ft	6 in
Breadth extreme	39 ft	4 in
Depth moulded	24 ft	
Draft	17 ft	

Sail area: 18,400 sq ft
Rig:
23 sails. 4 headsails, double topsails, single topgallants, royals. Jigger mast, lower and upper spanker
Masts:
height of mainmast over deck 98 ft 6 in
Engine: 4-stroke diesel built in 1942
Complement:
as a training ship of the pre-war German Navy, 46 officers and petty officers, 20 crew, 180 cadets
Use: sail training ship

After the German training ship *Niobe* had become a total loss during a thunder squall in the Fehmarn Belt on July 26, 1932, the Germany Navy was faced with the need to build a new training ship. *Gorch Fock* was the first sail training vessel of that type to be built for the Germany Navy. Of her sister-ships only one, the Romanian *Mircea* (built in 1939) is an exact replica. The others, i.e., *Eagle*, ex *Horst Wessel* (1936), *Sagres II*, ex *Albert Leo Schlageter* (1938), and the present *Gorch Fock II* of the German Federal Navy, are identical to the prototype in all respects ecxept that they are 26 ft longer.

The ship was built to Lloyds A1 classification. All decks are steel plated and covered with 60 mm (2¹/₂ inch) teak planking. The forecastle is joined to the forward deckhouse. As *Gorch Fock* the ship carried a stockless anchor on the starboard side and an old-fashioned stock anchor on the port side. Her figurehead in those days was a scroll and plaque bearing the national arms. Except for the arms this has remained unchanged. Only the two subsequent sail training ships of the German Navy carried the large eagle at the bow. Originally, a single spanker and gaff topsail were set on the mizzen mast. Until 1939 *Gorch Fock* used to make long voyages, as well as shorter trips in company with her sister-ships. In May 1945 she was sunk off Stralsund, to be salvaged in 1948 by the Soviet Union. After she had been refitted, which took till 1951, she became the Soviet Navy's training vessel *Tovaristsch II*. (*Tovaristsch I* was the four-masted bark ex *Lauriston*). Her external appearance has hardly changed. The stock anchor on the port side has been replaced by a stockless anchor. Her home port is now Odessa. She is registered in the Leningrad main shipping register under the number M-19053.

Georg Stage

Type: full-rigged ship. Steel

Country: Denmark

Owner:
Georg Stage Foundation,
Copenhagen

Home port: Copenhagen

Year of construction:
1934/35. Commissioned April, 1935

Builders:
Frederikshavn's Vaerft & Flydedok
A/S, Frederikshavn

Tonnage: 298 tons gross, 185 tons net

Dimensions:

Length hull	134 ft	6 in
Length between		
perpendiculars	123 ft	5 in
Breadth extreme	27 ft	6 in
Draft	12 ft	6 in

Sail area: 9,260 sq ft

Rig:
20 sails. 3 headsails, double topsails,
single topgallants, royals

Masts and spars:
all masts with top and topgallant
masts. Lower masts, lower yards
and topsail yards steel. Topmasts
and all other yards and spars wood.
Height of mainmast over waterline
98 ft

Engine:
122 hp diesel. Speed under power
5 knots

Complement:
captain, 1st, 2nd and 3rd officers,
purser, engineer, radio operator,
steward, doctor (only for the voyages
in the Atlantic), 4 petty officers,
80 boys

Use: sail training ship

In 1882 the Danish shipowner Carl Frederik Stage set up a foundation he called 'Georg Stage's Minde' (Georg Stage Memorial Foundation) and presented to it the fully-equipped, full-rigged ship *Georg Stage*. The ship and foundation were named after the shipowner's only son who had died shortly before. In 1935 the ship was replaced by the new and slightly larger *Georg Stage II*. (The old *Georg Stage* still exists under the name *Joseph Conrad*). *Georg Stage II* has two through decks, five watertight bulkheads and a double bottom. She carries 145 tons fixed ballast (iron, stones) and has room for 23 tons of water ballast. She carries 4 lifeboats slung outboard in davits, 1 motorboat and 1 dinghy. Her starboard anchor is of the old-fashioned type, her port anchor stockless. There is an anchor capstan on the forecastle deck. She is equipped with radio-telephone and a 0.1 kw transmitter, which has a 300-mile range. Lighting is by oil-lamps, heating by stoves. The figurehead is a bust of Georg Stage. Foresail, mainsail and spanker can be reefed. Boys for training are selected by the Board each year in February. Most of them pay the equivalent of £ 23 ($ 55) per season. The overall running costs of the ship, at the moment, amount to roughly £ 17,000 per annum. Some of the boys, who are between 15 and 18 years old, receive subsidies. In order to avoid differential treatment as far as possible, all boys are given numbers on board. They sleep in hammocks, which are rolled up and stowed in hammock nettings against the ship's bulwarks during the day. Courses begin annually in April.

Initially, the ship anchors each night; gradually the voyages become longer. By tradition, *Georg Stage* visits ports in Sweden, Norway and Scotland in sum-

mer. By the beginning of September she is normally back in Copenhagen, where the boys unrig her as part of their programme. During the winter the ship is laid up in the Royal Danish Naval Yard in Copenhagen, where she is rerigged the following spring. The boys continue their training on motor vessels the same autumn. About 30 boys transfer to the state-owned training ship *Danmark* each year. *Georg Stage* took part in the Tall Ships Race in 1956, 1960 and 1966.

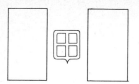

Palinuro

ex *Jean Marc Aline*
ex *Commandant Louis Richard*

Type: barkentine. Steel

Country: Italy

Owners:
Italian Navy. Nautical school at
La Maddalena, Sardinia

Home port: La Maddalena

Year of construction: 1934

Builders:
Anciens Chantiers Dubigeon,
Nantes

Tonnage:
858 tons gross, $\frac{1041}{1341}$ tons

displacement

Dimensions:
LOA	226 ft	2 in
Length between perpendiculars	164 ft	
Breadth extreme	33 ft	
Depth moulded	18 ft	9 in
Draft (fully equipped)		
aft	15 ft	10 in
forward	12 ft	5 in

Sail area: 9,675 sq ft

Rig:
14 sails. 3 headsails; foremast:
double topsails, single topgallant;
main- and mizzen masts: gaff sails,
gaff topsails

Masts:
all masts are pole masts. Height of
foremast 115 ft, mainmast 113 ft,
mizzen mast 98 ft 6 in

Engine: 375 hp diesel

Complement:
5 officers, 12 petty officers, 44 crew,
approx 50 boys

Use: sail training ship

Built in Nantes, the barkentine previously sailed under French colours as *Jean Marc Aline* and *Commandant Louis Richard*. In 1951 the Italian Navy bought her for her good sailing qualities. In 1954 and 1955 she was refitted and modernised to fit her for her role as a training vessel. On July 1, 1955 she was commissioned under her new name of *Palinuro*. (Palinuro was the steersman of the ship of Aeneas when he sailed to Italy.) She trains mainly cadet quartermasters, as well as future port authority staff. The barkentine is equipped with the most up-to-date navigation instruments. Her poop extends forward of the mainmast. She has bow and stern ornaments and a figurehead. Her sides below the deck-line are painted with a white gun-port strake in the manner of the English frigates. Training voyages are normally made in the Mediterranean.

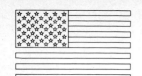

Eagle

ex *Horst Wessel*

Type: bark. Steel

Country: U.S.A.

Owners:
U.S. Coast Guard; Coast Guard Academy New London, Connecticut

Home port:
New London, Connecticut

Year of construction:
1936. Launched June 30, 1936

Builders: Blohm & Voss, Hamburg, Germany

Tonnage:
$\frac{1634}{1816}$ tons displacement

Dimensions:
LOA	294 ft	5 in
Length hull	265 ft	10 in
Breadth extreme	39 ft	4 in
Draft (equipped)	17 ft	
Freeboard	8 ft	10 in

Sail area: 21,345 sq ft

Rig:
22 sails. 4 headsails, double topsails, single topgallants, royals. Mizzen mast: spanker, gaff topsail

Masts and spars:
height of fore- and mainmasts over waterline 150 ft, mizzen mast 131 ft 6 in over waterline. Length of fore- and main yards 78 ft 6 in

Engine:
750 hp 8-cylinder M.A.N. 4 stroke diesel

Complement:
19 officers, 46 crew, approx 180 cadets

Use: sail training ship

In 1790 Alexander Hamilton, the first U.S. Secretary of the Treasury, founded the U.S. Coast Guard by requesting the commissioning of a number of boats whose main task was to prevent smuggling.
Until 1798 the Coast Guard fleet was the only navy the United States had. Today the Coast Guard generally looks after the coast, including all sea marks such as light-houses, light-ships, buoys, etc. In peacetime the Coast Guard is under Treasury control, in war time under the Department of the Navy.
In the Second World War the U.S. Coast Guard used the Danish full-rigged ship *Danmark* as their cadet training ship. *Danmark* had been caught by the war while on a visit in the United States, and was unable to return home. After the war the U.S. Coast Guard, as part of war reparations, took over from Germany the bark *Horst Wessel* and renamed her *Eagle. Horst Wessel* had been built as the German Navy's second sail training ship. She had only been on a few training voyages when the war broke out, but she was used extensively during the early war years for transporting men and supplies in the Baltic. She was handed over to the United States in 1946 in Bremerhaven. Her mizzen mast has been re-rigged to take a single spanker instead of the double one, and she now carries two stockless anchors, whereas *Horst Wessel's* port anchor had been of the old-fashioned kind.
The large eagle which was originally her figurehead has been replaced by a smaller eagle which blends rather better into her bow lines. The original eagle is now in the Marine Museum at Mystic Seaport, Connecticut.
For her main annual voyage from June to August *Eagle* sails to European or Central American waters with the Coast Guard Academy's 1st and 3rd classes on board. Following this, she leaves on another, shorter cruise to the Western Atlantic with the 2nd and 4th classes. All cadets sleep in hammocks. Stability is ensured by 344 tons of pig iron ballast. Three 75-kw diesel generators provide electric power.

Romance

ex *Thetis*
ex *Grethe*

Type: brigantine. Wood

Country: U.S.A.

Owner:
Capt. Arthur M. Kimberly,
Kimberly Cruises, Miami, Florida

Home port: St. Thomas, Virgin Islands

Year of construction: 1936

Builders:
J. Ring-Andersen, Svendborg,
Denmark

Tonnage:
approx 150 tons displacement,
82 tons gross, 64.63 tons net

Dimensions:
LOA	110 ft	
Length hull	86 ft	
Length between perpendiculars	75 ft	
Breadth extreme	21 ft	6 in
Depth in hold	6 ft	
Draft	9 ft	6 in

Sail area: 4,520 sq ft

Rig:
12 sails. 3 headsails; foremast: single topsail, single topgallant, royal; mainmast: gaff sail, gaff topsail, 3 staysails

Masts and spars:
height of mainmast over deck 75 ft. Foremast with top and topgallant masts. Mainmast with one topmast. Bowsprit with jib-boom, spritsail yard

Engine: 119 hp Burmeister & Wain diesel

Complement:
6 permanent crew, 18 passengers

Use: private charter vessel

The schooners and galeasses trading in the Baltic until a few years ago must be counted among the very last merchant sailers. Quite a number of these Baltic traders were built at the famous shipyard of J. Ring-Andersen at Svendborg on the Danish island of Fyn. Smaller fishing vessels are still being built there on classical lines, using oak frames. In 1936 J. Ring-Andersen launched the galeas *Grethe,* built for Hans Pilegaard of Hasle on the island of Bornholm, which was her first home port. In those days she traded mainly in Danish goods such as grain and foodstuffs. Under the same name she was later owned by the shipowner Knud Olsen of Rönne, Bornholm. Rönne became her new home port, and she sailed exclusively in the salt trade between Germany and Denmark. When Knud Olsen moved to Copenhagen, *Grethe* went with him. In 1964 the American film company United Artists bought the galeas and had her converted at Nielsen's shipyard at Holbaek, Denmark. United Artists were then about to make the film 'Hawaii,' after the book of the same title by James A. Michener (Mirish Corporation Production), in which a brigantine called *Thetis* plays an important part. In 1820 the Reverend Abner Hale and his wife had sailed in her from Boston to Hawaii on a missionary expedition.
At Holbaek *Grethe* was turned into an exact copy of the 19th century brigantine. All the work was done according to traditional shipbuilding methods. Shrouds and backstays were set up to outside channels with deadeyes and lanyards. Both cargo hatches remained as they had been. On January 18, 1965 *Thetis II* was launched. She was christened with Danish *aquavit* and Hawaiian *okolehao.* Captain Alan Villiers sailed her from Holbaek to Honolulu in ten weeks, passing through the Panama Canal under full sail. When the shooting of the film was finished, Capt. Arthur M. Kimberly bought *Thetis* in March 1966. He renamed her *Romance* and made St. Thomas in the Virgin Islands her new home port. She now sails for charter throughout the year. She makes three eight-day cruises per month from November to May and one long voyage from June to September. On the short cruises the passengers may take an active part in the handling of the ship if they wish. On the long voyage the crew, apart from the ship's officers, is made up of passengers only, so that they have to take watches. The engine is used as little as possible. The ship is equipped with self-inflating life-rafts, radio-telephone and other modern navigation instruments.

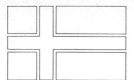

Christian Radich

Type: full-rigged ship. Steel

Country: Norway

Owners:
Østlandets Skoleskib, Oslo.
Merchant navy

Home port: Oslo

Year of construction: 1937

Builders:
Framnaes Mek. Verstad, Sandefjord

Tonnage: 696 tons gross, 207 tons net

Dimensions:
LOA	238 ft
Length hull	205 ft
Length between perpendiculars	174 ft
Breadth extreme	31 ft 10 in
Draft	14 ft 9 in

Sail area: 13,280 sq ft

Rig:
26 sails. 4 headsails, double topsails,
single topgallants, royals

Engine:
450 hp diesel. Speed under power
8 knots

Complement:
captain, 1st, 2nd and 3rd officers,
6 instructors, doctor, engineer,
cook, steward, approx 100 boys

Use: sail training ship

Christian Radich was built to replace the brig *Statsraad Erichsen* which belonged to the Kristiania Schoolship Association. She was named after her patron and sponsor. Before the Second World War the ship made two long voyages, the last of them to the New York World's Fair, together with the Danish ship *Danmark*. Late in 1939 *Christian Radich* left New York, while *Danmark* stayed behind. Back in Norway she joined the Norwegian fleet at the naval base of Hörten, where she was seized by German troops in April 1940.

The Norwegian Government having emphatically declined the German proposal to use the ship in the Baltic as a training vessel under Norwegian administration, she was used as a submarine depot ship until the end of the war. The end of the war found her lying at Flensburg, half-submerged and without masts or yards. After having been raised by the allied forces and returned to her owners, she spent some time at Sandefjord where she was repaired and refitted at a cost of £70,000. Since 1947 *Christian Radich* has been back in com-

mission. In 1956/57 she took part in the film 'Windjammer,' cruising from Oslo to Madeira, Trinidad, New York, Boston and back to Oslo.
In spring 1963 she had an extensive refit at the Naval Yard (Marinens Hovedverft) at Hörten, during which she had a more powerful engine installed, the galley modernised and the standing and running rigging renewed. The ship took part in the Tall Ships Race in 1956, 1958, 1960, 1964, 1966 and 1968.

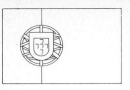

Sagres II

ex *Guanabara*
ex *Albert Leo Schlageter*

Type: bark. Steel

Country: Portugal

Owner: Portuguese Navy

Home port: Alfeite, near Lisbon

Year of construction:
1937. Launched October 30, 1937

Builders: Blohm & Voss, Hamburg

Tonnage: 1869 tons displacement

Dimensions:

LOA	293 ft 8 in
Length hull	266 ft 9 in
Length between perpendiculars	230 ft
Breadth extreme	39 ft 6 in
Draft	24 ft 9 in

Sail area: 19,132 sq ft

Rig:
23 sails. 4 headsails, double topsails, single topgallants, royals. Mizzen mast: double spanker, gaff topsail

Masts:
fore and main masts with one topmast. Mainmast truck approx 146 ft over the waterline

Engine: 750 hp M.A.N. diesel. Speed under power approx 10 knots

Complement:
10 officers, 19 petty officers, 131 crew, approx 90 cadets

Use: sail training ship

The last and most modern sail training vessel to be built for the former German Navy was *Albert Leo Schlageter*, built in 1937. She made only a few voyages before the war broke out. In those days the figurehead was a large eagle. She had a complement of 298.

During the war the bark was damaged by mines. At the end of the war she was taken over by the United States at Bremerhaven. Since they had no use for her, she was passed on to Brazil in 1948, where she was renamed *Guanabara* and used off and on as training vessel by the Brazilian Navy until 1961. In October 1961 she was bought by the Portuguese Navy to replace *Sagres I*, which had been taken out of commission, and was named *Sagres II* after her predecessor.

Sagres is the port in southern Portugal from which the famous Portuguese discoverers sailed. It is closely associated with Henry the Navigator who founded there the first college of navigation. His bust is *Sagres'* figurehead.

Sagres II sailed on her first voyage under the Portuguese flag on April 24, 1962 from Rio de Janeiro, which had been her home port until then, to Lisbon. Her captain was Lt. Cmdr. Henrique Alfonso Silva da Horta. Like her predecessor, *Sagres II* carries a large red cross on all her square sails (not on the spanker, unlike *Sagres I*). She normally makes two training voyages a year.

The ship took part in the Tall Ships Race in 1964.

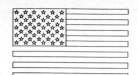

Swift of Ipswich

Type: 2-masted topsail schooner. Wood
Country: U.S.A.
Owner:
Swift Associates Ltd., Santa Barbara, California
Year of construction:
1937. Launched Spring, 1937
Home port: Santa Barbara, California
Builders:
William A. Robinson Inc.,
Ipswich, Massachusetts.
Designed by Howard I. Chapelle
Tonnage:
64 tons displacement (long tons)
Dimensions:
LOA	103 ft	6 in
Length hull	69 ft	4 in
Length between perpendiculars	63 ft	2 in
Breadth extreme	18 ft	4 in
Depth moulded	17 ft	6 in
Depth in hold	13 ft	6 in
Draft	9 ft	

Sail area: 5,702 sq ft
Rig:
7 sails. 3 headsails; foremast: square foresail, square topsail, gaff sail; gaff topsail, gaff sail; mainmast: gaff sail
Masts and spars:
height of mainmast over deck 70 ft 2 in. Bowsprit with jib-boom
Engine:
165 hp General Motors 671 diesel
Complement:
4 permanent crew, 42 passengers, 12 berths
Use: private charter vessel

She was built after the American privateer *Swift*, a brigantine built in 1778 in Baltimore. Her superstructure and ornaments are in keeping with the fashion of the time.
She has stern windows, and her shrouds are set up to outside channels with deadeyes and lanyards. Another typical feature is the large after cabin. Her present figurehead represents Mrs. Robinson, the builder's wife. The schooner is equipped with modern navigation aids such as radio-telephone and echo sounder.
From 1940 to 1958 *Swift of Ipswich* belonged to the actor James Cagney and was moored at Newport Beach opposite his house. Cagney sold her to the Newport Dunes Inc., who in turn sold her to Swift Associates Limited in 1963. She was converted to take passengers and now sails on short cruises in the waters off California.

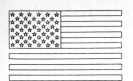

Topaz

ex *Greda*
ex *Dagny*

Type: 2-masted gaff schooner. Wood

Country: U.S.A.

Owner:
Capt. Omer Darr, Boston,
Massachusets

Home port:
registered at Boston, Massachusetts.
Home port will be Honolulu, Hawaii

Year of construction: 1937

Builders:
J. Ring-Andersen, Svendborg,
Denmark

Tonnage:
80 tons gross, 180 tons deadweight

Dimensions:
LOA	119 ft	6 in
Length hull	85 ft	4 in
Breadth extreme	20 ft	8 in
Depth in hold	8 ft	6 in
Draft	6 ft	10 in

Rig: 5 sails. 3 headsails

Masts and spars:
height of mainmast over deck 64 ft
Bowsprit with jib-boom

Engine: 200 hp Alpha diesel

Use: trading in copra in the
South Pacific

The Galeas *Dagny,* built in 1937 by the yard of J. Ring-Andersen at Svendborg, Denmark, was the sister-ship of the galeas *Grethe,* launched by the same yard in 1936. *Dagny* first belonged to an Aalborg shipowner, then, together with *Grethe,* to the shipowner Knud Olsen from Rönne, who moved both ships to Copenhagen. They were mainly engaged in the Baltic trade.

In May 1967 Omer Darr, an American from Boston, bought the galeas and in the same year had her converted into a two-masted schooner with a deckhouse and bridge aft. Initially *Topaz,* as she is now named, is to trade in copra from Tahiti. Later she is to sail from Honolulu.

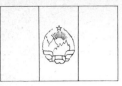

Mircea

Type: bark. Steel.

Country: Romania

Owner:
Mercantile Marine Nautical College, Constanta

Year of construction:
1938; launched September, 1938

Home port: Constanta

Builders: Blohm & Voss, Hamburg

Tonnage:
1760 tons displacement
(fully equipped: 1312 tons gross)

Dimensions:
Length overall	269 ft	6 in
Length hull	242 ft	
Length between perpendiculars	203 ft	6 in
Breadth extreme	39 ft	5 in
Depth moulded	24 ft	
Draft	17 ft	

Sail area: 18,815 sq ft

Rig:
23 sails. 4 headsails, double topsails, single topgallants, royals; mizzenmast: double spanker, gaff topsail

Masts:
height of mainmast over deck 133 ft 3 in, height of mainmast above bottom of keel 161 ft 4 in

Engine: 1100 hp MaK diesel

Complement:
40 officers and petty officers, 50 permanent crew, 120 apprentices

Use: sail training ship

Mircea was built in 1938 for Romania to precisely the same basic design as *Gorch Fock I*, now *Tovaristsch*. She replaced the brig *Mircea I* which had been taken out of commission. The other sailing ships of the former Germany Navy, *Horst Wessel* (1936), now *Eagle,* and *Albert Leo Schlageter* (1938), now *Sagres II,* as well as the present Federal German Navy's training ship *Gorch Fock II* (1958) were built to the same design except that they are 8 metres (26 ft 3 in) longer. It is not widely known that yet another sail-training vessel was built to the same plans by the same shipyard. She was launched in Hamburg but was never officially named. After the end of the war she was taken to Kiel, loaded with gas shells and sunk in the Baltic. This means that, in all, Blohm & Voss built six sail training ships to the same plans. *Mircea* was named after Prince Mircea of Romania who, in the 14th century, won back the Dobrugea region from Turkey after a long struggle and thereby gave Walachia access to the sea. The ship has a splendid bust of the Prince as her figurehead.

In April 1939 she sailed from Hamburg to the port of Constanta on the Black Sea and a little later made her maiden voyage to the Mediterranean. After the war *Mircea* was temporarily in Russian hands but was soon returned to Romania. From January to September 1966 she was laid up with her yard in Hamburg for a refit. This consisted of routine work, new standing and running rigging and sails, installation of a MaK diesel engine, new lifeboats and tenders, completely new accommodation (including new decks, panelling, furniture and washing facilities), replacement and modernisation of navigation aids and electrical installations, and redesigning

of the watertight compartments for increased safety.

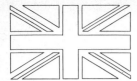

Centurion

ex *Aegean*
ex *Beegie*
ex *Centurion*

Type: brigantine. Wood

Country: Great Britain

Owner: John H. Miller, London

Home port:
Hamble, Hants.
Registered in Gibraltar

Year of construction:
Laid down in 1937, launched 1939/40.
completed 1945/46

Builders:
Langdon Bros., New Smyrna
(Florida)

Tonnage:
43 tons displacement, 26.72 tons gross,
21.82 tons net

Dimensions:
LOA	75 ft	
Length hull	60 ft	
Length between perpendiculars	51 ft	7 in
Breadth extreme	13 ft	6 in
Draft	8 ft	6 in

Sail area: 2583 sq ft

Rig:
8 sails. 4 headsails; foremast: fore
course, topsail; mainmast: gaff main,
gaff topsail

Masts:
height of mainmast above deck
75 ft 5 in

Engine: 60 hp Penta diesel

Complement:
16 as a participant in the S.T.A. race
from Falmouth to The Skaw in 1966

Use: private yacht

In the 1812 war between England and the United States the English captured the fast American customs cutter *Centurion*. She has long disappeared from the oceans of the world, but from her plans, which have been preserved by the British Admiralty, it was possible to build an exact replica. The original *Centurion* carried a gun forward of the foremast, which is why the foremast in the present *Centurion* is positioned further aft than would be normal. Building of *Centurion* was started for the American Major Cyrus Strong in 1937. After the Major's death in 1940 the ship was bought and taken to Annapolis, Maryland, by a person who can no longer be traced. In 1945 Mr. Winfield became her owner. He renamed her *Beegie* and sailed her from Nova Scotia to Bermuda, where she was bought by Mr. A. E. Guinness in 1947. She was registered in the Bermudas and cruised mainly in Bermudan waters. Mr. Guinness sold the ship to Mr. Richard de Graaf Hunter in 1949, who once logged 480 miles in 48 hours on a voyage to Aden. In 1956 the brigantine was bought by the American 'Hod' Fuller. She was registered in the United States under the name of *Aegean* but remained in Greece, being cruised by her owner in the Aegean and Mediterranean. Her present owner is Mr. John Millar of London, who acquired her in 1960 and gave her back her old name, *Centurion*.

For the 1966 Tall Ships Race from Falmouth to The Skaw Mr. Millar lent his ship to the British Sea Cadet Corps. By coming first in Group 2 of Class B the youthful crew gave an impressive demonstration of *Centurion*'s fine sailing qualities.

The two square sails are brailed up to the centre of the yards like curtains instead of being furled all along the yards. This means that, in theory, all sail can be set and taken in from the deck. All sails are of Terylene. *Centurion*'s figurehead is a gilt dolphin; her transom stern is decorated with carvings and bears her name and the initials R.Y.S. (Royal Yacht Squadron).

Seute Deern II

ex *Noona Dan*
ex *Havet*

Type: ketch. Wood.

Country: West Germany

Owner:
Deutscher Schulschiff-Verein,
foundation for training ships

Home port: Oldenburg

Year of construction: 1939

Builders: J. Ring-Andersen, Svendborg

Tonnage:
425 tons displacement,
105.36 tons gross, 25.72 tons net.

Dimensions:
LOA	118 ft	11 in
Length hull	98 ft	1 in
Length between perpendiculars	87 ft	1 in
Breadth extreme	23 ft	5 in
Moulded depth	9 ft	6 in
Depth in hold	7 ft	3 in
Draft	10 ft	

Sail area: 2,960 sq ft

Rig:
7 sails. 3 headsails; main and mizzen
masts: gaff sails and gaff topsails

Masts:
both masts with one topmast; height
of mainmast above waterline 86 ft

Engine:
165 hp Burmeister & Wain
diesel (1961)

Complement:
8 permanent crew, 24 boys,
2 instructors

Use: sail training ship

Seute Deern was built by a Danish yard as the galeas *Havet*. After the war she was bought by the shipping firm of Lauritzen, Copenhagen, who renamed her *Noona Dan*. In 1961 she took a Danish expedition to the Solomon Islands and the Australian coast. Not long after her return the Deutsche Schulschiff-Verein in conjunction with the Stiftung für Ausbildungsschiffe (Schoolship Foundation) bought her and converted her into a ketch-rigged training vessel. In memory of the former training ship *Seute Deern* of the T. Essberger Line she was given the same name.

She was officially commissioned on July 22, 1964. In the summer season she makes weekly cruises from Travemünde to the western Baltic. These are to give boys from the nautical training establishments at Bremen, Bremerhaven, Elsfleth, Hamburg, Leer and Lübeck the opportunity to complement their theoretical training by practical seamanship. Occasionally boys from the *Schulschiff Deutschland* join her for cruises. Her home port is Oldenburg, as is traditional for all ships of the Deutsche Schulschiff-Verein. Her winter quarters are in Bremen. Her training equipment includes radio-telephone, radio direction finder, echo sounder, Decca and radar.

Mariusz Zaruski

Varua

ex *Mloda Gwardia*
ex *General Zaruski*

Type: ketch
Country: Poland
Owners:
Liga Obrony Kraju (National Defence League and League for Sports and Technology)
Home port: Gdansk
Year of construction: 1939
Builders: B. Lund at Ekenäs near Kalmar, Sweden
Tonnage: 71 tons gross
Dimensions:

LOA	91 ft 10 in
Length between perpendiculars	82 ft
Breadth extreme	19 ft
Draft	11 ft 6 in

Sail area: 3337 sq ft
Rig: 7 sails
Engines:
2 150 hp 6 cylinder Albin diesels. Twin screw
Complement: 3 permanent crew, 25 boys
Use: sail training vessel

Type:
brigantine. Composite construction
Country: Tahiti
Owner:
William Albert Robinson, Papeete, Tahiti
Home port: Papeete
Year of construction:
1942; launched March 19, 1942
Builders:
W. A. Robinson, Ipswich, Massachusetts
Tonnage:
50 tons displacement, 43 tons gross, 37 tons net
Dimensions:

LOA	88 ft 6 in
Length hull	69 ft 7 in
Length between perpendiculars	59 ft 10 in
Breadth extreme	16 ft 1 in
Depth in hold	6 ft 7 in
Draft (fully equipped)	7 ft 10 in

Sail area: 1614 sq ft
Rig:
8 sails. 2 headsails; foremast: square foresail, square topsail; mainmast: 3 staysails, bermudan main.
Masts:
height of mainmast above deck approx. 52 ft 6 in
Engine:
47 hp 2 stroke Deutz diesel
Complement: 2 to 5
Use: private yacht

The ketch was built by a Swedish yard for Poland after the plans of the yacht *Kaparen* belonging to the Svenska Seglar Skolan. Since the war prevented delivery to Poland, Sweden used her under the name of *Kryssaren* until 1945, when she was commissioned by Poland as the training ship *General Zaruski*. In 1948 her name was changed to *Mloda Gwardia* (Young Guard), and again, in 1957, to *Mariusz Zaruski*. Mariusz Zaruski was a pioneer of Polish offshore yachting.

During the Second World War W. A. Robinson of Ipswich, Mass., owned a shipyard which built mainly mine-sweepers and landing craft. This is where *Varua* was built, as a side-line, so to speak. The well-known yacht designer Starling Burgess had a hand in her design. *Varua* in Tahitian means 'sprit' or 'soul.' In 1951 Robinson cruised in her all over the Southern Sea, along the west coast of South America as far as Panama. From there he returned to Tahiti via the Galapagos Islands. His book *To the Great Southern Sea* describes the voyage and the ship in detail.

Pollux

Type: bark. Steel

Country: Netherlands

Owners:
 Matrozen-Instituut Amsterdam.
 Merchant navy school for seamen

Location: Oosterdok, Amsterdam

Year of construction:
 1940; launched April, 1940,
 commissioned January, 1941

Builders: Verschure, Amsterdam

Tonnage:
 746.89 tons gross, 272.86 tons net

Dimensions:
Length hull	201 ft	5 in
Breadth extreme	36 ft	2 in
Depth in hold	9 ft	10 in
Draft	2 ft	

Rig:
 upper and lower topsail yards,
 single topgallant yards.

Masts and spars:
 height of mainmast 103 ft 4 in,
 fore and main masts with topmast
 and topgallant mast, mizzen mast
 with one topmast, bowsprit with
 jib-boom 32 ft 10 in

Complement:
 commandeur, bosun, 2 bosun's mates,
 cook, instructor, about 80 boys

Use: stationary schoolship

As early as 1849 a sea training association was founded in Amsterdam with the aim of giving seamen a professional status. The government supported the scheme by providing the retired troop transporter Z. M. *Dordrecht* for the purpose. Several retired Navy vessels have since served in the same way. The last of them was H. M. *Pollux,* who served till 1940. The name of *Pollux* had become so closely connected with the Merchant Navy that any new ship was bound to inherit it. Because of the change in the educational system it later became necessary to rename the whole of the training establishment Lagere Zeevaartschool Pollux (Elementary Seaschool Pollux).

The present *Pollux* was built specially for use as a stationary schoolship. She is, in fact, incapable of going to sea because she is flat-bottomed. At the same time, this feature gives her very generous room below. Her figurehead is a mermaid. The boys, who join the school at 14 to 16 years of age, go through a one-year training period and are then taken over by the various shipping lines. Many of them sit for their mate's certificate. The title of *Commandeur* for the captain is a left-over from the days of the old whalers. In 1943 *Pollux* was towed to Ymuiden by the German occupation forces, where she was completely unrigged and used by the German Navy. 1945 found her in very poor condition. For some time afterwards she was used as living accommodation by the British and Dutch Navy. Late in 1945 she returned to Amsterdam and was taken in hand for an extensive refit by the Stoomvaart Maatschappij "Nederland" (Netherlands Steamship Company).

Albatross

Type:
4-masted motor schooner. Steel
(4-masted bermudan schooner)

Country: Sweden

Owners: Broström, Gothenburg

Home port: Gothenburg

Year of construction:
1942; launched June 18, 1942,
taken over December 7, 1942

Builders: Lindholm Shipyard, Gothenburg

Tonnage:
2215 tons displacement,
1049 tons gross, 556.41 tons net

Dimensions:

LOA	259 ft	1 in
Length hull	235 ft	2 in
Length between perpendiculars	206 ft	7 in
Breadth extreme	37 ft	5 in
Depth in hold	16 ft	5 in
Draft	14 ft	9 in

Sail area:
working rig 9558 sq ft;
in addition running square-sail of
1830 sq ft (not in use at present)

Rig:
a total of 10 sails. 3 headsails
(boomed fore staysail); all masts with
bermudan sails; only main sail and
spanker have booms; main staysail;
jigger staysail

Masts:
all masts of equal height, without
separate topmasts, approx
61 ft above the waterline

Engine:
1200 hp Klöckner-Humboldt-Deutz
diesel. Speed under power 11 knots

Complement:
20 permanent crew of which 7 are
engineers. 20 cadets when operating
as a training vessel

Use: sail training ship (at present laid up)

Built as a cargo-carrying sail-training ship for a private firm in 1942 *Albatross* had to meet the standards of a modern cargo ship in design and construction. Profitability being the main concern, *Albatross* was not given a square rig, which would have needed a large crew, but a schooner rig. She is of the three-island type, with a poop, midship structure and forecastle. The navigating bridge and wheelhouse are on the poop. To make her suitable for northern waters her hull was specially reinforced against ice. Her masts appear slight in relation to her size because of the absence of spreaders and cross-trees. She carries the following boats: 2 lifeboats in davits, 1 workboat, 2 sailing dinghies for the cadets, and 2 self-inflating life-rafts. Her original figurehead, a large albatross, was destroyed when the ship collided with a fishing vessel in 1949 and has never been replaced. There is now a stylised figure of an albatross on either side of the bow.

During most of the war *Albatross* was moored in Gothenburg as a stationary schoolship. On September 16, 1943 she made her first short trip to Karlshamn, returning to Gothenburg on October 13, 1943, where she was once again moored till 1945. On December 18, 1945, after a short trip to England, the schooner sailed for Rio de Janeiro, Buenos Aires, and Cape Town. Before returning home she made three more voyages between South Africa and South America. In 1947 she was chartered by the Gothenburg Academy of Sciences and from July 4, 1947 to October 3, 1948 sailed all the way round the world engaged in oceanographic research. Following this, she returned to normal training service. The training in *Albatross* concentrated mainly on navigation and marine engineering. After a 6-months

course the apprentices transferred to one of the company's cargo liners. After a number of trips in the Mediterranean, *Albatross* frequently carried timber in north European waters. Since 1965 she has been moored in the Lundbyhamn in Gothenburg, and there has been talk of selling her to Peru.

Bel Espoir II

ex *Prince Louis II*
ex *Peder Most*
ex *Nette S.*

Type: 3-masted gaff schooner. Wood

Country: France

Owners:
Les Amis de Jeudi Dimanche, Paris

Home port:
L'Aber Wrac'h, Brittany.
Registered at Brest

Year of construction: 1944

Builders: J. Ring-Andersen, Svendborg

Tonnage: 189 tons gross, 79.75 tons net

Dimensions:
LOA	120 ft
Length hull	90 ft
Breadth extreme	23 ft
Depth in hold	7 ft
Draft	8 ft 6 in

Sail area:
(without running square-sail)
5005 sq ft

Rig:
9 sails. 3 headsails;
foremast: gaff sail, gaff topsail
(running squaresail); mainmast:
gaff sail, gaff topsail; mizzen: spanker

Masts:
all masts with one topmast;
height of mainmast above deck 80 ft

Engine: 170 hp diesel

Complement:
captain, instructor, bosun,
engineer, cook, 24 boys

Use: sail training vessel

In 1944 the Danish shipping company of A.C. Sørensen had the *Nette S.* built, later to be called *Peder Most*. She was designed and equipped for cattle transport. Plying betwen Copenhagen and Hamburg she carried up to 200 head of cattle a trip.

The schooner has a typically Scandinavian round stem and stern. The sails are bent to the masts with hoops. All gaffs are lowered. The tender is not slung over the stern in davits as it frequently seen in craft of this type, but lashed down athwartships between chocks on the quarter deck aft of the wheelhouse.

In 1955 the schooner was bought by the Outward Bound Trust, London, to replace its retired *Prince Louis I*. The main aim of the Outward Bound Trust, which runs a number of schools in Britain, is not to turn boys into seamen but to foster a spirit of comradeship, adaptability and courage among the boys who sail in its training ships.

Before the vessel embarked on her new career she had an interior refit and was given a new deck to fill in the large hatches no longer needed. On June 30, 1955, during a renaming ceremony in Glasgow, H.R.H. The Duke of Edinburgh dedicated her to her new duties under a new flag.

As *Prince Louis II* she belonged to the Outward Bound Moray Sea School at Burghead, Elgin, Scotland. In 1967 she was moved to Dartmouth, Devon, because she had become too small as a training vessel. On May 9, 1968 she was sold to the French enterprise Les Amis De Jeudi-Dimanche, which renamed her *Bel Espoir*.

This French youth organisation is concerned with providing recreational facilities for children. It takes its names from the fact that French school children, in addition to Sunday, have half of Thursday off. The *Bel Espoir* will give children from modest homes the opportunity to enjoy the open sea and see foreign countries. Spain and Sweden are among her chief destinations.

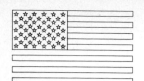

Caribee

Type:
2-masted topsail schooner. Wood

Country: U.S.A.

Owner:
Windjammer Cruises Inc.,
Miami Beach, Florida.
(Capt. Mike Burke)

Home port:
Miami Beach, Florida. Registered in
Ipswich, Massachusets

Year of construction: 1942

Builders:
at Ipswich, Massachusetts. Designed by
Howard I. Chapelle

Tonnage:
250 tons displacement,
180 tons gross, 102 tons net

Dimensions:

LOA	119 ft 8 in
Length between perpendiculars	92 ft 7 in
Breadth extreme	24 ft 3 in
Draft	11 ft 10 in

Sail area: 4,844 sq ft

Rig:
9 sails. 3 headsails; foremast:
running square-sail, single topsail,
fore trysail; mainmast:
main staysail: gaff mainsail,
gaff topsail

Masts:
height of mainmast above deck
98 ft 5 in; both masts have one
topmast

Engine: 180 hp petrol

Complement:
8 permanent crew.
Accommodation for 20 persons

Use: private charter vessel

In the 18th and early 19th century
sleek-hulled, fast sailing craft were frequently used as coastal privateering
vessels and slave traders. Even if they
were of moderate size, these vessels were
fairly heavily armed. The same type of
craft was used by customs authorities
and as coastal patrol vessels (cf. *Centurion*).
In outward appearance and rig *Caribee*
is a faithful copy of one of these craft.
Her painted gun-ports are an attractive
feature. Together with *Yankee Clipper*
and *Polynesia* she belongs to Windjammer Cruises of Miami Beach. Capt.
Mike Burke, the initiator of the scheme,
bought her after the Second World War.
He now sails her on 10-day charter
cruises from Miami Beach to the Bahamas throughout the year.

Henryk Rutkowski

Type: ketch

Country: Poland

Owners: Liga Obrony Kraju (National Defence League and League for Sports and Technology)

Home port: Gdansk

Year of construction: 1944

Builders: built by a German yard

Tonnage: 70 tons gross

Dimensions:
LOA	89 ft	6 in
Length between perpendiculars	76 ft	9 in
Breadth extreme	21 ft	1 in
Draft	8 ft	10 in

Sail area: 2519 sq ft

Rig:
4 sails. 2 headsails, gaff sails

Engine:
135 hp 3-cylinder Burmeister & Wain diesel

Complement: 3 permanent crew, 15 boys

Use: sail training vessel

The ship is named after a popular hero of the Polish Resistance Movement from 1939 to 1945.

Zew Morza

Type: 2-masted gaff schooner

Country: Poland

Owner:
Polski Zwiazek Zeglarski
(Polish Yachting Association)

Home port: Szczecin

Year of construction: 1945

Builders: yard at Dziwnów

Tonnage: 70 tons gross

Dimensions:
LOA	102 ft	8 in
Length between perpendiculars	89 ft	6 in
Breadth extreme	21 ft	
Draft	11 ft	2 in

Sail area: 3875 sq ft

Rig:
7 sails. 3 headsails, gaff sails, gaff topsails

Masts: each with one topmast

Engine:
150 hp 6-cylinder Hercules diesel

Complement:
9 permanent crew, 20 boys

Use: sail training vessel

The schooner was acquired by her present owners in 1949 and fitted out as a training vessel at the shipyard of Stocznia Pólnocna at Gdańsk. *Zew Morza* means 'Call of the Sea'. She is a sister-ship to *Janek Krasicki*.

The rig

The earliest known picture of a sailing vessel is on an Egyptian urn of the 4th century B.C., but it is safe to assume that Man had found means of harnessing the wind for the propulsion of boats and rafts long before that time. The sight of objects driven along by the wind must have given him ideas for making something specific to catch the wind, although it could not have been a sail as we know it today. It was not until the art of weaving cloth was discovered that proper sails could be made. Branches with dense foliage, large leaves, skins or mats must have served the purpose in those early days. These simple craft sailed before the wind, with the wind pushing them from behind, but as time went by, ways were found to trim the sails in such a way that they would pull even with the wind from abeam. The original type of sail was a square sail bent to a yard, a horizontal spar hung from the mast at right angles to the ship's centreline. In this basic position the sail offers the maximum resistance to a following wind. By changing the angle of the sail with the help of braces the ship can be sailed with the wind from over the quarter to forward of the beam. Until somewhere round the middle of the 5th century A.D. all ships had square sails, the Nordic ships as well as the ships of the Egyptian Queen Hatshepsut, the Phoenician dromons, the Greek triremes and the Roman warships and merchantmen. Warships did not usually set sails in battle, however, because they were much faster and more manoeuvrable under oars.

Whereas much is known about the further development of shipbuilding in northern Europe, almost no evidence is left of Mediterranean shipbuilding from the 5th to 9th centuries A.D. It is all the more surprising to find an entirely new type of rig appearing in pictures of Mediterranean vessels after that period: the lateen rig. This undoubtedly originated in the Mediterranean, although nothing is known about who invented it. In contrast with the square sail the lateen sail was triangular and was set on a sloping yard lashed to the mast parallel to the ship's centreline. Thus, the lateen sail was the first fore-and-aft sail, and from it all the other fore-and-aft sails developed. Typical of lateen-rigged vessels are the 15th and 16th-century galleys and galeasses, Columbus' caravels and the large Arab dhows which can still be seen today.

From the 14th century the square sail appeared once again in the Mediterranean. Towards the end of the century vessels in both northern and southern countries combined both rigs by setting square sails on the forward masts and lateen sails on the after masts. At the beginning of the 15th century this type of rig was fairly universal.

In the 16th century Holland became the most important seafaring nation. The best known shipwrights of the time made this the country's Golden Age of shipbuilding. One of the most important innovations to the rig was the adoption of the staysail, which initially was only set as headsail on the forestay but later appeared on the other mast and topmast stays. The jib belongs to this category of sails. From about 1660 onwards all large sailing ships set staysails.

From the middle of the 17th century the gaff rig came into use. In this the sail is bent to a spar the lower end of which rests against the mast, gripping it with a kind of prong, or gaff, hence

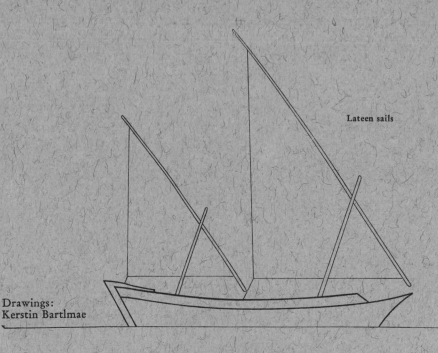

Lateen sails

Drawings:
Kerstin Bartlmae

the name. Fast vessels such as the Dutch
yachts started to set gaff sails as their
main sails as early as the 17th century.
The rig enabled vessels to sail close to the
wind and thus be largely independent of
the wind direction. A large number of
multi-masted merchant schooners of the
19th and early 20th centuries and nearly
all yachts at the beginning of the century
were gaff-rigged. Since then the Bermudan rig has been adopted almost
universally by yachts. However, even
today all the rigs that have ever been
designed are still to be found on the
world's oceans.

As ships grew steadily in size over the
centuries so the sail area, too, had to be
increased. Even in ships with many
masts the square sails eventually became
so large that in heavy weather they
could only be handled with great difficulty. Neither several rows of reef
points nor additional panels of canvas,
called bonnets, which could be laced to
the foot of the sail, solved the problem.
The sail area had to be split up into
more and smaller sails.

Columbus' *Santa Maria* is the first ship
which we know for certain to have set a
main topsail over the mainsail. The
pyramid of sails grew. The topsail was
followed by the topgallant and, in the
second half of the 18th century, by the
royal. Finally, in the 19th century, skysails and the odd moonsail topped the
pyramid, but these were of very little
practical significance. In the 1860s the
topsail was divided into lower and
upper topsails, a little later the topgallant
into lower and upper topgallants. Under
optimum conditions the following sails
could be set on a square-rigged mast:
course (fore, main or mizzen), lower topsail, upper topsail, lower topgallant,
upper topgallant, royal, skysail,
moonsail.

Studding sails have presumably been in
use for as long as staysails. These are
square sails set on small extra spars
extending from the yard-arms. They
were widely used in light winds. Warships, which had to catch every breath of
air to remain manoeuvrable when
attacking or escaping, nearly always set
studding sails.

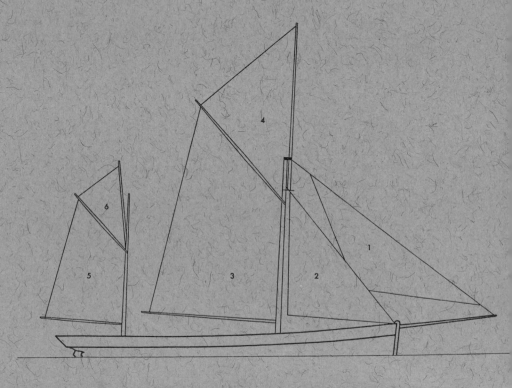

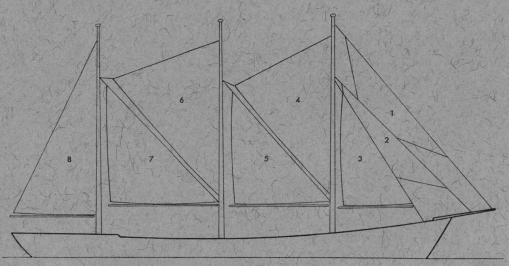

Topsail Schooner
1 Flying jib
2 Outer jib
3 Inner jib
4 Fore staysail
5 Foresail
6 Fore lower topsail
7 Fore upper topsail
8 Main topmast staysail
9 Mainsail
10 Main gaff topsail
11 Mizzen sail
12 Mizzen gaff topsail

Brigantine
1 Flying jib
2 Outer jib
3 Inner jib
4 Fore topmast staysail
5 Fore staysail
6 Foresail
7 Fore lower topsail
8 Fore upper topsail
9 Fore topgallant sail
10 Fore royal
11 Main staysail
12 Lower main topmast staysail
13 Upper main topmast staysail
14 Main topgallant staysail
15 Mainsail
16 Main gaff topsail

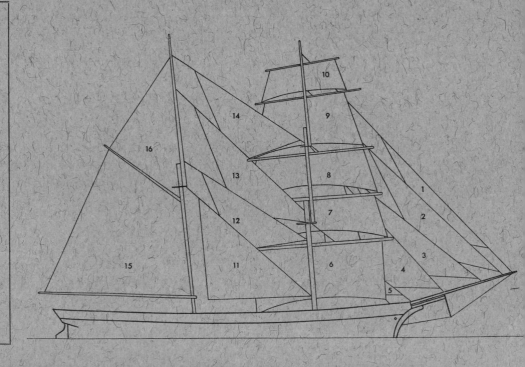

Brig
1 Flying jib
2 Outer jib
3 Inner jib
4 Fore topmast staysail
5 Foresail
6 Fore lower topsail
7 Fore upper topsail
8 Fore topgallant
9 Fore royal
10 Main topmast staysail
11 Main topgallant staysail
12 Main royal staysail
13 Mainsail
14 Main lower topsail
15 Main upper topsail
16 Main topgallant
17 Main royal
18 Trysail

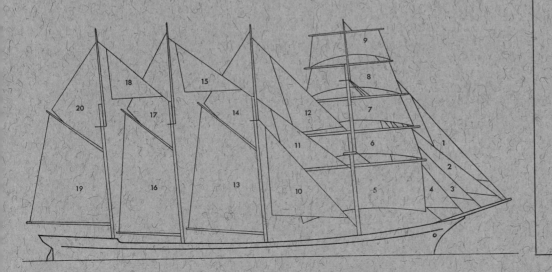

Barkentine
1 Flying jib
2 Outer jib
3 Inner jib
4 Fore topmast staysail
5 Foresail
6 Fore lower topsail
7 Fore upper topsail
8 Fore lower topgallant sail
9 Fore upper topgallant sail
10 Main staysail
11 Main topmast staysail
12 Main topgallant staysail
13 Mainsail
14 Main gaff topsail
15 Mizzen topmast staysail
16 Mizzen sail
17 Mizzen gaff topsail
18 Jigger topmast staysail
19 Spanker
20 Gaff topsail

Bark
 1 Flying jib   2 Outer jib
 3 Inner jib
 4 Fore topmast staysail   5 Foresail
 6 Fore lower topsail
 7 Fore upper topsail
 8 Fore topgallant sail   9 Fore royal
10 Main topmast staysail
11 Main topgallant staysail
12 Main royal staysail   13 Mainsail
14 Main lower topsail
15 Main upper topsail
16 Main topgallant
17 Main royal
18 Mizzen staysail
19 Mizzen topmast staysail
20 Mizzen topgallant staysail
21 Lower spanker   22 Upper spanker
23 Gaff topsail

Full-rigged ship (optimum rig)
 1 Flying jib
 2 Outer jib
 3 Inner jib
 4 Fore topmast staysail
 5 Fore staysail
 6 Foresail
 7 Fore lower topsail
 8 Fore upper topsail
 9 Fore topgallant
10 Fore royal
11 Main staysail
12 Main topmast staysail
13 Main topgallant staysail
14 Main royal staysail
15 Mainsail
16 Main lower topsail
17 Main upper topsail
18 Main topgallant sail
19 Main royal
20 Main skysail
21 Main spencer
22 Lower mizzen topmast staysail
23 Upper mizzen topmast staysail
24 Mizzen topgallant staysail
25 Mizzen royal staysail
26 Crossjack
27 Mizzen lower topsail
28 Mizzen upper topsail
29 Mizzen topgallant sail
30 Mizzen royal
31 Spanker

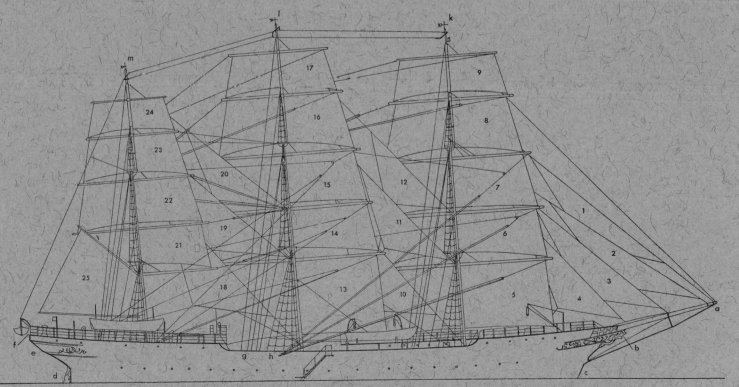

The Portuguese Grand Banks schooners

For the last 500 years, ever since the Portuguese Diogo de Teive discovered the rich fishing grounds of the Grand Banks off Newfoundland, Portuguese fishermen have sailed there after cod. During this long period the ships which carried the fishermen to the area have altered frequently. Wooden ships gave way to steel hulls, square-rigged vessels gave way to schooners, which needed a far smaller crew to work them, and today the greater part of the fleet consists of motor vessels. In 1966 only eight large schooners were still sailing to the Grand Banks and their number is diminishing all the time.

Fishing methods, however, have not changed. It makes no difference whether the fishermen arrive aboard motor vessels or sailing schooners. Now, as then, the fisherman fishes with hand-lines, quite alone in his small 13 ft. dory. Dories are flat-bottomed wooden boats; the word comes from the Portuguese 'pescadores' meaning fishermen.

The demands made on the doryman are exceptional: an excellent sense of direction, great experience of sea and weather, courage and presence of mind are the most important essentials for successful fishing.

As early as the sixteenth century the owners of cod-fishing boats banded together to form a guild responsible for catching and selling fish, as well as caring for the families of the fishermen, above all those lost at sea. Since the 1930's the 'Gremio', the Sociedade Nacional dos Armadores de Bacalháo (National Society of cod-fishing vessel owners) has looked after the interests of the Grand Bank fleet and their relatives in every way. The fishermen themselves come from nearly every coastal town and village in Portugal.

In March the Grand Banks fleet assembles in Lisbon. On the hill of San Jeronimo above Belem roads, where Vasco Da Gama spent his last night, the Archbishop of Mytilene holds a special Mass for the fishermen. The President of the Republic is also present to bid farewell to the fleet. It takes the ships eight or ten days to cover the 1,900 miles to the Grand Banks off Newfoundland. In accordance with age-old tradition, when the helmsman is relieved he is greeted with the words 'Praise be to God and our Lord Jesus Christ, now and for ever' after which the course is given and repeated.

Depths on the Banks average between 10 and 30 fathoms. The cod gather in these shallow waters in great numbers to feed on their plentiful prey, notably schools of herring coming inshore to spawn. Herring, therefore, is the main bait used by the doryman.

The vessels anchor at the fishing grounds. The dories, which are stored in nests of four to six boats on the main deck, are launched and manned by a single fisherman. With the help of a small sail he sets off for a likely spot — often out of sight of the mother ship. He throws out a line about 1300 ft. long on which there are about 400 baited hooks. After one and a half to two hours he pulls in the line and loads the fish into the dory. The boats often spend the whole day out fishing.

There are still about 2,500 dories fishing off Newfoundland today. The Portuguese fleet is supervised and looked after by the auxiliary and hospital ship *Gil Eanes* which provides all necessities. In 1966, as well as the motor vessels, the schooners *Adelia Maria, Argus, Gazela Primeiro, Brites, Creoula, Dom Deniz, José Alberto* and *Santa Maria Manuela* sailed to the Grand Banks. All the ships are equipped with modern navigational aids, electric generators and refrigeration. The fishermen are well looked after and have heated cabins, but such modern amenities only accentuate the contrast with the age-old traditional method of fishing and underline the intrepidity with which these men go about their work. The fleet returns to Portugal in September after six months' fishing, interspersed with short trips to Labrador and Greenland.

For details of nine Portuguese Grand Banks schooners see pages 218 to 221

Janek Krasicki

Type: 2-masted gaff schooner

Country: Poland

Owners:
  Liga Obrony Kraju (National Defense League and League for Sports and Technology)

Home port: Gdansk

Year of construction: 1945

Builders:
  yard at Nowe Warpno (formerly Neuwarp, in the Stettiner Haff)

Tonnage: 70 tons gross

Dimensions:
LOA	102 ft	8 in
Length between perpendiculars	89 ft	6 in
Breadth extreme	21 ft	
Draft	11 ft	2 in

Sail area: 3875 sq ft

Rig:
  7 sails. 3 headsails, gaff sails, gaff topsails

Masts: each with one topmast

Engine: 75 hp 3-cylinder Cullesen diesel

Use: sail training vessel

The schooner was acquired by her present owners in 1950 and refitted as a training vessel by the shipyard of Stocznia Rybacka at Ustka. Janek Krasicki was a popular fighter in the Polish Resistance Movement from 1939 to 1945. The vessel is a sister-ship to *Zew Morza*.

Cruz del Sur

ex *Clorinda*
ex *Cruz del Sur*

Type:
full-rigged ship. Wood.
(Ex 3-masted schooner)

Country: U.S.A.

Owner:
Mills B. Lane Jr., Atlanta, Georgia

Home port: Savannah, Georgia

Year of construction: 1945/47

Builders:
Lacomba Shipbuilding Yard,
Valencia, Spain

Tonnage: approx 200 tons gross

Dimensions:
LOA	171 ft	6 in
Length hull	138 ft	
Length between		
perpendiculars	125 ft	
Breadth extreme	27 ft	
Depth in hold	8 ft	10 in
Draft	11 ft 10 in - 14 ft	9 in

Sail area: 16,146 sq ft

Rig:
25 sails. 4 headsails, double topsails,
single topgallants, royals

Masts and spars:
height of mainmast above deck 105 ft;
topmasts and topgallant masts;
bowsprit with jib-boom

Engine: GMC 671 diesel

Complement:
12 permanent crew, 8 passengers

Use: private yacht

In 1939 the big Spanish shipping company Empresa Nacional Elcano bought the Danish three-masted schooner *Rømø* to use as training vessel for its officer cadets and renamed her *Estrella Polar*. The company's second training ship, the wooden three-masted schooner *Cruz del Sur* was built in 1945—47 at Valencia. Unlike the *Estrella Polar* she carried no cargo. The two schooners sailed as the company's training ships for many years. Later the *Cruz del Sur* was sold to Portugal, who in turn sold her to the American millionaire Huntington Hartford of New York. He sailed her to Nassau in the Bahamas, where she lay for some time without being put to any particular use.

In 1963 and 1964 the 20th Century Fox film company made preparations for filming Richard Hughes' novel *A High Wind In Jamaica,* written in 1929. This is the story of six children from Jamaica who are sent to school to England in the sailing ship *Clorinda*. On the way the ship is attacked by pirates, the crew is killed and the children are taken as hostages. But they contrive to outwit the pirates and return home safely.

Thus, in 1964, *Cruz del Sur* was converted into a barkentine by Merrill-Stevens, Miami, Florida, renamed *Clorinda,* and got ready for shooting. After work on the film was finished she spent nine months lying idle at the end of her chain in Kingston, Jamaica, having been impounded by the Cuban Government. In September 1965 the President of the Citizens and Southern National Bank in Atlanta, Georgia, Mills B. Lane Jr., bought the barkentine. After a hazardous trip in tow via Fernandina, Florida, she safely reached the harbour of Savannah, Georgia. Once again named *Cruz del Sur,* the barkentine was re-rigged as a full-rigged ship by a Savan-

nah shipyard during 1965/66. In the course of this refit she had new masts, topmasts, yards, standing and running rigging. Her owner now cruises her as a luxury pleasure yacht. When moored she is a major tourist attraction.

Falken
and Gladan

Type: 2-masted gaff schooners. Steel
Country: Sweden
Owners: Royal Swedish Navy
Home port: Karlskrona
Year of construction:
1946 (*Falken*), 1947 (*Gladan*)
Builders: naval shipyard, Stockholm
Tonnage: 220 tons displacement
Dimensions:
LOA	128 ft 11 in
Length hull	112 ft 10 in
Length between	
perpendiculars	92 ft 10 in
Breadth extreme	23 ft 7 in
Draft	13 ft 9 in

Sail area: 5586 sq ft (working rig).
In addition there is a fisherman's
staysail of 1044 sq ft and a running
square sail of 936 sq ft
Rig:
a total of 9 sails. 3 headsails: fore
and main masts: gaff sails, gaff
topsails; running squaresail,
main fisherman's staysail
Masts:
both masts have one topmast;
height of mainmast above waterline
103 ft
Engine:
128 hp 6-cyliner Scania-Vabis diesel
Complement:
15 permanent crew, of which three
or four are officers, 38 boys
Use: sail training ships

Together with her sister-ship *Gladan*
(= kite), *Falken* (= falcon) was built
by the Swedish Navy as replacement for
the full-rigged ships *Jarramas* and *Najaden*. For six months in 1952 *Falken*
was on charter as training ship to the
Rydberg Foundation. In both ships the
galley is in the forward deckhouse, the
officers' mess in the after deckhouse.
Boys sleep in both berths and hammocks. The gaffs are lowered for
handing sail. Stability is ensured by 60
tons of permanent ballast. *Falken* trains
officer cadets of both the Navy and
Mercantile Marine. She cruises mainly
in the North Sea and the Baltic.
Participation in Tall Ships Races: *Falken*
1956 and 1968, *Gladan* 1956, 1960
and 1968.

Right: Gladan, *far right:* Falken

The Portuguese Grand Banks schooners

The Portuguese Grand Banks schooners have a long tradition. For 500 years they have been sailing to the banks off Newfoundland to catch cod. Their story is told in more detail on page 212.

In 1966 eight schooners were still sailing to the Grand Banks: *Gazela Primeiro* and *José Alberto*, *Creoula II* and *Brites*, *Santa Maria Manuela* and *Argus*, *Dom Deniz* and *Adelia Maria*.

All these ships are equipped with up-to-date navigation instruments, electric generators and refrigeration. The crew's quarters are heated.

Hortense belonged to the fleet until a short while ago, but at the time of going to press negotiations are in progress with the Outward Bound Trust in London who are considering her acquisition as a schoolship to replace the schooner ex *Prince Louis II*.

Gazela Primeiro

Type: barkentine (topsail schooner). Wood
Country: Portugal
Owners: Parceria Geral de Pescarias, Lisbon. Fishing vessel
Home port: Lisbon
Year of construction: 1883
Builders: at Cacilhas
Tonnage: 324 tons gross, 221 tons net. Fish hold capacity 5193 quintals = 701,053 lbs
Dimensions:

Length hull	135 ft
Breadth extreme	26 ft 7 in
Depth in hold	16 ft 5 in

Rig: 13 sails. 4 headsails; foremast: jib, upper and lower topsails, single topgallant, gaff foresail; mainmast: gaff topsail. Hoisting gaffs
Masts and spars: foremast equipped with topmast and topgallant mast, main and mizzen masts with one topmast each. Height of foremast over deck 93 ft 4 in, Height of mizzenmast over deck 91 ft
Engine: 180 hp Benz diesel
Complement: 42 men. 31 dories carried

José Alberto

Type: 4-masted gaff schooner. Steel
Country: Portugal
Owner: Sociedade de Pesca Oceana Lda., Figueira da Foz. Fishing vessel
Home port: Figueira da Foz
Year of construction: 1923
Builders: at Marstal, on the island of Ärö, Denmark
Tonnage: 687 tons gross, 443 tons net. Fish capacity 11,061 quintals = 1,463,370 lbs
Dimensions:

Length hull	193 ft 6 in
Breadth extreme	32 ft 10 in
Depth in hold	13 ft 2 in

Rig: 8 sails. 4 headsails. Hoisting gaffs
Masts and spars: all masts with one topmast (shortened). Height of foremast over deck 75 ft 4 in. Height of mizzenmast over deck 75 ft 4 in. Bowsprit
Engines: 2 250 hp Deutz diesels
Complement: 74 men. 55 dories carried

Left to right:
Gazela Primeiro, José Alberto, Creoula II

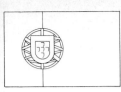

Hortense

Type: 3-masted gaff schooner
Country: at time of writing, Portugal
Owners: will probably be owned by the
Outward Bound Trust, London
Home port: still undecided
Year of construction: 1929
Builders:
M. Maria Monica, Gafanha, Aveiro,
Portugal
Tonnage: 373 tons gross, 284 tons net
Dimensions:

LOA	170 ft
Length between perpendiculars	138 ft 10 in
Breadth extreme	32 ft 6 in
Depth moulded	16 ft 9 in

Engine: 147 hp 6-cylinder Sulzer diesel
Complement: 43 when fishing for cod
Use: sail training vessel, after she has
been taken over by the Outward
Bound Trust

Brites

Type: 4-masted gaff schooner. Wood
Country: Portugal
Owners: Brites, Vaz & Irmaos Lda.,
Aveiro. Fishing vessel
Home port: Aveiro
Year of construction: 1936
Builders: at Gafanha, near Aveiro
Tonnage:
423 tons gross, 291 tons net.
Fish capacity 8265 quintals =
1,106,689 lbs
Dimensions:

Length hull	141 ft 4 in
Breadth extreme	33 ft 6 in
Depth in hold	17 ft

Rig: 7 sails. 3 headsails, fore staysail with
boom. Hoisting gaffs
Masts and spars:
all masts with one topmast.
Height of foremast over deck 94 ft.
Height of mizzen mast over deck
99 ft. Bowsprit
Engine: 300 hp Deutsche-Werke diesel
Complement: 52 men. 38 dories carried

Creoula II

Type: 4-masted gaff schooner. Steel
Country: Portugal
Owner: Parceria Geral de Pescarias,
Lisbon. Fishing vessel
Home port: Lisbon
Year of construction: 1937
Builders: Companhia Uniao Fabril,
Lisbon
Tonnage:
664 tons gross, 390 tons net.
Fish capacity 9295 quintals =
1,297,285 lbs
Dimensions:

Length hull	189 ft 6 in
Breadth extreme	32 ft 7 in
Depth in hold	16 ft 6 in

Rig: 7 sails. 3 headsails, fore staysail with
boom. Hoisting gaffs
Masts and spars:
all masts with one topmast. Height
of foremast over deck 113 ft 3 in.
Height of mizzen mast over deck
118 ft 2 in. Bowsprit
Engine: 480 hp Benz diesel
Complement: 73 men. 54 dories carried

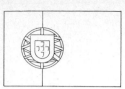

Santa Maria Manuela

Type: 4-masted gaff schooner. Steel

Country: Portugal

Owners: Empresa de Pesca Ribau Lda., Gafanha da Nazaré, Aveiro. Fishing vessel

Home port: Viana do Castelo

Year of construction: 1937

Builders: Companhia Uniao Fabril, Lisbon

Tonnage: 666 tons gross, 390 tons net. Fish capacity 10,139 quintals = 1,341,389 lbs

Dimensions:

Length hull	189 ft 7 in
Breadth extreme	32 ft 7 in
Depth in hold	16 ft 6 in

Rig: 7 sails. 3 headsails; forestaysail with boom, hoisting gaffs

Masts and spars: all masts with one topmast. Height of foremast over deck 116 ft. Height of jiggermast over deck 121 ft; bowsprit

Engine: 380 hp Burmeister & Wain diesel

Complement: 74 men. 55 dories carried

Argus

Type: 4-masted gaff schooner. Steel

Country: Portugal

Owner: Parceria Geral de Pescarias, Lisbon. Fishing vessel

Home port: Lisbon

Year of construction: 1938

Builders: De Haan & Oerlmans, Heusden, Holland

Tonnage: 696 tons gross, 413 tons net. Fish capacity 11,093 quintals = 1,467,337 lbs

Dimensions:

Length hull	188 ft 11 in
Length between perpendiculars	170 ft
Breadth extreme	35 ft 6 in
Depth in hold	16 ft 10 in
Draft	16 ft

Rig: 7 sails. 3 headsails, boomed fore staysail, hoisting gaffs

Masts and spars: all masts with one topmast; height of foremast over deck 112 ft, height of jiggermast over deck 117 ft 6 in; bowsprit

Engine: 475 hp Sulzer diesel

Complement: 72 men. 53 dories carried

Dom Deniz

Type: 3-masted gaff schooner. Wood

Country: Portugal

Owners: Pascoal & Filhos Lda., Aveiro.
Fishing vessel.

Home port: Aveiro

Year of construction: 1940

Builders: at Gafanha near Aveiro

Tonnage: 530 tons gross, 328 tons net. Fish capacity
7988 quintals = 1,056,620 lbs

Dimensions:

Length hull	147 ft 1 in
Breadth extreme	33 ft 7 in
Depth in hold	13 ft 8 in

Rig: 6 sails. 3 headsails, boomed fore staysail,
hoisting gaffs

Masts and spars: all masts with one topmast;
height of foremast above deck 93 ft 6 in;
height of mizzen mast above deck 101 ft 8 in;
no bowsprit

Engine: 275 hp Deutz diesel

Complement: 59 men. 44 dories carried

Adelia Maria

Type: 4-masted gaff schooner. Wood

Country: Portugal

Owner: José Maria Vilarinho, Aveiro.
Fishing vessel

Home port: Aveiro

Year of construction: 1948

Builders: at Gafanha, near Aveiro

Tonnage: 623 tons gross, 400 tons net.
Fish capacity 10,099 quintals = 1,363,365 lbs

Dimensions:

Length hull	147 ft 4 in
Breadth extreme	35 ft 6 in
Depth in hold	17 ft

Rig: 6 sails. 2 headsails, boomed fore staysail,
hoisting gaffs

Masts and spars: all masts in one piece; height of
foremast above deck 82 ft; height of jiggermast
90 ft 10 in. No bowsprit

Engine: 425 hp Famo-Kiel diesel

Complement: 69 men. 54 dories carried

Alpha

Kapella

Type: barkentine
Country: U.S.S.R.
Owners:
   Ministry of Mercantile Marine,
   Moscow
Home port: Leningrad
Year of construction: 1948
Builders: yard in Finland
Tonnage:
   322 tons gross, 41 tons net,
   55 tons deadweight
Dimensions:

LOA	144 ft	4 in
Breadth extreme	29 ft	2 in
Moulded depth	13 ft	1 in
Draft	10 ft	10 in

Engine:
   4-stroke diesel engine built in
   East Germany 1958.
   Speed under power 7 knots
Use: sail training ship

Type: barkentine
Country:
   U.S.S.R. (Latvian Soviet Socialist
   Republic)
Owners:
   Ministry of Mercantile Marine,
   Moscow. Sea school at Riga
Home port: Riga
Year of construction: 1948
Builders: yard at Åbo (Turku), Finland
Tonnage:
   322 tons gross, 41 tons net, 57 tons
   deadweight, 300 tons displacement
Dimensions:

LOA	126 ft	10 in
Breadth extreme	29 ft	2 in
Moulded depth	13 ft	1 in
Draft	9 ft	2 in

Rig:
   9 sails. 3 headsails; foremast: fore
   course, double topsails, single
   topgallant, royal; main and mizzen
   masts: gaff sails (hoisting gaffs)
Masts:
   foremast with top and topgallant
   masts, main and mizzen masts with
   topmasts
Engine:
   2-stroke Finnish diesel (1958).
   Speed under power 7.5 knots
Use: sail training ship

Kapella is the training ship of the nautical training establishment at Riga. Her signal letters are URFE. She is entered in the Leningrad main shipping register under the number M-16560. She cruises mainly in the Baltic. Like several other Soviet training vessels she was built by Finland as part of that country's war reparations after the Second World War.

Right Kapella *as sail training ship, below as cargo schooner*

Alpha, like a number of other Soviet training ships, was built after the Second World War by Finland as part of war reparations to Russia. Her signal letters are UOJV. She is entered in the Leningrad main shipping register under the number M-16566.

Meridian, Sekstant and Tropik

Type: barkentine

Country: U.S.S.R.

Owners:
Ministry of Fisheries, Moscow
(*Meridian* is also the Kaliningrad
Sea School)

Home ports:
Meridian, Kaliningrad, *Tropic*, Riga
Sekstant Nachodka nr Vladivostok

Builders: a Finnish yard

Tonnage:
322 tons gross, 41 tons net,
55 tons deadweight

Dimensions:

		Tropik
LOA	129 ft 4 in	144 ft 5 in
Breadth extreme	29 ft 2 in	
Moulded depth	13 ft 1 in	
Draft	11 ft 2 in	10 ft 10 in

Engines:
2-stroke and 4-stroke diesels.
Speed under power 6.5 knots
(*Tropik* 7 knots)

Use: sail training ships

Like several other Soviet training ships,
Meridian, Sekstant and *Tropik* were
built by Finland as part of war reparations after the Second World War. Their
signal letters are UTCW, UZUU and
UWLZ respectively, and their respective
numbers in the Leningrad main shipping
register are M-16574, M-16551 and
M-16577.

Horisont

Type: barkentine

Country: U.S.S.R.

Owners: merchant navy

Year of construction: 1948

Builders: Laivateollisuus, Turku, Finland

Tonnage:
322 tons gross, 41 tons net,
55 tons deadweight

Dimensions:

LOA	129 ft	4 in
Breadth extreme	29 ft	2 in
Depth moulded	13 ft	1 in
Draft	11 ft	2 in

Rig:
14 sails. 3 headsails; foremast: fore
course, double topsails, single
topgallant, royal; mainmast: gaff sail,
gaff topsail, main staysail, main
topmast staysail; mizzen: gaff sail,
gaff topsail

Engine: diesel

Use: sail training vessel

Lilla Dan

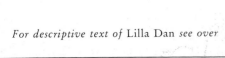

Type: 2-masted topsail schooner. Wood

Country: Denmark

Owners: Kogtved Søfartskole, Kogtved, near Svendborg

Home port: Kogtved

Year of construction:
1950. Keel laid May 1950, launched October 28, 1950

Builders: J. Ring Andersen, Svendborg

Tonnage:
95 tons gross, 12 tons net, 140 tons deadweight

Dimensions:

LOA	106 ft	8 in
Length hull	84 ft	8 in
LWL	78 ft	6 in
Breadth extreme	20 ft	7 in
Depth moulded	10 ft	2 in
Depth in hold	7 ft	9 in
Draft approx.	8 ft	2 in

Sail area: 3013 sq ft

Rig:
10 sails. 4 headsails; foremast: double topsails, gaff sail; mainmast: gaff sail, gaff topsail, topmast staysail

Masts:
height of mainmast above waterline 75 ft 5 in; both masts have topmasts

Engine:
90/100 hp/2-cylinder Alpha diesel. Speed under power 7.5 knots

Complement:
captain, quartermaster, 16 boys

Use: sail training ship

For descriptive text of Lilla Dan see over

Wilhelm Pieck

Lilla Dan is run by the Kogtved Nautical School to teach its pupils practical seamanship. Originally built for the shipping company of J. Lauritzen, Copenhagen, as a sail training ship for their officer cadets, she was bought in 1967 by the Kogtved Nautical School (Kogtved Søfartsskole). She cruises mainly in the waters off Fyn. The boys' living and sleeping quarters are in what would be the hold. There are eight berths each to port and starboard. The saloon and captain's cabin are aft, the chart and navigating rooms in the deckhouse aft of the mainmast. Aft of this there is a raised quarter-deck. The hull, with its bluff bow and transom stern , was built of Danish oak. Two lifeboats are carried in davits on the quarterdeck, one dinghy is carried across the stern. The gaff sails, on hoisting gaffs, are bent to the mast with hoops. The ship carries a ballast of 10 tons of lead and 2 tons of stones. Training includes the use of all modern navigation aids.

Originally a shield with the badge of the Lauritzen Line decorated each bow. These were removed by her present owners and are now part of the very sizeable collection of figureheads and name plaques of the shipyard of J. Ring-Andersen at Svendborg. Only the ship's lower topsail still bears the Lauritzen badge.

Type: brigantine. Steel
Country: German Democratic Republic
Owners:
  Gesellschaft für Sport und Technik (League for Sports and Technology), Department for Watersports
Home port: Greifswald
Year of construction: 1951, launched 1950
Builders: Warnow-Werft, Warnemünde
Tonnage: 290 tons displacement
Dimensions:

LOA	164 ft	1 in
Length hull	114 ft	11 in
Length between perpendiculars	105 ft	
Breadth extreme	24 ft	3 in
Draft	11 ft	10 in

Sail area: 5382 sq ft
Rig:
  13 sails. 4 headsails; foremast: single topsail, single topgallant, royal; mainmast: gaff sail, gaff topsail, staysail, topmast staysail, topgallant staysail
Masts:
  both masts have one topmast; height of mainmast above the waterline 105 ft
Engine:
  106 hp diesel. Speed under power approx 8 knots
Complement:
  11 permanent crew, 35 boys
Use: sail training ship

The ship is the last true brigantine ever to be built and one of the very few still sailing. This racy type of sailing ship was much used by 19th century smugglers. It goes without saying that it was equally popular with the authorities for coastal patrol. Since a brigantine needs only a small crew for sail handling, plenty of hands could be spared for manning the guns.

The ship is named after the first president of East Germany. The deckhouse on the maindeck houses mainly the galley, apart from a number of smaller store rooms. On the raised quarterdeck, forward of the chartroom, there is the main steering wheel and the compass. The stockless anchors are handled solely by means of the capstan on the forecastle. In addition to two self-inflating life-rafts the ship carries two tenders slung in davits. The main staysail is boomed. For her training trips the brigantine cruises mainly in the Baltic.

Kodor

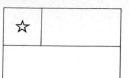

Esmeralda

Type: 3-masted schooner
Country: U.S.S.R.
Owner: Ministry of Fisheries, Moscow
Home port: Leningrad
Year of construction: 1951
Builders: a Finnish yard
Tonnage:
339 tons gross, 93 tons deadweight
Dimensions:

LOA	129 ft	4 in
Breadth extreme	29 ft	2 in
Depth moulded	13 ft	1 in
Draft	11 ft	2 in

Engine:
2-stroke diesel (Finnish, 1950).
Speed under power 7 knots
Use: sail training ship

---

ex *Juan D'Austria*

Type: 4-masted barkentine. Steel
Country: Chile
Owners: Chilean Navy
Home port: Valparaiso
Year of construction:
keel laid 1946, launched 1952,
commissioned 1954
Builders:
Echevarrieta y Larrinaga, Cadiz
Tonnage:
3500 tons displacement (equipped)
Dimensions:

LOA	370 ft	10 in
Length hull	308 ft	6 in
Length between		
perpendiculars	260 ft	
Breadth extreme	42 ft	8 in
Depth in hold	28 ft	6 in
Draft	19 ft	8 in

Sail area: 30,700 sq ft
Rig:
21 sails. 6 headsails; foremast: fore course, double topsails, single topgallant, no gaff sail; mainmast: gaff sail, gaff topsail, staysail, topmast staysail, topgallant staysail; mizzen mast and jigger: gaff sail, gaff topsail, topgallant staysail
Masts:
lower jigger mast serves as engine exhaust; height of mainmast above waterline 159 ft
Engine:
1500 hp, 6-cylinder Fiat diesel.
Speed under power 12 knots
Armament: four 5.7 cm rapid fire guns
Complement:
332 officers, petty officers, crew and cadets
Owner: Chilean Navy (training vessel)
Armament: 4 5.7 cm quick-firing guns
Use: sail training ship

Like several other Soviet sail training ships *Kodor* was built by Finland after the Second World War as part of war reparations to the Soviet Union. Her signal letters are UQFW, and she is entered in the Leningrad main shipping register under the number M-16732.

In the 1879 Nitrate War against Bolivia and Peru, the Chilean warship *Esmeralda* emerged victorious from several battles against the enemy fleet. It was after her that the present Chilean sail training ship has been named. The barkentine was laid down in 1946, as *Juan d'Austria*, for the Spanish Navy. During building a large part of the ship was destroyed by fire, which delayed the launching until 1952. In 1954 the Chilean Navy bought the ship as training vessel for its officer cadets and renamed her *Esmeralda*. In common with her almost identical sister-ship *Juan Sebastian de Elcano*, she carries the old, genuine schooner rig in which all gaffs are hoisted and lowered. The sails are bent to the masts by hoops. In a number of points concerning the superstructure and the way the foremast is rigged *Esmeralda* differs from her sistership. *Esmeralda* sets no gaff sail on the foremast and must, therefore, be termed a barkentine. Her square sails are brailed up to the yard arms instead of being gathered against the mast, as in her sister-ship. Her poop extends forward as far at the mizzen mast; her forecastle, which is very long, stops just short of the mainmast. There is a small navigating bridge on top of the deckhouse, situated roughly amidships.
Esmeralda is equipped with the most modern of navigation instruments. In addition to the boats in davits and chocks the ship carries eight fully equipped inflatable boats lashed to the lower shrouds above the bulwark and rail. The figurehead is a massive, handsomely painted condor holding the Chilean coat-of-arms in its claws. The ship's training cruises take her to all parts of the globe. *Esmeralda* participated as a guest in the procession from St. David's Head to New York during the 1964 Tall Ships Race.

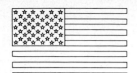

Black Pearl

Type: barkentine. Wood

Country: U.S.A.

Owners:
Barclay H. Warburton, Boston, Massachusetts

Home port:
Philadelphia, Pennsylvania

Year of construction:
1951; launched April 18, 1951

Builders:
C. Lincoln Vaughn, Wickford, Rhode Island

Tonnage:
36 tons displacement, 27 tons gross, 23 tons net

Dimensions:

LOA	72 ft	6 in
Length hull	59 ft	
Length between perpendiculars	38 ft	
Breadth extreme	15 ft	6 in
Depth moulded	16 ft	
Depth in hold	7 ft	4 in
Draft	8 ft	3 in

Sail area: 1991 sq ft

Rig:
10 sails. 2 headsails: foremast: double topsails, single topgallant; mainmast: gaff sail, gaff topsail, staysail, topmast staysail

Masts:
foremast with topmast and topgallant mast; mainmast with one topmast; height of mainmast above the deck 55 ft

Engine: 150 hp Hercules diesel

Complement: 6, including 4 boys

Use: private yacht

The brigantine, which is rather yachty in appearance, was built by C. Lincoln Vaughn as his private yacht. In the summer he used to cruise her mainly along the central section of the United States' east coast. Her present owner, Barcley H. Warburton of Boston, who bought her in August 1959, cruises her between the West Indies and Nova Scotia. Although she continues to be a private yacht she is used occasionally for training courses for boys.
During the summer of 1962 *Black Pearl* was moored for one month in Boy's Harbor, a boys' youth camp at East Hampton, Long Island. She was the only private sailing ship to join the ranks of the Tall Ships during 'Operation Sail 1964' at New York, on which occasion she had three officers and five cadets on board. During a 1,160-mile summer cruise in 1965 she logged an average of 8.1 knots. If need be, the ship can be handled under sail by two men only. In all, there is room for nine persons on board. Her up-to-date equipment includes a 3-kw generator, deep freeze, radio-telephone, radio direction finder and echo sounder. She can carry 265 gallons of fuel oil and 400 gallons of fresh water in tanks.
Black Pearl has proved herself as an outstanding sailer.

Zarja

Type: 3-masted gaff schooner. Wood

Country: U.S.S.R.

Owner:
thought to be the Leningrad Oceanographic Institute

Home port: thought to be Leningrad

Year of construction: 1952

Builders: a Finnish yard

Tonnage:
333 tons gross, 580 tons displacement

Rig:
9 sails (including topsails, see below). 3 headsails (fore staysail with boom); foremast: gaff sail, square running sail gathered to the middle of the yard and made fast to the lower mast); main and mizzen masts: gaff sail (topsails are not carried, but are provided for)

Masts and spars:
all mast have one topmast. Hoisting gaffs

Engine:
300 hp diesel. Speed under power 9 knots

Use: sail training ship

Zarja was built in Finland as part of Finnish war reparations to the Soviet Union. She carries a civilian crew and, being non-magnetic, is used for oceanographic research. On October 28, 1964 she entered the Thames Estuary on her return from a research cruise and spent six days moored up alongside Tower Stairs Pier. On November 3 she continued her voyage to Leningrad via Bergen. In 1965 she paid a short visit to Copenhagen.

Zawisza Czarny II

Type: 3-masted staysail schooner. Steel

Country: Poland

Owner: Zwiazek Harcerstwa Polskiego (Polish Sea Scouts)

Home port: Kolobrzeg

Year of construction: 1952

Builders: Stocznia Pólnocna, Gdánsk

Tonnage: 164 tons gross

Dimensions:

LOA	137 ft 10 in
Length hull	116 ft 6 in
Length between perpendiculars	108 ft 4 in
Breadth extreme	22 ft 4 in
Draft	15 ft

Sail area: 5,920 sq ft

Rig: 10 sails (including running square-sail). 4 headsails (boomed fore stay-sail); foremast: fore trysail, running squaresail; mainmast: boomed main staysail, main trysail; mizzen mast: boomed mizzen staysail, bermudan mizzen sail

Masts: pole masts

Engine: 300 hp DWK diesel

Complement: 5 permanent crew, 47 boys

Use: sail training ship

The present *Zawisza Czarny* should not be confused with the wooden three-masted gaff schooner of the same name, ex *Petrea,* which was built in 1902 at the yard of Holm & Gustafsson at Raa, Sweden. That ship operated under Polish colours from 1934 and after the occupation of Poland in August 1939 is thought to have been taken to Lübeck, renamed *Schwarzer Husar* (Black Hussar), painted black and used for training purposes by the marine division of the Hitler Youth. In 1946 she was returned to Poland but she was in such poor condition that she had to be broken up in 1947.

Zawisza Czarny II was built in 1952 as a fishing vessel and converted in 1961 to become a training vessel for the Sea Scouts. In the winter of 1967 she underwent a further conversion during which her length was increased by 3 metres (9 ft 10 in).

Zawisza Czarny is rigged as a staysail schooner, which in a three-master is extremely rare these days. Another unusual feature is the way each of her trysails are set between two curved gaffs. This wishbone-rig improves the efficiency of the sails. Staysails do away

with the need for heavy gaffs and also make sail handling easier.

Zawisza was the name of a 15th-century noble family, and 'Czarny', meaning 'The Black One', was a famous member of the family, who fought against the Teutonic Knights. A bust of him clad in armour stands on a kind of plinth at the bow of the ship.

Dewarutji

Type: barkentine. Steel

Country: Indonesia

Owners: Indonesian Navy

Home port: Djakarta

Year of construction:
1953; keel laid October 15, 1952; launched January 24, 1953

Builders:
H. C. Stülcken & Sohn, Hamburg

Tonnage: 886 tons displacement

Dimensions:

LOA	191 ft	3 in
Length hull	163 ft	
Length between perpendiculars	136 ft	2 in
Breadth extreme	31 ft	2 in
Depth moulded	23 ft	1 in
Draft	13 ft	3 in

Sail area:
11,840 sq ft; fore course 1,162 sq ft; mainsail 1,560 sq ft

Rig:
16 sails. 4 headsails; foremast: fore course, double topsails, single topgallant, royal; mainmast, mizzen: gaff sail, gaff topsail, mainsail without boom

Masts:
all masts with one topmast (wood); height of mainmast above deck 115 ft

Engine:
600 hp 6-cylinder M.A.N. diesel. Speed under power 10.4 knots

Complement:
captain, 8 officers, 8 petty officers, doctor, bosun, sailmaker, 6 sailors, engineer, cook, 4 stewards, 78 cadets

Use: sail training ship

For descriptive text on Dewarutji see over

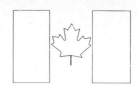

In 1932 the shipyard of H. C. Stülcken & Sons at Hamburg built the sail training ship *Jadran* for the Yugoslav Navy. When the Indonesian Navy wanted a similar ship for the training of its cadets it turned to the same yard.

Dewarutji, in Indonesian mythology, is the ruler and patron of the sea, roughly the same as our Neptune. *Dewarutji's* wooden figurehead is a representation of the god.

The barkentine has three decks. The uppermost is a continuous spar-deck joining poop and forecastle, at the same time taking in the midshiphouse. The true poop and forecastle are on the second deck down. This is where all of the permanent crew have their quarters: the officers in the poop, the petty officers and staff in the midshiphouse, which also houses the galley. The cadets live and sleep (in hammocks) in two separate flats on the tween-deck. The air-conditioned stores rooms are on the after tween-deck. To make her suitable for the tropics, the whole ship is fully ventilated and air-conditioned. The radio and chart rooms are on the poop, forward of which there is the manually operated, double steering wheel. The stock anchor to starboard is stowed on a riding chock, the stockless anchor to port in a hawsepipe.

The only power-operated machinery on deck is a combination windlass (operated by hand or electricity) for weighing the anchors.

Dewarutji carries 1 motor jollyboat, 3 cutters, 3 dinghies and 1 gig (over the stern). She is equipped with every modern navigational aid. Mainsail and mizzen sail can be set and handed either by hoisting and lowering the gaffs or by means of brails, outhauls and down-hauls. These two sails have slides along

their luff and head which run in T-tracks on the masts and gaffs. The gaff topsails are fitted with hoops along the luff. To enable the boat davits to be operated while the ship is sailing the lower yard braces lead to brace gallows nearly 8 ft high. During trials the ship sailed as close as $5^1/2$ points off the wind. She carries 200 tons of permanent ballast.

Dewarutji cruises mainly in East Asian waters. In 1964 she sailed to New York to take part in 'Operation Sail'.

Type: brigantine. Steel

Country: Canada

Owners:
Brigantine Incorporated, Kingston. Royal Canadian Sea Cadet Corps "St. Lawrence"

Home port: Kingston, Ontario

Year of construction:
1953; launched December 5, 1953; commissioned July, 1957

Builders:
Kingston Shipyards Ltd., designed by F. A. MacLachlan

Tonnage:
$\frac{39}{42}$ tons displacement, 34.30 tons gross, 30.87 tons net

Dimensions:

LOA	71 ft	6 in
Length hull	59 ft	8 in
Length between perpendiculars	45 ft	
Breadth extreme	15 ft	2 in
Depth in hold	8 ft	6 in
Depth moulded	10 ft	10 in
Draft	7 ft	6 in

Sail area: 2,490 sq ft

Rig:
8 sails. 2 headsails; foremast: fore course, single topsail; mainmast: gaff sail, gaff topsail, staysail, topmast staysail

Masts:
height of mainmast above waterline 53 ft

Engine: 72 hp diesel

Complement: 22 officers and cadets

Use: sail training ship

St. Lawrence

The Royal Canadian Sea Cadet Corps "St. Lawrence" was established in 1942. It is sponsored jointly by a civilian body and the Navy, but the ship does not train naval cadets exclusively. The Corps' main objective is not to train boys (between the ages of 13 and 18) for a naval career, but to teach them to live in a restricted space as a community in which one member is dependent on the other. So far, well over 10,000 Canadian boys have attended the courses and graduated as sea cadets. In 1952 the Corps decided to have a ship of its own built. She was named after the 112-canon three-decker H. M. S. *St. Lawrence* built in 1814 by the Navy Shipyard at Point Frederick, Kingston, Ontario.

Each season the 'permanent crew', who act as ship's officers, are selected from among the senior boys. They must commit themselves to remaining with the ship throughout one full sailing season. The courses usually last 15 days, and the boys graduate with different ranks according to their aptitude and ability. A boy must partake in several courses before he may take a leading position on board. The brigantine carries three 11 ft dories which are used as tenders. She has painted gun-ports on a white band. *St. Lawrence II* sails exclusively on Lake Ontario and during the winter month is laid up at Kingston.

In July 1964 the ship took part in 'Operation Sail' at New York. On that occasion she was un-rigged and motored to New York via the Oswego Canal and the Hudson River.

Libertad

Type: full-rigged ship. Steel

Country: Argentina

Owner: Argentinian Navy

Home port: Buenos Aires

Years of construction:
1953/56; keel laid December 11, 1953; launched May 30, 1956, commissioned May 28, 1960

Builders:
A.F.N.E. Astilleros Navales, Rio Santiago (Argentinian state shipyard)

Tonnage: $\frac{3765}{2740}$ tons displacement

Dimensions:

LOA	338 ft	
Length hull	301 ft	1 in
Length between perpendiculars	262 ft	7 in
Breadth extreme	44 ft	4 in
Depth moulded	36 ft	1 in
Draft (fully equipped)	21 ft	10 in

Sail area: 28,450 sq ft

Rig:
27 sails. 5 headsails, double topsails, single topgallants, royals

Masts:
all masts with one topmast; height of foremast 159 ft 6 in, mainmast 163 ft, mizzen 142 ft

Engines:
2 1200 hp Sulzer diesels, driving one shaft through a Vulcan hydraulic coupling. Speed under power 13.5 knots

Complement:
351, consisting of 24 officers, 49 cadets, 39 engineer cadets, 239 petty officers and crew

Use: sail training ship

The full name of this remarkable training ship built recently is Fragata A. R. A. *Libertad* (A. R. A. = Armada República Argentina). It was in the summer of 1963 that the ship sailed from Buenos Aires on her 6-month maiden voyage, during which her main ports of call were San Juan, Bermuda, Lisbon, Le Havre, Hamburg, London, Cadiz, Dakar. During her 15-day stay in Hamburg 30,000 visitors came on board.

Libertad conforms to all the requirements of modern nautical instruction. She has a flush deck and a bridge with wings, of the type which is common on motor vessels, between the foremast and the mainmast. There is a funnel between the mainmast and the mizzen mast. In addition to the main engines the ship has two 500 kwh 380 v generators and one 85 kwh 380 v auxiliary generator. Her radar has a range of 48 nautical miles. She has an echo sounder and two transmitters, an emergency receiver, a high frequency receiver, three receivers for the lifeboats, five emergency receivers for the lifeboats, three R. A. I. receivers and two Hammer-Lund receivers.

The following boats are carried: two wooden jollyboats with a metal cabin (equipped with a 4-cyl. 40 hp Thornycroft engine; each has room for 15 persons); one wooden landing launch with a 4-cyl. 40 hp Thornycraft engine (holds 30 persons); one boat with sails and oars and one boat with sails. In addition, there are several self-inflating life-rafts. Since the sails are fairly flat-cut they do not belly out very much when full. Because of this, and because the long deck enables the three masts to be sufficiently spaced out, the stays do not have to be dressed with baggywrinkle against chafing. Originally, the ship's only ornament was the arms of the Argentine Navy on the stern. Later a female figure was added as a figurehead at the bow.

In July 1964 *Libertad* took part in the Tall Ships Race from Lisbon to the Bermudas, from where she continued to New York to participate in 'Operation Sail.'

Mayflower II

Type: bark (gallion). Wood

Country: U.S.A.

Owner:
Plimoth Plantation Inc.,
Plymouth, Massachusetts

Location: Plymouth, Massachusetts

Year of construction:
1955/56. Keel laid July, 1955.
Launched September, 1956

Builders:
Stuart Upham, Brixham, Devon,
England. Designed by William Avery
Baker

Tonnage:
260.12 tons gross, 223.29 tons net,
365 tons displacement (on the
voyage made in 1957), 181 tons
burden (in 1620)

Dimensions:

Length hull	106 ft	8 in
LOA	approx 131 ft	10 in
LWL	79 ft	9 in
Breadth extreme (wales)	25 ft	10 in
Depth in hold	10 ft	11 in
Depth moulded	18 ft	4 in
Draft (1957 voyage)	12 ft	9 in
Freeboard (1957 voyage)	6 ft	7 in

Sail area: 5,065 sq ft

Rig:
6 sails. Bowsprit with square spritsail; fore- and mainmasts: courses,
deep-setting single topsails; mizzen
mast: latteen sail

Masts:
fore- and mainmasts with one
topmast

Complement: 33 (1957 voyage)

Use: museum ship

In 1620, 105 Puritans, known as the Pilgrim Fathers, sailed from England in the *Mayflower* in order to settle in New England. Including the crew, there must have been 125 to 130 persons on board the *Mayflower,* which was a normal Elizabethan cargo-galleon, by no means specially built for the purpose.

In 1947 the Plimoth Plantation of Plymouth, Massachusetts started to think about building a replica of *Mayflower* which was to be moored in Plymouth harbour as a museum and memorial. Eventually two Englishmen, Mr. Charlton and Mr. Lowe, took up and realized the idea, promising to present the ship to the Plimoth Plantation after she had successfully crossed the Atlantic.

There were no original plans to work from. All that was known about her were her approximate dimensions and what type of ship she had been. The original dimensions would not have allowed for standing headroom, so the replica, which was to be open to the public, and to be built higher. *Mayflower II* was built on the slip as far as the tween-deck and completed in the yard's dry dock. Only English oak was used for the hull, Canadian pine for the masts and yards. Ropes and sailcloth were made in Scotland. 135 tons of pig iron ballast ensured stability; in fact, she proved slightly too stiff on the crossing. For greater safety it was decided to steer her with a wheel instead of the tiller.

The standing rigging and the masts were subjected to great strain because the bowsprit, on account of the spritsail, could not be stayed and the braces were led to the stays. But this is how it had been in the days of the Pilgrim Fathers. Staysails and jibs were not introduced till later. The yards of the lower sails could be lowered on deck. None of the sails could be reefed.

In 1620 *Mayflower* had taken 67 days to cross the Atlantic under the command of Captain Christopher Jones. In 1957 Alan Villiers managed to do it in 53 days. The average speed on this voyage, lasting from April 20, to June 12, 1957, was 7.7 knots, the average day's run 106 nautical miles and the distance covered 5,420 nautical miles.

Following her triumphant arrival at the Pilgrims' Rock at Plymouth, *Mayflower II* continued to New York and then visited several American east-coast ports in turn. At the end of June 1958 she returned to her permanent mooring in the harbour of Plymouth, Massachusetts.

Gorch Fock II

Type: bark. Steel

Country: West Germany

Owners: German Navy

Home port: Kiel

Year of construction:
1958; launched August 23, 1958,
commissioned December 17, 1958

Builders: Blohm & Voss, Hamburg

Tonnage: 1760 tons displacement

Dimensions:

LOA	293 ft
Length hull	266 ft 6 in
Length between perpendiculars	230 ft 5 in
Breadth extreme	39 ft 4 in
Depth moulded	32 ft 10 in
Draft	16 ft 5 in

Sail area: 21,011 sq ft

Rig:
23 sails. 4 headsails, double topsails,
single topgallants, royals; mizzen
mast: double spanker, gaff topsail

Masts:
height of fore and mainmasts over
designed waterline 148 ft, height
of mizzen mast over DWL 131 ft

Engine:
800 hp M.A.N. diesel. Speed under
power approx 10 knots

Complement:
269, consisting of captain, 9 officers,
doctor, meteorologist, 36 petty
officers, 21 crew, 200 officer and
petty officer cadets

Use: sail training ship

When the new German training ship *Gorch Fock II* was built, the builders could draw on the experience gained with the former German Navy's *Gorch Fock, Horst Wessel* and *Albert Leo Schlageter,* which had all been built to the same basic design, except for slight differences in their dimensions. Safety was the prime consideration in all of them, and they all had exceptional stability due to the careful stowage of fixed ballast. If one includes *Mircea,* built for Romania, there are now five ships of the same design afloat, *Gorch Fock II's* sister-ships still being in service.

The bark was named after the German writer of sea stories, Hans Kinau, whose pen name was Gorch Fock. He was killed in the Skagerrak in 1916.

The deckhouse and forecastle in *Gorch Fock II* are joined. On the starboard side she carries a stockless anchor, on the port side an old-type anchor with stock. The anchor capstans can be either power driven or manually operated. To enable the cadets to take frequent turns at the helm, the main wheel, on the poop forward of the chartroom, actually consists of three large wheels. A total of four boats are carried: two on the poop slung in davits, two lashed down on the deckhouse, one of which is a motor launch. In addition there are a number of self-inflating life-rafts. The bow ornament, which cannot be called a figurehead, is a stylised albatross. The ship makes two training cruises annually. The shorter of the two normally takes her to North Sea ports, the longer one into the Atlantic (Canaries, Bermudas, Antilles, New York etc.). During the winter she is laid up in Kiel. She took part in the Tall Ships Race in 1960, 1962, 1964, 1966 and 1968.

Bounty II

Type:
full-rigged ship. Wood (constructed on the lines of a merchant ship of the 18th century)

Country: U.S.A.

Owner:
Metro-Goldwyn-Mayer Inc., New York, New York

Location:
Vinoy Basin, St. Petersburg, Florida

Year of construction:
1960. Keel laid February, 1960. Launched August 27, 1960

Builders:
Smith & Rhuland Ltd., Lunenburg, Nova Scottia, Canada

Tonnage:
120 tons displacement, 415 tons gross, 111 tons net

Dimensions:

LOA	169 ft	
Length hull	133 ft	
Length between perpendiculars	114 ft	9 in
Breadth extreme	30 ft	5 in
Depth moulded	20 ft	8 in
Depth in hold	27 ft	9 in
Draft	13 ft	9 in

Sail area: 10,225 sq ft

Rig:
18 sails. 2 headsails, single topsails, single topgallants, royals

Masts and spars:
height of mainmast above deck 103 ft 8 in; all masts with topmast and topgallant mast; bowsprit with jib-boom

Engines:
2 220 hp Caterpillar marine diesels driving twin screws

Complement:
a total of 26 men for the film 'Mutiny on the Bounty'. Originally she had a crew of 45 (1789)

Armament:
the original ship of 1789 had 4 4-pounders and 10 ½-pounders mounted on the rails

Use: museum ship

Of the many ship mutinies that have occurred through the centuries, none has fired the imagination so much or provided material for as many books and films as the mutiny on H. M. S. *Bounty* in 1789. This may be due to several unusual and interesting facts: the events took place in the South Pacific; the mutineers were not found until many years later; Captain Bligh, by an outstanding feat of seamanship, managed to cover over 3,600 miles in an open boat, to return to England and bring some of the mutineers to justice.

In one of his accounts, Captain James Cook had described the fruit of the bread-fruit tree (artocarpus) which grows on the Polynesian islands as being a very tasty and nourishing food. This prompted the settlers in the British possessions in the West Indies to submit a petition to King George III in which they asked that breadfruit be introduced to the West Indies as food for the negro slaves. In 1787 the British Admiralty bought the merchantman *Bethia*, built in 1785 and previously owned by Duncan Campbell, for £ 1,950. In Deptford on the Thames the ship was refitted and armed at a cost of £ 4,456.

Lieutenant William Bligh was put in command and given the order to sail to Otaheite (Tahiti) and from there take young bread-fruit plants to the West Indies. This attempt to improve the lot of the slaves being considered a deed of remarkable human kindness, the ship was given the name *Bounty*. The irony of it all was that the West Indian slaves later rejected bread-fruit as a food because they did not like it. Bligh sailed from Spithead on December 23, 1787. Having had to abandon the plan to sail round Cape Horn because

of persistent bad weather, he did not reach Tahiti until October 26, 1788. He left Tahiti with 1,105 plants on board on April 4, 1789, bound for Jamaica. On April 28, 1789, off the island of Tofua, not far from the Tonga Islands, mutiny broke out. Fletcher Christian, 24 years of age and first mate, took over the command and set Bligh and 18 other men adrift in a 23 ft open boat. After 41 days, and having covered 3,618 miles, the boat reached Timor. On his return to England, Bligh succeeded in having the frigate *Pandora* sail to Tahiti in search of the mutineers. He himself was court-martialled, and although he was acquitted he was reprimanded for his ruthless, cruel and inhuman command. Bligh went on to be the Governor of New South Wales from 1805 to 1808 and was later promoted to the rank of Vice Admiral. The whole incident did much to improve conditions for seamen on board British Naval vessels.

Fletcher Christian returned at first to Tahiti, but left again with several natives, including women, on board. They eventually reached the uninhabited island of Pitcairn in January 1790 and burnt the *Bounty* shortly afterwards. It was not till 18 years later, in 1808, that the American seal hunter *Topaz* from Boston happened to find the few survivors. Direct descendents of the mutineers still live on the island today. Of its roughly 150 inhabitants about one-third bear the family name of Christian.

In 1957 Louis Marden of the National Geographic Society discovered the remains of the *Bounty* and salvaged an anchor, pigs of ballast, fastenings, etc.

For the film 'Mutiny of the Bounty,' Metro-Goldwyn-Mayer Inc. had a

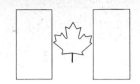

Bluenose II

replica of the *Bounty* built from the original plans preserved in London. In all, the replica, which had to be made longer by 30 ft to accommodate the big film cameras and had to have an auxiliary engine installed, cost $ 700,000 to design and build. The carved figurehead, which represents a lady in riding costume, corresponds to old descriptions of the original.

When the film was finished *Bounty* visited a number of American ports, then in October 1962 sailed to London and in 1964 was present at the World's Fair in New York. Wherever she went she attracted much attention and was viewed by many thousands of people. She is now permanently on show in the harbour of St. Petersburg, Florida.

Type: 2-masted gaff schooner. Wood

Country: Canada

Owners:
Oland & Son Ltd., Halifax, Nova Scotia

Year of construction:
1963; keel laid February 27, 1963; launched July 24, 1963

Builders:
Smith & Rhuland Ltd., Lunenburg, Nova Scotia

Tonnage:
285 tons displacement, 191 tons gross, 96 tons net

Dimensions:

LOA	143 ft
Length hull	112 ft
LWL	111 ft 7 in
Breadth extreme	27 ft
Depth moulded	17 ft
Draft	15 ft 10 in

Sail area: 10,901 sq ft

Rig:
8 sails. 3 headsails; foremast: gaff sail, fore gaff topsail; mainmast: gaff sail, gaff topsail, fisherman's staysail

Masts:
height of mainmast above deck 127 ft

Engines:
two 180 hp diesels. Speed under power 10 knots

Complement:
12. Additional cabin space for 12 guests

Use: private charter vessel

The schooner *Bluenose* was built in 1921, a typical Banks fishing schooner from Nova Scotia. In those days a schooner's sole objective was no longer to get her cod to market quickly in order to realize a good price: her main concern was a good performance in the big International Fishermen's Races between Canada and the U. S. A. *Bluenose* won the Cup for Canada several times and became so famous that, like the maple leaf, she was depicted on stamps and coins as a national emblem. Later she had to be sold and continued to sail as a trader in the West Indies, where she ran on a coral reef in 1946 and became a total loss.

Bluenose II was built in her memory in 1963, from the original plans and by the same yard. The only difference lies in the accommodation plan. The space of the hold is taken up by comfortable cabins for passengers and crew. The navigation instruments are of the most up-to-date type.

During the winter months *Bluenose II* cruises on charter in the Caribbean, in the summer in Canadian waters. 'Bluenose' is the nickname given to the fishermen of Nova Scotia by their rivals from Gloucester, Massachusetts. It was between these two rival groups that the keenest races used to be sailed.

Santa Maria

Type:
reconstruction of a *Nao* (merchant vessel of the late 15th century). Wood

Country: Spain/U.S.A.

Owner:
Smithsonian Institution, Washington, D. C.
Location:
Potomac River, Washington, D. C.

Year of construction: 1963

Tonnage:
105 tunns (toneles) burthen, 148 tons displacement, 87 tons gross

Dimensions:

LOA	101 ft 9 in
Length hull	91 ft 3 in
Length on deck	77 ft 6 in
Length between perpendiculars	65 ft 7 in
Length keel	51 ft 10 in
Breadth extreme	25 ft 11 in
Depth in hold	12 ft 6 in
Draft	9 ft 10 in

Sail area: approx 3,550 sq ft

Rig:
5 sails. Bowsprit with spritsail; foremast: square foresail; mainmast: main course, topsail; mizzen mast: lateen sail

Masts and spars:
height of mainmast from keel to truck 85 ft; length of mainyard 53 ft 9 in; mainmast has a very light topmast; fore-, main- and lateen yards made from two pieces lashed together

Complement: in 1492, 40 men

Use: museum ship

Columbus set out on his first voyage in 1492 in order to reach India by sea. He died believing that he had found India, and so did his contemporaries, when, in fact, he had discovered America. Columbus sailed from Palos with his three ships *Santa Maria, Pinta,* and *Nina* on August 3, 1492 and on October 12, 1492 reached an island called Guanahani by the Indians, which he named San Salvador. It can be assumed that this was Watling Island in the Bahamas. No illustrations, excact dimensions or plans of any of these ships were handed down. Ships were not built to plans until the 17th century. *Santa Maria* was Columbus' flagship (he was an admiral), and as such became one of the most famous ships in maritime history. Numerous efforts have been made to reconstruct her, of which the most recent, and certainly the most successful, has been that of Capitan de Corbeta José Maria Martinez-Hidalgo, Director of the Museo Maritimo at Barcelona.

The present *Santa Maria* was built in 1963 as an exhibit in the New York World's Fair and shipped to America on board the German cargo-ship Neidenfels. After the close of the Fair she was taken to Washington where she is now moored in the Potomac as the principal exhibit of the Museum for American History of Exploration. A second ship built to the same plans for Venezuela is under construction at the moment at the same yard.

Santa Maria was an ordinary merchant ship when Columbus chose her for his voyage. He deliberately selected small ships because they were easier to handle and would tack better into the predominant Westerlies.

Strangely enough, many of the attempted reconstructions and descriptions ignored the fact that *Santa Maria* was a *nao,* not a *caravel.* The resulting errors and misinterpretations are obvious. Columbus referred to her as a *nao* eighty-one times in his journals, while he insists on calling *Pinta* and *Nina caravels.*

The *nao,* in Columbus' day, was the most fully rigged of large sailing vessels, setting five sails in all: square spritsail, fore course, main course, main topsail, and a lateen mizzen. The *nao* had a 'round tuck' stern and a high forecastle. Very probably there was a shelter on the quarterdeck. In those days the traditional ratio for extreme breadth — keel length — length on deck was 1 : 2 : 3 (as-dos-tres). This produced what to our standards are rather slow, cumbersome ships, and Columbus himself said so, too. The caravels were rather more lively ships. They had a flat stern and no forecastle, and in the beginning these vessels, which had two or three masts, were entirely lateen-rigged. Commander Martinez-Hidalgo based his calculation of dimensions on the information to be found in various sources that she was a little over 100 tuns *(toneles)* burden. This is a measurement of capacity and indicates the number of tuns or barrels, of wine of a certain size the ship could load, 1 tun being equal to roughly 5/6 of 1 registered ton. From exhaustive experiments with models and careful study of all relevant graphic material and previous models, there finally emerged a ship of 105 tuns (toneles) burden, and the dimensions listed. These results formed the basis of Martinez-Hidalgo's reconstruction of the *Santa Maria.*

Santa Maria carried two boats, a launch and a smaller yawl. Four bombards firing stone shot stood on the quarterdeck. There were no covers to the gun ports. Light-guns called falconets were

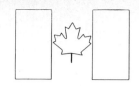

Pathfinder

mounted on the rails. In addition the crew was equipped with the usual hand-weapons of the time.

The main topsail was rectangular, not trapezoidal as frequently depicted, and it was sheeted to the round top, not the main yardarms. The spritsail was furled to the yard which was then hauled alongside the bowsprit and lashed down. It can be assumed that *Santa Maria* had large red crosses painted on her square sails as was common in Spanish and Portuguese ships at that time.

A ship of her type could sail within roughly 7 points of the wind. Speeds of up to 9.5 knots have been entered in her log, even over long distances.

* Publisher's note: In 1969, while en route to an exhibition in St. Louis, the ship capsized and sank during a storm on the Mississippi River.

Type: brigantine. Steel
Country: Canada
Owner:
  Toronto Brigantine Incorporated
Home port: Toronto
Year of construction:
  1963; launched May 6, 1963
Builders:
  Kingston Shipyard Ltd.
  Designed by F. A. MacLachlan
Tonnage:
  $\frac{39}{42}$ tons displacement, 36 tons
  gross, 32 tons net
Dimensions:

LOA	71 ft	6 in
Length hull	59 ft	8 in
Length between		
perpendiculars	45 ft	
Breadth extreme	15 ft	2 in
Depth in hold	8 ft	6 in
Depth moulded	10 ft	10 in
Draft	7 ft	6 in

Sail area: 2,490 sq ft
Rig:
  8 sails. 2 (3) headsails; foremast: fore course, single topsail; main-mast: gaff sail, gaff topsail, staysail, topmast staysail
Masts:
  height of mainmast above waterline 53 ft
Engine: 110 hp Palmer diesel
Complement: 30 officers and cadets
Use: sail training ship

This brigantine is the identical sister-ship to *St. Lawrence II* of Kingston, except that her accommodation plan is slightly different, *Pathfinder* having room for a larger number of boys. The Toronto Brigantine Incorporated is a civilian body made up of Toronto citizens. Any boy or girl between the ages of 14 and 18 can join the courses. They normally last one week in the summer season, while in the autumn the ship sails on day cruises only. During the winter she is laid up in Toronto. She cruises exclusively on Lake Ontario, visiting ports along the shore.

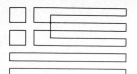

Carita

Type:
3-masted staysail schooner. Steel

Country: Greece

Owner: A. Lusi Ltd., London

Home port: Piraeus

Year of construction:
1959; launched April, 1959

Builders:
Amsterdamsche Scheepwerf, G. De
Vries Lentsch jr., Amsterdam

Tonnage:
485 tons displacement, 336.18 tons
gross, 154.42 tons net

Dimensions:

LOA	170 ft	4 in
Length between perpendiculars	121 ft	
Breadth extreme	27 ft	10 in
Depth moulded	19 ft	8 in
Depth in hold	13 ft	9 in
Draft	15 ft	5 in

Sail area:
9,354 sq ft (mainsail 2,475 sq ft)

Rig:
7 sails. 2 (3) headsails; foremast:
bermudan sail; mainmast: bermudan
sail, staysail; mizzen mast:
bermudan sail

Masts and spars:
height of mainmast above waterline
132 ft; fore and main staysails with
booms. No bowsprit

Engine:
2 597 hp Davey-Paxman diesels

Complement: 14

Use: private yacht

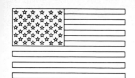

Mary Day

Type: 2-masted gaff schooner. Wood

Country: U.S.A.

Owner:
Capt. Havilah S. Hawkins.
Sedgwick, Maine

Home port: Sedwick, Maine

Year of construction: 1962; launched
January 20, 1962

Builders: at South Bristol, Maine

Tonnage:
approx 100 tons displacement,
86 tons gross

Dimensions:

Length between perpendiculars	83 ft	
Breadth extreme	23 ft	6 in
Depth in hold	6 ft	
Draft	6 ft	6 in

Sail area: 3,600 sq ft

Rig:
4 sails. 2 headsails, gaff sail on each
mast

Masts:
height of mainmast above deck 64 ft.
Topmasts are provided for but
are not carried

Engine: no auxiliary

Complement:
4 permanent crew, captain, quartermaster, cook, assistant cook and
28 passengers

Use: private charter vessel

Mary Day was the first sailing vessel of this type and size to be built in Maine for thirty years. She was designed by the owner, Capt. H. S. Hawkins, previously the owner of *Alice S. Wentworth*. Outwardly, *Mary Day* looks very much like the old coastal schooners, but down below she was designed as a cruising vessel from the beginning. She has two one-berth cabins, six double-berth cabins, two three-berth cabins and two four-berth cabins. The large 'saloon' aft is the passengers' common room. The schooner was named after Capt. Hawkins' wife.

Mary Day carries a large motor tender slung in davits across the transom stern. This is also used for towing, since the schooner herself has no engine. During the summer she sails from Camden, Maine, on one-week cruises starting every Monday.

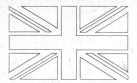

Sir Winston Churchill

Type:
3-masted topsail schooner. Steel

Country: Great Britain

Owner:
Sail Training Association (S.T.A.)

Home port:
Portsmouth. Registered at Hull

Year of construction:
1965; keel laid November 21. 1964;
launched February 5, 1966;
commissioned March 3, 1966

Builders:
Richard Dunston (Hessle) Ltd.,
Haven Shipyard, Hessle, Yorks
Designed by Camper & Nicholson
Ltd.

Tonnage:
281 tons displacement, 300 tons
Thames Measurement

Dimensions:

LOA	150 ft	4 in
Length hull	135 ft	
Length between perpendiculars	100 ft	
Breadth extreme	26 ft	8 in
Moulded depth	18 ft	8 in
Draft	15 ft	9 in

Sail area:
8,750 sq ft; mizzen 1,378 sq ft;
mainsail 927 sq ft; running square
sail 1,260 sq ft

Rig:
14 sails. 4 headsails, foremast: running
square sail, single topsail, raffee,
gaff sail, gaff topsail; mainmast:
gaff sail, gaff topsail, topmast staysail;
mizzen mast: bermudan sail, topmast staysail

Masts:
height of mainmast above deck:
97 ft 9 in. All masts aluminium,
pole masts

Engines:
2 120 hp Perkins diesels.
Speed under power 9½ knots

Complement:
6 permanent crew, 40 boys or girls

Use: sail training ship

In 1954 the Englishman Bernard Morgan had the idea that all the large sailing ships ought to meet regularly for a Tall Ships Race. The idea met with a sympathetic response in Britain, and in 1955 a committee was formed which initially called itself The Sail Training Race Committee and was later renamed Sail Training Association (S. T. A.). It organizes the Tall Ships Races, which were initiated with the 1956 Torbay to Lisbon race.

Since then races have been held at two-yearly intervals: 1958 Brest to Las Palmas, 1960 Oslo to Ostend, 1962 Cannes to Naples, 1964 Lisbon to Bermuda, followed by 'Operation Sail' in New York, 1966 Falmouth to The Skaw, followed by a joint visit of all participants to Copenhagen and a return race from The Skaw to Den Helder, and 1968 Gothenburg to the Orkneys and back to Kristiansand. The 1970 race will be from Plymouth to Santa Cruz, Tenerife.

Entry in the Tall Ships Race is open to all ships at least 50 per cent of whose crew are cadets or boys between the ages of 16 and 21.

The idea of the Tall Ships Races was born in Britain, and it was a British association that organized them, but Britain herself no longer possessed a sail training ship. For several races she chartered foreign ships, usually keeping on the permanent crew and making up the complement by the required number of British boys. But the cry for a British ship became ever louder, and eventually, in 1964, the S. T. A., under the patronage of H. R. H. The Duke of Edinburgh, commissioned the schooner *Sir Winston Churchill* to be built.

A large number of firms and organizations all over the country spontaneously offered their support. Her launching, scheduled originally for November 9, 1965, was delayed until February 1966 because the ship fell over on the slip during a heavy gale on October 31, 1965. Her aluminium masts broke, but the rest of the damage was not too serious, and she was put into service in March 1966 as planned.

The training ship is, above all, considered a means of enabling a large number of boys and girls from all parts of the country and all classes of society to live together in a community in which everything they do is part of a team effort. Character training is the main objective. Boys are taken irrespective of whether they later intend to follow a naval career. The response among young people in Britain has been so enthusiastic that courses are always booked out for months in advance, and another ship, the *Malcolm Miller,* has had to be built only one year after the *Sir Winston Churchill.* *Sir Winston Churchill* is, of course, equipped with the most up-to-date navigation instruments and safety equipment. She has a central heating system for use during winter cruises. Her figurehead is a red lion holding the Sail Training Association's shield with the initials S. T. A.

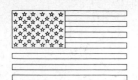

Shenandoah

Type:
2-masted topsail schooner. Wood

Country: U.S.A.

Owner:
Capt. Robert S. Douglas, Coastwise Packet Co., Vineyard Haven, Massachusetts

Home port:
Vineyard Haven, Martha's Vineyard, Massachusetts

Year of construction:
1964. Launched February 15, 1964

Builders:
Harvey F. Gamage, South Bristol, Maine

Tonnage:
172 tons displacement, 85 tons gross

Dimensions:
LOA	152 ft
Length hull	114 ft
Length between perpendiculars	100 ft
Breadth extreme	23 ft
Depth in hold	7 ft
Draft	11 ft

Sail area: 6,788 sq ft

Rig:
8 sails. 3 headsails; foremast: double topsails, gaff sail; mainmast: gaff sail, gaff topsail

Masts and spars:
height of mainmast above deck 90 ft 6 in; both masts have top masts; bowsprit with jib-boom

Engine: no auxiliary

Complement:
8, additional accomodation for guests

Use: private charter vessel

In recent years it has become very popular in the United States to spend one's holidays on board a large sailing ship, which has led to a steadily rising demand for suitable ships. It was with this in mind that *Shenandoah* was built, a fine-looking schooner which has accommodation for a crew of 8 and 37 passengers. She makes one-month cruises off Cape Cod.

Shenandoah was built from the plans of the fast U. S. customs cutter *Joe Lane* built in 1849.

The vessels engaged in coastal smuggling in those days were not all of one and the same type, but they had certain things in common: manoeuvrability, speed and a firstclass crew. Since the 'hot' cargoes rarely took up much space, smallish ships were preferred, which could negotiate narrow channels, if need be. The ships sent out to catch them had to have equal qualities and, in addition, had to be big and strong enough to carry the necessary guns. *Shenandoah* is a classic example of this excellent type of ship.

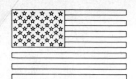

America II

Type:
  2-masted schooner. Wood (replica)

Country: U.S.A.

Owner:
  F. & M. Schaefer Brewing Co.,
  New York, New York

Home port: New York, New York

Year of construction:
  1967. Launched May 3, 1967

Builders:
  Goudy & Steven, East Boothbay,
  Maine

Tonnage:
  149 tons displacement, 92.24 tons
  gross, 66 tons net

Dimensions:

LOA	130 ft
Length hull	104 ft 10 in
LWL	90 ft 8 in
Length on keel	80 ft 10 in
Breadth extreme	22 ft 10 in
Draft (max)	11 ft 6 in

Sail area: 5,387 sq ft

Rig:
  4 sails. One headsail (with boom);
  foremast: gaff sail; mainmast: gaff
  sail, gaff topsail

Masts:
  height of mainmast above deck 74 ft.
  Mainmast with topmast

Engine:
  350 hp General Motors 8 V - 71 diesel

Complement: 7

Use: private yacht

The story of the schooner *America* is one of the most thrilling in the history of yachting. On the occasion of the Great Exhibition of 1851 in London it was decided to sail a yacht race off the British coast and invite the newly-founded New York Yacht Club to enter. Britain in those days was the stronghold of yachting and was expected to win the race from the outset, whereas the Americans could hope to enter but a single boat, and that was not even built. Her keel was laid in the winter of 1850 at the yard of William Brown in New York City, and as she took shape she incorporated all the experience which had so far been gained in the buildings of fast ships. She was launched on May 3, 1851 and, since she was to represent her country, was named *America.*

The Royal Yacht Squadron put up as trophy a silver cup which was later to become world-famous as the America's Cup. The historic race took place on August 22, 1851, starting at 10 a. m. The Royal Yacht Squadron had entered 14 yachts in all, schooners and cutters. The United States was represented by the *America* only, but this yacht achieved the seemingly impossible: she covered the 58-mile course round the Isle of Wight in 10$\frac{1}{2}$ hours and crossed the finishing line 8 minutes before her nearest rival. When Queen Victoria, who was watching the race from the Royal Yacht *Victoria and Albert,* asked who was second, she was given the reply: "There is no second, Your Majesty."

So the Cup went to the United States and has remained there ever since. Twenty challenges, the last of them in 1967, have so far been mounted by British, Canadian and Australian 12-metres, but none has succeeded in winning back the coveted trophy. It is estimated that a total of roughly £ 10 million has been spent to date on building yachts and training crews for the America's Cup Race. Many a sponsor has lost a fortune in the process. The enormous sums involved can nowadays only be raised by syndicates of millionaires. The cost of the 1967 race to the American syndicate, for example, was $ 3.7 million.

The schooner *America* had cost $ 20,000 when she was built. She was preserved as a national monument until 1944. On May 3, 1967, exactly 116 years after the original, *America II*, a precise replica, was launched in Maine. The cost of this copy, built for R. J. Schaefer, President of the T. & M. Schaefer Brewing Co. of New York, was no less than $ 500,000!

During the 1967 America's Cup Race off Newport, Rhode Island, *America II* was among the spectator fleet. It is planned that she should cruise all along the American coast and during stays in port be open to public viewing.

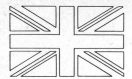

Malcolm Miller

Type:
 3-masted topsail schooner. Steel

Country: Great Britain

Owner:
 Sail Training Association (S.T.A.)

Home port: Portsmouth

Year of construction:
 1967; keel laid March 23, 1967;
 launched October 5, 1967;
 commissioned March 10, 1968

Builders:
 John Lewis & Sons Ltd., Aberdeen

Tonnage:
 244 tons displacement; 300 tons
 Thames Measurement, 219.16 tons
 gross, 40.33 tons net

Dimensions:

LOA	150 ft
Length hull	135 ft
Length between	
perpendiculars	100 ft
Breadth extreme	25 ft
Depth moulded	18 ft 7 in
Draft	15 ft 6 in

Sail area:
 7,104 sq ft (working area), 8,798 sq ft
 with running square sail

Rig:
 14 sails. 4 headsails; foremast: running
 square sail, single topsail, raffee,
 gaff sail, gaff topsail; mainmast:
 gaff sail, gaff topsail, topmast staysail;
 mizzen mast: bermudan sail, topmast staysail

Masts:
 height of mainmast above deck
 97 ft 9 in. All masts in one piece,
 of equal height and in aluminium

Engines:
 2 120 hp Perkins diesels.
 Speed under power 9.5 knots

Complement:
 7 permanent crew, 40 boys or girls

Use: sail training vessel

The main function of sail training vessels has always been to train future officers and seamen for the navy and merchant marine. Surprisingly enough, Britain, as one of the leading maritime nations, did not have a real, large sailing schoolship in commission for several decades. When, eventually, the *Sir Winston Churchill* was built it was not exactly with the idea of resuming the old tradition of naval sail-training but to give it a new lease of life under different aspects. The principal objective of the Sail Training Association, who owns the two schooners, is not to prepare boys for a naval career but to put them through a school of general character building.

The lively interest which the training courses on board *Sir Winston Churchill* aroused and the great enthusiasm with which both boys and girls joined in, led to the building of her sister-ship just one year after she had been launched. The two schooners are absolutely identical, except that in *Malcolm Miller* the accommodation has been enlarged and improved. Their figureheads are different, too. The red Scottish lion on *Malcolm Miller's* bow, holding in its claws the coat-of-arms of Sir James Miller, was carved by the well-known sculptor of wooden figureheads, Jack Whitehead of Wootton, Isle of Wight. Sir James Miller was a former Lord Major of London and Lord Provost of Edinburgh. It was a generous donation by his family, covering half of the total building costs of £175,000, which made it possible for the ship to be built. She is named after Malcolm, son of Sir James, who was killed in a car crash in 1966.

The new schooner sailed on her maiden voyage from Leith on March 10, 1968. In August 1968 both ships took part in the Tall Ships Race from Gothenburg to the Orkneys and back to Kristiansand. Between them the two ships made thirty cruises in 1968 in which 1,260 boys and girls took part.

Nonsuch

Type:
square-rigged ketch. Wood (oak)

Country: Canada

Owner:
Manitoba Museum, Winnipeg,
Manitoba

Location: Winnipeg

Year of construction: 1968; launched
August 1968

Builders:
J. Hinks & Son, Appledore,
Devon, England

Tonnage:
65 tons displacement

Dimensions:

LOA	74 ft 10 in
Length hull	53 ft 6 in
Length between perpendiculars	50 ft 3 in
Breadth extreme	15 ft 6 in
Depth moulded	6 ft 10 in
Depth in hold	6 ft 10 in
Draft	6 ft 10 in

Sail area: 1,894 sq ft

Rig:
6 sails. 2 headsails. Mainmast: main
course, topsail; mizzenmast: square
topsail, lateen sail

Masts:
height of mainmast above deck
73 ft 10 in

Engine: 95 hp Perkins diesel

Complement: approx 12

Use: museum ship

The original *Nonsuch* was built in 1650 by Page of Wivenhoe, Essex, and the first ship of what was later to become known as the Hudson's Bay Company. In 1668 she crossed from England to North America to trade with the Indians. She got as far as James Bay, where her crew spent the winter in a hut they built on land and returned to England the following year with a cargo of beaver skins. Upon her return, in May 1670, King Charles II granted a group of interested noblemen the right to trade with the Hudson Bay territory.

To celebrate the third centenary of the Hudson's Bay Company, the shipyard of J. Hinks & Son at Appledore, Devon, was commissioned to build a precise replica of the *Nonsuch* from plans carefully prepared by the National Maritime Museum. This particular shipyard was chosen because its shipwrights still use the old-fashioned adze and are skilled in the traditional methods of shipbuilding.

The replica was built in a traditional manner, using only large tree nails as fastenings. The result is a very fine ship indeed, a ship of the past in its lines and decorations and an impressive testimony to the Company's pioneering deeds. There were, of course, much bigger ships in those days, but it was in the wake of the *Nonsuch* that the Hudson's Bay Company extended its trading territory far into the interior of western Canada until, in 1869, it surrendered its lands to Canada.

The carved decorations on the present *Nonsuch* are the work of the well-known carver of figureheads, Jack Whitehead of Wootton, I. O. W., among them some fine stern ornaments and mermaids supporting the catheads. After visiting North America in 1969 and 1970 *Nonsuch* will be presented to the Manitoba Museum in Winnipeg.

The Tall Ships Race

The idea of getting the last remaining sailing ships to race together at regular intervals was originally a British idea and was realized in 1956 when the first Tall Ships Race, from Torbay to Lisbon, took place. Ever since then the British Sail Training Association has been organising a Tall Ships Race every two years. Participation is open to any sailing vessel which is used for training purposes and is crewed by young people. For the purpose of the race the ships are divided into several classes. Since the starting and finishing points are different for every race, the youngsters have an excellent opportunity to get to know foreign countries and peoples. It is to be hoped that one day the Iron Curtain countries with their many splendid schoolships will be among the participants, and this would certainly be welcomed with great enthusiasm by all the youngsters. Our picture shows the start of the 1960 race from Oslo to Ostend (and for some participants from there to Lisbon and Naples) while the fleet is still close together.

In 1968 nine square-riggers and large schooners participated in the race from Gothenburg to the Orkneys and back to Kristiansand. The next race will be held in 1970, starting from Plymouth on July 29 and finishing in Santa Cruz de Tenerife.

The birth of a wooden ship

The Danish town of Svendborg is known not only for its nautical college but also for its important shipyards. The biggest of them builds large steel ships, but it is not this which attracts the lover of traditional wooden shipbuilding. It is the smaller yard of J. Ring-Andersen, just across the way. Although it appears modest by comparison, fascinating things go on behind its walls, for it is one of the very few remaining yards where seagoing wooden ships are craftsman-built by hand. In the picture we can see a fishing vessel on the stocks being built for British account for operation in the North Sea. The keel, stem, stern-post and frames have already been assembled. The timber used is oak. Not until the 19th century was it possible to bend straight timbers into any desired shape by the use of steam. Until then builders relied entirely on grown timbers, i.e. timbers with a natural curvature. Even today builders prefer grown timbers because they 'work' less and thus put less strain on the fastenings.

The vast quantities of timber that were needed for building ships (it is estimated that it took 4,000 sound oak-trees to build a ship-of-the-line) and the fact that only certain parts of a tree could be used, led to widespread deforestation of Great Britain in the 18th century. A similar thing happened to what is now the Lüneburg Heath in Northern Germany. In the end shipyards had to turn to America for timber.

This is, very roughly, how a wooden ship is built: to start with the keel is laid on blocks on the slip. Then the previously assembled stem and sternpost are connected to the wooden keel. The ribs are either set up on the keel *in situ* or, which is commoner, assembled

in frames on the loft floor and erected on the keel. Finally the deck beams are fastened across the tops of the frames. Now the bottom, side and deck planks are laid over this skeleton to make a hollow vessel, the hull.

All wooden ships at the yard of J. Ring-Andersen are built in this way. The hull under construction in the picture has reached the stage where the skeleton is about to be planked up inside and out.

A number of the larger sailing ships built at this yard are still afloat, the oldest of them having been in commission for over sixty years without interruption: *Bel Espoir, Carthaginian, Lilla Dan, Regina Maris* (1908), *Romance, Seute Deern II, Topaz.* Wooden ships of this size have an important advantage over steel or iron ships in that they are more supple, more resistant to impact and, above all, safe from rust.

267

Pamir and Passat

It was with great difficulty and virtually at the eleventh hour that the shipowner Heinz Schliewen and Captain Helmut Grubbe succeeded in rescuing the two large four-masted barks from the breaker's yard in Antwerp. They had them towed to Travemünde, where they arrived on June 20, 1951. A little later they were taken to Kiel where the Howaldt-Werke, at considerable cost, converted them into cargo-carrying training ships. Amongst other things this meant the installation in each ship of an auxiliary engine, watertight bulkheads, two deckhouses, gangways, etc. Brace and halyard winches were transferred to the upper deck for safety reasons. The work was finished late in 1951, and the ships were given A1 classifications.

This picture, taken in August 1951, shows them lying next to each other in Kiel.

Pamir sailed from Hamburg on her first post-war voyage under the German flag on January 10, 1952. She had loaded 4,000 tons of cement for Brazil, a quantity approximately equal to 400 railway goods trucks. *Passat* sailed from Brake on the River Weser on February 12, 1952, also bound for Brazil with cement.

With a few exceptions both ships sailed on this route until 1957. They were the last big cargo-carrying sailing ships to ply the oceans.

Ships for which no details are available

The following is a list of sailing ships about which no detailed information is available at this moment. Many of them are now hulks; some are only planned and not yet built.

Bulgaria

Assen, *Burgas* and *Kamica*, 2-masted gaff schooners, sail training vessels of the Bulgarian Navy.

Canada

Briton, steel hulk. 2700 tons displacement, length 230 ft 8 in. Built in 1883 as the bark H.M.S. *Calypso*. She was steam-powered and armed with guns. Since 1952 she has been used as store vessel in Lewisport, Newfoundland.

Federal Republic of Germany

Aar, 3-masted gaff schooner, steel, built in 1932, 330 tons gross. Owner W. Tietjen, marine brokers in Hamburg. The ship had her length increased in 1952. Today she is usually seen without sails, carrying bulk cargo between Finland and Great Britain. She is manned by a crew of seven.
Mariann (ex *Britanie*), 3-masted gaff schooner, wood. Built at Malmö, Sweden, in 1903. Owner Peter v. Sucker, Keitum, Sylt. Length over all appr. 130 ft, length between perpendiculars appr. 105 ft, breadth extreme appr. 26 ft, draft (unloaded) appr. 8 ft.
At the moment the schooner is lying idle at Keitum-Munkmarsch (Isle of Sylt) waiting to be converted to a private schoolship on plans drawn up by the owner.

France

The Association Pour un Grand Voilier-Ecole Francais at Paris ist planning to build a 3-masted schooner (possibly a staysail schooner). Likely yard: Dubigeon-Normandie, Nantes. Design: M. Yves Marechal. Proposed tonnage and dimensions: 788 tons gross, length about 217 ft, beam 33 ft, sail area about 13,000 sq. ft. Permanent crew of 16, approximately 90 boys.
As with the ships of the Sail Training Association this vessel is to be made available to all young people interested in sailing. According to the Association's Secretary, finance is the main problem at the moment.
Amphitrite, barkentine, 161 tons gross. Built in England in 1887 as 3-masted. schooner yacht. Now run as sail training vessel under the French flag.

Great Britain

Kathleen & May, 3-masted gaff schooner, wood. Early in 1968 she was still laid up near Appledore, Devon. Future use uncertain.
Mercury (ex H.M.S. *President*, ex H.M.S. *Gannet*), hulk, composite construction, 1130 tons displacement, length between perpendiculars 169 ft 8 in. She was built in 1878 as a gunboat and armed with six guns. From 1904 she served as training vessel to the Royal Naval Reserve in London. From 1916 to 1968 she lay in the Hamble River near Southampton as a stationary training vessel under the name of H.M.S. *Mercury*. Her destiny is as yet uncertain.
Wan Fu, brigantine, steel. Length between perpendiculars 109 ft 7 in. Ten sails. Built in 1959, designed by William Garden. She is owned by the Hilton Hotel in Hong Kong and used as a yacht.

Italy

Ebe, brigantine, wood. 600 tons gross. Built in 1921 in Viareggio. From 1952 to 1955 used as a training ship of the Italian Navy. Now on show in the Science Museum in Milan.

Netherlands

Abel Tasman, hulk, iron. Built in Rotterdam in 1876 as the armed barkentine *Bonaire* for the Royal Dutch Navy. Now houses the Delfzijl Sailing School.

Nigeria

Dynomene, hulk, iron. 1900 tons gross. Length between perpendiculars 269 ft 6 in. Built in 1882 by W. H. Potter for Fernie to sail as a full-rigged cargo-ship under the British flag. Since 1910 her hulk has been lying in the river Niger.

Sweden

Ellen, 3-masted gaff schooner, wood. Built in 1908 in Thuro (Sweden). Motorized since 1930. Last seen in San Pedro, California, in December 1967. Used as cargo-carrier in the Pacific, calling mainly at Californian and Central American ports.

U.S.A.

Buccaneer, hulk, wood. 2043 tons displacement. Length 253 ft 4 in. Built in 1918 in Orange, Texas, as the 5-masted barkentine *City of Beaumont*. Now used as a breakwater at Hastings, N.Y.
Independence, 2-masted topsail schooner. Length 88 ft 7 in. Pleasure yacht cruising in the Caribbean.
Rendezvous, brigantine. Built in 1934 in Seattle. Her home port is in California and she is used as a yacht.

Ships which no longer exist

These are sailing ships which still appear on registers but which are no longer in existence (I), or whose existence is doubtful (II), or which operate as motor vessels (III).

I

Brazil

Albatroz (ex *Wishbone*) 2-masted gaff schooner. Built in 1920. Withdrawn from service and broken up in the sixties.

Chile

General Baquedano, bark (steam-powered corvette), built in 1898. Broken up in the fifties.

Ecuador

Beagle II (ex *Swift*), brigantine, built around 1922. Named after Darwin's famous *Beagle*. From 1964 to 1967 run by the Charles Darwin Research Station at Santa Cruz, Galapagos. After being taken out of service she was sunk off Santa Cruz on November 23, 1967.

Great Britain

Clipper Cutty Sark (ex *Estrella Polar*), 3-masted topsail schooner, built in 1939. She sank on June 11, 1964.
H.M.S. *Conway*, ship of the line, built 1832. Ran aground in the Menai Strait, North Wales, in 1954 on her way to the breakers. Broken up in 1956.
New Endeavour (ex *Cito*), 3-masted topsail schooner. Built in Denmark as a ketch. Rerigged as schooner in 1965. According to a semi-official report she became a total loss off the Australian coast in 1967.

Portugal

Dom Fernando E Gloria, bark, (formerly warship, frigate), built in 1857. Last used as a stationary schoolship (hulk). Completely destroyed by fire in about 1963.

Sweden

Gerda, brig, built 1869. Last used as a floating museum in Gävle. Broken up in 1951.

Spain

Baleares (ex *Sant Mus*), barkentine, built 1919. Broken up in 1952.

Uruguay

Aspirante (ex *Exir Dallen*, ex *Parodi*, ex *Trinidad*, ex *Gelmirez*), 3-masted schooner. Said to be last used as a stationary schoolship. According to the Commander-in-Chief of the Uruguayan Navy the ship has ceased to exist.

U.S.A.

Emery Rice (ex *Bay State*, ex *Nantucket*), bark, built 1876. The ship was sold on March 7, 1958 to the Boston Metal Company, Baltimore, Maryland, to be broken up,
Verona (ex *Xarifa*), 3-masted staysail schooner with topsails (frequently called a barkentine), built 1912. Completely destroyed by fire on the West African coast in the summer of 1967, shortly after leaving Fernando Póo.

II

Dominican Republic

Duarte (ex *Nueva Tioditie*), gaff schooner, built in 1943. Sank in May 1965. Efforts to repair her are being made, but she looks like a write-off.

Great Britain

Vindicatrix (ex *Arranmore*), full-rigged ship, built 1893. The hulk was last used as a stationary schoolship by the Gravesend Sea School, and finally delivered to the breaker's yard of John Cashmore Limited, Newport, Monmouthshire, on January 13, 1967. Her fate has not yet been decided.

Italy

Patria (ex *Susanne Vinnen*), 5-masted square-rigged schooner, built 1922. Converted into a pure motor vessel in 1947. Her future is uncertain.

Mexico

Seven Seas (ex *Abraham Rydberg II*), full-rigged ship, built 1912. Presumed to have been renamed and to be operating in the banana trade as a pure motor vessel under the Mexican flag.

Poland

Lwow (ex *Nest*, ex *Lucco*, ex *Chinsura*), bark, built 1869. Last used as hulk at Gdynia.

Yugoslavia

Vila Velebita, brigantine, built 1908. Probably replaced by *Jadran*. Continued existence questionable.

III

Norway

Kjeöy (ex *Statsraad Erichsen*), built as brig in 1858. Now operating as coastal motor vessel.

Russian ships

Several barkentines were built by the Laivateollisuus yard at Turku, Finland for the Soviet Union. Their dimensions and tonnage are the same as those of *Alpha, Meridian* etc. see page 222/224.

Sirius (1948)
Zenit (1948)

A series of three-masted gaff-rigged cargo schooners, were built for the Russians by Laivateollisuus at Turku, Finland with the same dimensions and of the same type as *Kapella* (Schooner!—page 223).

Perlmutr (1949)
Chaika (1949)
Sprut (1949)
Utritsa (1949)
Krab (1949)
Jantar (1949)
Kometa (1949)
Saira (1949)
Ambra (1949)
Sardina (1949)
Kaira (1949)
Vostok (1949)
Keta (1949)
Akula (1950)
Kupy (1950)
Myntu (1950)
Takhuna (1951)
Ristna (1951)

A considerable number of similar vessels had not been named when they were delivered to the Soviet Union, but their builders numbers were 22, 23, 24, 25, 26, 30, 31, 33, 35, 37, 38, 39 and 40. These ships were built in 1950—51. Further three-masted gaff-rigged sail training schooners were also built by the

Laivateollisuus yard in Turku for the Russians, all with the same measurements and of the same type as *Kapella*. (Schooner!—page 223).

Ivan Mesjatsev (1950)
Georgij Ratmanov (1950)

Several similar vessels had not been named when they were delivered to the Soviet Union. Their construction numbers were 42, 43, 44 and 45 and they were built in 1951-52.

Several sailing vessels were built by Hammars yard, Finland for Russia, but their present employment is not known. Their measurements are:

Length hull	147 ft.
Length between perpendiculars	123 ft.
Breadth extreme	28 ft. 8 in.
Draft	11 ft. 4 in.
Displacement	626 tons
Deadweight	300 tons
Sail area	8848 sq. ft.
Propulsion: 3-cylinder June-Munktell Diesel engine	225 h.p.

Lama (gaff-rigged)

Keel laid	June 1, 1945
Launched	June 20, 1946
Delivered	September 25, 1946

Polarnaja (gaff-rigged)

Keel laid	August 28, 1945
Launched	July 20, 1946
Delivered	September 25, 1946

Venera (Bermuda-rigged)

Keel laid	June 29, 1946
Launched	April 30, 1947
Delivered	July 14, 1947

Chemtjug (Bermuda-rigged)

Keel laid	August 20, 1946
Launched	July 10, 1947
Delivered	October 13, 1947

Globus (gaff-rigged)

Keel laid	May 20, 1947
Launched	December 20, 1947
Delivered	July 7, 1948

Svesda (Bermuda-rigged)

Keel laid	July 24, 1947
Launched	July 23, 1948
Delivered	October 21, 1948

Osjminog (Bermuda-rigged)

Keel laid	December 13, 1947
Launched	November 17, 1948
Delivered	July 20, 1949

Two barkentines were built at F. W. Hollming's yard in Raumo, Finland. They are used as training ships, and their dimensions are probably much the same as those of *Alpha, Meridian* etc., see page 222/224.

Junga

Keel laid	April 15, 1946
Launched	May 9, 1947
Delivered	August 13, 1947

Sturman

Keel laid	April 17, 1946
Launched	December 22, 1946
Delivered	August 13, 1947

List of ships in chronological order of construction

1628 *Vasa*, two-decker, Sweden
1765 *Victory*, ship of the line, Great Britain
1797 *Constellation*, frigate, U.S.A.

1797 *Constitution*, frigate, U.S.A.
1813 *Niagara*, brig., U.S.A.
1817 *Foudroyant*, frigate, Great Britain

1824 *Unicorn*, frigate, Great Britain
1841 *Charles W. Morgan*, full-rigged ship, U.S.A.

1853 *Edwin Fox*, full-rigged ship, New Zealand
1857 *Jylland*, frigate, Denmark
1863 *Alice S. Wentworth*, 2-masted gaff schooner, U.S.A.

1863 *Star of India*, bark, U.S.A.
1864 *Carrick*, full-rigged ship, Great Britain
1869 *Cutty Sark*, full-rigged ship, Great Britain

1874 *Meiji Maru*, full-rigged ship, Japan
1874 *Boys Marine Training Establishment*, bark, U.A.R.

1878 *Falls of Clyde*, 4-masted, full-rigged ship, U.S.A.
1882 *Joseph Conrad*, full-rigged ship, U.S.A.
1882 *Dolphin*, hulk, ex bark, Great Britain

1883 *Gazela Primeiro*, barkentine, Portugal
1885 *Polly Woodside*, bark, Australia
1885 *Wavertree*, hulk, ex full-rigged ship, U.S.A.

1886 *Balclutha*, full-rigged ship, U.S.A.
1887 *Moby Dick*, frigate, Great Britain
1887 *Sigyn*, barkentine, Finland

1888 *Af Chapman*, full-rigged ship, Sweden
1892 *Fram*, 3-masted topsail schooner, Norway
1895 *C.A. Thayer*, 3-masted gaff schooner, U.S.A.

1896 *Giorgio Cini*, barkentine, Italy
1896 *Santo Andre*, bark, Portugal
1896 *Galatea*, bark, Spain

1897 *Najaden*, full-rigged ship, Sweden
1897 *Wawona*, 3-masted gaff schooner, U.S.A.
1898 *Presidente Sarmiento*, full-rigged ship, Argentinia

1899 *Andalucia*, 4-masted bark, Chile
1899 *Jarramas*, full-rigged ship, Sweden
1899 *Kaiulani*, bark, U.S.A.

1900 *Victory Chimes*, 3-masted gaff schooner, U.S.A.
1901 *Duchesse Anne*, full-rigged ship, France

1901 *Discovery*, bark, Great Britain
1902 *Suomen Joutsen*, full-rigged ship, Finland

1902 *Champigny*, 4-masted bark, U.S.A.
1903 *Pommern*, 4-masted bark, Finland
1903 *Duenna*, brigantine, Great Britain

1904 *Moshulu*, 4-masted bark, Finland
1904 *Worcester*, ship of the line, Great Britain
1906 *Viking*, 4-masted bark, Sweden

1908 *Arken*, 2-masted topsail schooner, Denmark
1908 *Regina Maris*, barkentine, Norway
1909 *Dar Pormorza*, full-rigged ship, Poland

1909 *Unyo Maru*, bark, Japan
1911 *Passat*, 4-masted bark, F.R.G.
1911 *Arethusa*, 4-masted bark, Great Britain

1914 *Statsraad Lehmkuhl*, bark, Norway
1914 *Alve*, 3-masted gaff schooner, F.R.G.
1914 *Tabor Boy*, 2-masted topsail schooner, U.S.A.

1917 *Lucy Evelyn*, 3-masted gaff schooner, U.S.A.
1917 *Iskra*, 3-masted gaff schooner, Poland

1918 *Norlandia*, 3-masted topsail schooner, Great Britain
1919 *Seute Deern*, bark, F.R.G.

1921 *Sedov*, 4-masted bark, U.S.S.R.
1921 *Bowdoin*, 2-masted gaff schooner, U.S.A.
1921 *Carthaginian*, bark, U.S.A.

1921 *L. A. Dunton*, 2-masted gaff schooner, U.S.A.
1923 *Shintoku Maru*, formerly 4-masted barkentine, Japan

1923 *José Alberto*, 4-masted gaff schooner, Portugal
1923 *Vema*, 3-masted schooner, U.S.A.

1926 *Krusenstern*, 4-masted bark, U.S.S.R.
1926 *Adventure*, 2-masted gaff schooner, U.S.A.
1927 *Schulschiff Deutschland*, full-rigged ship, F.R.G.

1927 *Creole*, 3-masted staysail schooner, Greece
1927 *Fantome*, 4-masted gaff schooner, Greece
1927 *Sørlandet*, full-rigged ship, Norway

1927 *Juan Sebastian de Elcano*, 4-masted topsail schooner, Spain
1927 *Yankee Clipper*, 2-masted staysail schooner, U.S.A.

1928 *Urania*, ketch, Netherlands
1928 *St. Roch*, 2-masted gaff schooner, Canada
1928 *Dunay*, full-rigged ship, U.S.S.R.

1928 *Polynesia*, 2-masted staysail schooner, U.S.A.

1929 *Hortense*, 3-masted gaff schooner, Portugal
1929 *Eugene Egenides*, 3-masted topsail schooner, Greece

1930 *Kaiwo Maru*, 4-masted bark, Japan
1930 *Nippon Maru*, 4-masted bark, Japan
1931 *Amerigo Vespucci*, full-rigged ship, Italy

1931 *Jadran*, 3-masted topsail schooner, Yugoslavia
1931 *Patria*, 4-masted bark, U.S.A.

1932 *Mercator*, barkentine, Belgium
1932 *La Belle Poule*, 2-masted topsail schooner, France

1932 *L'Etoile*, 2-masted topsail schooner, France
1933 *Almirante Saldanha*, formerly 4-masted topsail schooner, Brazil

1933 *Danmark*, full-rigged ship, Denmark
1933 *Tovaristsch*, bark, U.S.S.R.
1934 *Georg Stage*, full-rigged ship, Denmark

1934 *Palinuro*, barkentine, Italy
1936 *Brites*, 4-masted gaff schooner, Portugal
1936 *Eagle*, bark, U.S.A.

1936 *Romance*, brigantine, U.S.A.
1937 *Christian Radich*, full-rigged ship, Norway
1937 *Creoula*, 4-masted gaff schooner, Portugal

1937 *Sagres*, bark, Portugal
1937 *Santa Maria Manuela*, 4-masted gaff schooner, Portugal

1937 *Swift of Ipswich*, 2-masted topsail schooner, U.S.A.
1937 *Topaz*, 2-masted gaff schooner, U.S.A.

1938 *Argus*, 4-masted gaff schooner, Portugal
1938 *Mircea*, bark, Romania
1939 *Centurion*, brigantine, Great Britain

1939 *Mariusz Zaruski*, ketch, Poland
1939 *Seute Deern*, ketch, F.R.G.
1940 *Dom Deniz*, 3-masted gaff schooner, Portugal

1940 *Pollux*, bark, Netherlands
1942 *Albatross*, 4-masted motor schooner, Sweden

1942 *Caribee*, 2-masted topsail schooner, U.S.A.
1942 *Varua*, brigantine, France
1944 *Henryk Rutkowski*, ketch, Poland

1944 *Bel Espoir*, 3-masted gaff schooner, France
1945 *Cruz Del Sur*, full-rigged ship, U.S.A.
1945 *Janek Krasicki*, 2-masted gaff schooner, Poland

1945 *Zew Morza*, 2-masted gaff schooner,
     Poland
1946 *Falken*, 2-masted gaff schooner, Sweden

1947 *Gladan*, 2-masted gaff schooner, Sweden
1948 *Adelia Maria*, 4-masted gaff schooner,
     Portugal

1948 *Alpha*, barkentine, U.S.S.R.
1948 *Horisont*, barkentine, U.S.S.R.
1948 *Kapella*, barkentine, U.S.S.R.

1948 *Meridian*, barkentine, U.S.S.R.
1948 *Sekstant*, barkentine, U.S.S.R.
1948 *Tropik*, barkentine, U.S.S.R.

1950 *Lilla Dan*, 2-masted topsail schooner,
     Denmark
1951 *Black Pearl*, brigantine, U.S.A.

1951 *Wilhelm Pieck*, brigantine, G.D.R.
1952 *Kodor*, 3-masted schooner, U.S.S.R.
1952 *Esmeralda*, 4-masted barkentine, Chile

1952 *Zarja*, 3-masted gaff schooner, U.S.S.R.
1952 *Zawisza Czarny*, 3-masted staysail
     schooner, Poland

1953 *Dewarutji*, barkentine, Indonesia
1953 *St. Lawrence*, brigantine, Canada
1956 *Libertad*, full-rigged ship, Argentina

1956 *Mayflower*, galleon, U.S.A.
1958 *Gorch Fock*, bark, F.R.G.
1959 *Carita*, 3-masted staysail schooner, Greece

1960 *Bounty II*, full-rigged ship, U.S.A.
1962 *Mary Day*, 2-masted gaff schooner, U.S.A.
1963 *Santa Maria II*, nao, U.S.A.

1963 *Bluenose*, 2-masted gaff schooner, Canada
1963 *Pathfinder*, brigantine, Canada
1964 *Shenandoah*, 2-masted topsail schooner,
     U.S.A.

1965 *Sir Winston Churchill*, 3-masted topsail
     schooner, Great Britain
1967 *America*, 2-masted schooner yacht, U.S.A.

1967 *Malcolm Miller*, 3-masted topsail schooner,
     Great Britain
1968 *Nonsuch*, square-rigged ketch, Canada

List of ships by nationality

Argentina
1898 *Presidente Sarmiento*, full-rigged ship
1956 *Libertad*, full-rigged ship

Australia
1885 *Polly Woodside*, bark

Belgium
1932 *Mercator*, barkentine

Brazil
1933 *Almirante Saldanha*, formerly 4-masted
topsail schooner

Canada
1928 *St. Roch*, 2-masted gaff schoner
1953 *St. Lawrence*, brigantine
1963 *Bluenose*, 2-masted gaff schooner
1963 *Pathfinder*, brigantine
1968 *Nonsuch*, square-rigged ketch

Chile
1899 *Andalucia*, 4-masted bark
1952 *Esmeralda*, 4-masted barkentine

Denmark
1857 *Jylland*, frigate
1908 *Arken*, 2-masted topsail schooner
1933 *Danmark*, full-rigged ship
1934 *Georg Stage*, full-rigged ship
1950 *Lilla Dan*, 2-masted topsail schooner

Federal Republic of Germany
1911 *Passat*, 4-masted bark
1914 *Alve*, 3-masted gaff schooner
1919 *Seute Deern*, bark
1927 *Schulschiff Deutschland*, full-rigged ship
1939 *Seute Deern*, ketch
1958 *Gorch Fock*, bark

Finland
1887 *Sigyn*, barkentine
1902 *Suomen Joutsen*, full-rigged ship
1903 *Pommern*, 4-masted bark
1904 *Moshulu*, 4-masted bark

France
1901 *Duchesse Anne*, full-rigged ship
1932 *La Belle Poule*, 2-masted topsail schooner
1932 *L'Etoile*, 2-masted topsail schooner
1942 *Varua*, brigantine
1944 *Bel Espoir*, 3-masted gaff schooner

German Democratic Republic
1951 *Wilhelm Pieck*, brigantine

Great Britain
1765 *Victory*, ship of the line
1817 *Foudroyant*, frigate
1824 *Unicorn*, frigate
1864 *Carrick*, full-rigged ship
1869 *Cutty Sark*, full-rigged ship
1882 *Dolphin*, hulk, ex bark
1887 *Moby Dick*, frigate
1901 *Discovery*, bark
1903 *Duenna*, brigantine
1904 *Worcester*, ship of the line
1911 *Arethusa*, 4-masted bark
1918 *Norlandia*, 3-masted topsail schooner
1939 *Centurion*, brigantine
1965 *Sir Winston Churchill*,
3-masted topsail schooner
1967 *Malcolm Miller*, 3-masted topsail schooner

Greece
1927 *Creole*, 3-masted staysail schooner
1927 *Fantome*, 4-masted gaff schooner
1929 *Eugene Eugenides*, 3-masted topsail schooner
1959 *Carita*, 3-masted staysail schooner

Indonesia
1953 *Dewarutji*, barkentine

Italy
1896 *Giorgio Cini*, barkentine
1931 *Amerigo Vespucci*, full-rigged ship
1934 *Palinuro*, barkentine

Japan
1874 *Meiji Maru*, full-rigged ship
1909 *Unyo Maru*, bark
1923 *Shintoku Maru*, formerly 4-masted
barkentine
1930 *Kaiwo Maru*, 4-masted bark
1930 *Nippon Maru*, 4-masted bark

Netherlands
1928 *Urania*, ketch
1940 *Pollux*, bark

New Zealand
1853 *Edwin Fox*, full-rigged ship

Norway
1892 *Fram*, 3-masted topsail schooner
1908 *Regina Maris*, barkentine
1914 *Statsraad Lehmkuhl*, bark
1927 *Sørlandet*, full-rigged ship
1937 *Christian Radich*, full-rigged ship

Poland
1909 *Dar Pomorza*, full-rigged ship
1917 *Iskra*, 3-masted gaff schooner
1939 *Mariusz Zaruski*, ketch
1944 *Henryk Rutkowski*, ketch
1945 *Janek Krasicki*, 2-masted gaff schooner
1945 *Zew Morza*, 2-masted gaff schooner
1952 *Zawisza Czarny*, 3-masted staysail schooner

Portugal
1883 *Gazela Primeiro*, barkentine
1896 *Santo Andre*, bark
1923 *José Alberto*, 4-masted gaff schooner
1929 *Hortense*, 3-masted gaff schooner
1936 *Brites*, 4-masted gaff schooner
1937 *Creoula*, 4-masted gaff schooner
1937 *Sagres*, bark
1937 *Santa Maria Manuela*, 4-masted gaff
schooner
1938 *Argus*, 4-masted gaff schooner
1940 *Dom Deniz*, 3-masted gaff schooner
1948 *Adelia Maria*, 4-masted gaff schooner

Romania
1938 *Mircea*, bark

Spain
1896 *Galatea*, bark
1927 *Juan Sebastian de Elcano*, 4-masted
topsail schooner

Sweden
1628 *Vasa*, two-decker
1888 *Af Chapman*, full-rigged ship
1897 *Najaden*, full-rigged ship
1899 *Jarramas*, full-rigged ship
1906 *Viking*, 4-masted bark
1942 *Albatross*, 4-masted motor schooner
1946 *Falken*, 2-masted gaff schooner
1947 *Gladan*, 2-masted gaff schooner

U.A.R.
1874 *Boys Marine Training Establishment*, bark

U.S.A.
1797 *Constellation*, frigate
1797 *Constitution*, frigate
1813 *Niagara*, brig
1841 *Charles W. Morgan*, full-rigged ship
1863 *Alice S. Wentworth*, 2-masted gaff schooner
1863 *Star of India*, bark
1878 *Falls of Clyde*, 4-masted full-rigged ship
1882 *Joseph Conrad*, full-riged ship
1885 *Wavertree*, hulk, ex full-rigged ship

274

1886 *Balclutha*, full-rigged ship
1895 *C. A. Thayer*, 3-masted gaff schooner
1897 *Wawona*, 3-masted gaff schooner
1899 *Kaiulani*, bark
1900 *Victory Chimes*, 3-masted gaff schooner
1902 *Champigny*, 4-masted bark
1914 *Tabor Boy*, 2-masted topsail schooner
1917 *Lucy Evelyn*, 3-masted gaff schooner
1921 *Bowdoin*, 2-masted gaff schooner
1921 *Carthaginian*, bark
1921 *L. A. Dunton*, 2-masted gaff schooner
1923 *Vema*, 3-masted schooner
1926 *Adventure*, 2-masted gaff schooner
1927 *Yankee Clipper*, 2-masted staysail schooner
1928 *Polynesia*, 2-masted staysail schooner
1931 *Patria*, 4-masted bark
1936 *Eagle*, bark
1936 *Romance*, brigantine
1937 *Swift of Ipswich*, 2-masted topsail schooner
1937 *Topaz*, 2-masted gaff schooner
1942 *Caribee*, 2-masted topsail schooner
1945 *Cruz Del Sur*, full-rigged ship
1951 *Black Pearl*, brigantine
1956 *Mayflower II*, galleon
1960 *Bounty II*, full-rigged ship
1962 *Mary Day*, 2-masted gaff schooner
1963 *Santa Maria II*, nao
1964 *Shenandoah*, 2-masted topsail schooner
1967 *America*, 2-masted schooner yacht

U.S.S.R.
1921 *Sedov*, 4-masted bark
1926 *Krusenstern*, 4-masted bark
1928 *Dunay*, full-rigged ship
1933 *Tovaristsch*, bark
1948 *Alpha*, barkentine
1948 *Horisont*, barkentine
1948 *Kapella*, barkentine
1948 *Meridian*, barkentine
1948 *Sekstant*, barkentine
1948 *Tropik*, barkentine
1951 *Kodor*, 3-masted schooner
1952 *Zarja*, 3-masted gaff schooner

Yugoslavia
1931 *Jadran*, 3-masted topsail schooner

Acknowledgements

It would have been impossible to compile this book without the extremely generous assistance I have received from all parts of the world. Only in this way has it been possible to obtain authentic material. I should like to express my sincere thanks to all those concerned for their interest and support.

Argentina
Embassy of the German Federal Republic, Buenos Aires.
Embassy of the Republic of Argentina, Bonn.
Consulate General of the Republic of Argentina, Hamburg.

Australia
The Adelaide Steamship Company Limited, Adelaide.
I. Hawrylow, Melbourne.
National Trust of Australia (Victoria), Melbourne.

Brazil
Ministerio Da Marinha, Rio de Janeiro.

Canada
Brigantine Incorporated, Kingston, Ontario.
Oland & Sons Limited, Halifax.
Toronto Brigantine Incorporated, Adelaide, Toronto.

Chile
Armada De Chile, Buque Escuela *Esmeralda*, Commandante, Talcahuano.
Ministerio De Defensa Nacional, Santiago.

Denmark
Holbaek Skibs & Baadebyggeri, Holbaek.
Kogtved Søfartsskole, Kogtved.
Reederei J. Lauritzen, Copenhagen.
Kaj Lund, Copenhagen.
Navigations-Uddannelseradet Statensskoleskib *Danmark*.
Orlogsmuseet, Copenhagen.
J. Ring-Andersen, Skibsvaerft, Svendborg.
Sømandshøjskolen, Svendborg.
Stiftelsen *Georg Stage Minde*, Copenhagen.
O. Stoltenberg, Kalundborg.

Dominican Republic
Embassy of the Dominican Republic, Bonn.
Secretaria De Estado De Las Fuerzas Armadas, Santo Domingo.

Ecuador
Charles Darwin Foundation for the Galapagos Isles, Isla Santa Cruz.

Federal Republic of Germany
Blohm & Voss AG, Schiffswerft, Hamburg.
Deutscher Schulschiff-Verein, Bremen.
Deutsche Werft, Hamburg.
Der Hafenkapitän im Wasser- und Schiffahrts-amt, Emden.
Der Kommandant des Segelschulschiffs *Gorch Fock*.
Howaldtwerke, Kiel.
The Senate of the Hanseatic Town of Lübeck.
MCS-Film, Munich.
Morgenstern-Museum, Bremerhaven.
Schleswig-Holsteinische Seemannsschule, Lübeck-Travemünde.
H. C. Stülcken Sohn, Schiffswerft, Hamburg.
Reederei Zerssen & Co., Rendsburg.

Finland
Ålands Sjöfarts Museum, Mariehamn.
Lars Grönstrand, Turku.
Valtion Merimie-Sammattikuolu, Turku.

France
Association Pour Un Grand Voilier-Ecole Francais, Paris.
Marine National, Ecole Navale, Lanveoc-Poulmic (Brest).
Ministère Des Armées (Marine), Paris.

German Democratic Republic
Gesellschaft für Sport und Technik, Berlin.

Great Britain
Camper & Nicholson Limited, Southampton.
The Dulverton Trust, London.
Training Ship *Foudroyant*, Gosport.
General Register and Record Office of Shipping and Seamen, Cardiff.
J. Hinks & Son, Yacht and Boat Builders, Appledore.
Capt. Stephen Gibb, N. Ferriby, E. Yorks.
F. P. V. Latham, Arcadian Restaurant, Morecambe.
Lawrie D. Johns, Emsworth, Hampshire.
Lloyd's Register of Shipping, London.
Ministry of Defence (Naval), Royal Naval Reserve, Dundee.
Ministry of Tourism, Nassau, Bahamas.
National Maritime Museum, Greenwich.
Outward Bound Moray Sea School, Burghead.
Outward Bound Trust, London.
The Sail Training Association, Petersfield, Hampshire.

Commander H. F. M. Scott, Tunbridge Wells.
R. Simper, Ramsholt.
Thames Nautical Training College, Greenhithe.

Greece
Messrs. A. Lusi Limited, London.
Ministry of Merchant Marine, Seamen's Training Division, Piraeus.
Niarchos (London) Limited, London.

Italy
Adriatic Mercantile & Trading, Trieste.
Italian Consulate, Stuttgart.
Marina Militare, Accademia Navale, Livorno.
Ministero Della Difesa-Marina, Ufficio Storico M. M., Rome.
Stato Maggiore Della Marina, Ufficio Propaganda, Rome.

Japan
Institute for Sea Training, Capt. K. Sano, Tokyo.

Netherlands
Koninklijk Institut voor de Marine, Den Helder.
Maritiem Museum "Prins Hendrik", Rotterdam.
Matrozen-Opleidingsschip *Pollux*, Amsterdam.
Zuiderzee-Museum, Enkuizen.

New Zealand
New Zealand Information Service, Wellington.

Norway
Bergens Skoleskib, Bergen.
Fram Museum, Bygdøy.
Østlandets Skoleskib, Oslo.
Sørlandets Seilende Skoleskibs Institution, Kristiansand.
Wilson Shipping Company, Arendal.

Panama
Embassy of the German Federal Republic, Panama.
Olympic Maritime S.A., Succursale De Monte-Carlo.

Poland
Maritime Branch of Polish Chamber of Foreign Trade, Gdynia.
Polnische Militärmission, Berlin.
Wydawnictwo Morskie, Gdynia.

Portugal
Brites, Vaz & Irmaos, Ld., Gafanha-Aveiro.
Comissao Consultiva Nacional Das Pescarias Do Noroeste Do Atlântico, Lisbon.

Grémio Dos Armadores De Navios Da Pasca Do
Bacelhau, Lisbon.
Ministério Da Marinha, Lisbon.
Pascoal & Filhos, Lda., Aveiro.

Spain

Empresa Nacional *Elcano* De la Marina
Mercante, Madrid.
Escuela Maniobra *Galatea*, Comandancia,
El Ferrol del Caudillo.
Juan Sebastian De Elcano, Buque Escuela De
Guardias Marinas, Comandante.
Museo Maritimo, Barcelona.

Sweden

Broströms Tekniska AB, Göteborg.
K. Carlsson, Karlskrona.
Halmstads Stad, Fastighetskontoret, Halmstad.
Royal Swedish Embassy, Copenhagen.
Rederiaktiebolaget *Clipper*, Malmö.
Sjömansskolan *Viking*, Göteborg.
Statens Sjöhistoriska Museum, Wasavarvet,
Stockholm.
Svensk Sjöfarts Tidning, Göteborg.
Vandrarhemmet *af Chapman*, Stockholm.

Tahiti

W. A. Robinson, Papeete.

U.A.R.

Boys Marine Training Establishment Ras-El-Tin,
Alexandria.
The United Arab Company for Maritime
Transport, Cairo.

Uruguay

Embassy of the Federal Republic of Germany,
Montevideo.

U.S.A.

W. A. Baker, Naval Architect, Hingham, Mass.
Bounty Exhibit, St. Petersburg, Fla.
Capt. M. Burke, Windjammer Cruises Inc.,
Miami Beach, Fla.
U.S. Frigate *Constellation*, Mr. Leon D. Polland,
Baltimore, MD.
Commanding Officer U.S.S. *Constitution*,
Boston, Mass.
U.S. Coast Academy, New London, Conn.
Thomas J. Coughlin, Boston, Mass.
Department of Commerce, Harrisburg, Penn.
Department of Conservation and Economic
Development, Trenton, N. J.
R. S. Douglas, Coastwise Packet Company,
Vineyard Haven, Mass.
Mr. Harry Dring, San Francisco Maritime State
Historic Park.

Goudy & Stevens, Dockyard, East Boothbay,
Maine.
Capt. F. B. Guild, Maine Coast Cruises, Castine,
Maine.
Capt. Richard Headley, Santa Barbara, Calif.
Capt. H. S. Hawkins, Coastal Cruises, Edgwick,
Maine.
Mr. Gordon Jones, Seattle, Washington.
Capt. A. M. Kimberly, Kimberly Cruises,
St. Thomas, U.S. Virgin Islands.
Mills B. Lane, Jr., Bank President, Atlanta,
Georgia.
Larmont Geological Observatory,
Pallisades, N.Y.
Long Beach Island Board of Trade, Ship
Bottom. N.Y.
Marine Historical Association, Inc., Mystic
Seaport, Mystic, Conn.
The Maritime Museum Association,
San Diego, Calif.
Metro-Goldwyn-Mayer International Inco.,
New York, N.Y.
The Mirish Corporation, Hollywood, Calif.
Jerry Mac Mullen, San Diego, Calif.
National Geographic Society, Washington, D.C.
National Maritime Historical Society,
Washington, D.C.
Pennsylvania Historical and Museum
Commission, Harrisburg, Penn.
Plimoth Plantation, Plymouth, Mass.
San Francisco Maritime Museum, San Francisco,
Calif.
F. & M. Schaefer Brewing Company,
New York, N.Y.
Capt. Jim Sharp, Camden, Maine.
Smithsonian Institution, Washington, D.C.
South Street Seaport Museum, New York, N. Y.
Star of India, San Diego, Calif.
Tabor Academy, Marion, Mass.
United States Merchant Marine Academy,
Kings Point, N.Y.
Lawrence H. M. Vineburgh, Washington, D.C.
B. H. Warburton, Nassau, Bahamas.
Yachting Magazine, New York, N.Y.

U.S.S.R.

Ministry of Fisheries of the U.S.S.R., Moskow
Soviet Transport Publishing Department,
Moskow.
Soviet General Register and Record Office,
Leningrad.

Bibliography

Albatros, Der — All volumes (Bremen).
Antoniadis, X., and Paissios, G. C.: National Merchant Marine Academies (Piraeus, 1965).
Arethusa Magazine (London, 1961).

Baker, W. A.:The New Mayflower, Her Design and Construction (Barre, Massachusetts, 1958).
Blöss, H.: Glanz und Schicksal der Potosi und Preussen (Kiel, 1960).
Bowness, E.: Modelling the Cutty Sark (London, 1959).
Bowness, E.: The Four-Masted Barque (London, 1955).
Busch, F.O.: Niobe, Ein deutsches Schicksal (Leipzig, 1932).

Carr, F. G. G.: Cutty Sark (London, 1954).
Carr, F. G. G.: Maritime Greenwich (London, 1965).
Carr, F. G. G.: The Cutty Sark And The Days Of Sail (London).
Colledge, J. J.: British Sailing Warships (London).
Colton, J. F.: Last of the Square-rigged Ships (New York, 1937).
Colton, J. F.: Windjammers Significant (Flaggstaff, 1954).

Discovery, H.M.S. (London, 1959).
Dluhy, R.: Schiffstechnisches Wörterbuch (Bremen - Hannover, 1956).
Domizlaff, H.: Die Viermastbark Passat (Bielefeld - Berlin, 1960).

Eichler, O.: Vom Bug zum Heck (Bielefeld - Berlin, 1954).

Franzén, A.: The Warship Vasa (Stockholm, 1960).

Gramoll, Ed.: 'Jadran, Segelschulschiff mit Hilfs-motorantrieb' (published in the magazine Schiff-bau, Schiffahrt und Hafenbau, Berlin, 34. Jahr-gang, Heft 22).

Horgan, Th. P.: Old Ironsides (Boston, Mass., 1963).
Hurst, A. A.: The Sailing Schoolships (London, 1962).
Hycke, H. D.: The Great Star Fleet (Yachting, New York, 1960).

Jebens, H.: Passat im Novembersturm (Kassel)

Klemme, H.: Segelschulschiff Gorch Fock (Oldenburg, 1961).

Lacroix, L.: Les Derniers Grands Voiliers (Paris, 1950).
Lächler, P., and Wirz, H.: Die Schiffe der Völker

(Olten and Freiburg, 1962).
Landström, B.: The Ship (London, 1961).
Longridge, C. N.: The Anatomy of Nelson's Ships (London, 1955).
Lore of the Ship, The (London, 1963).
Lund, K.: Søens Verden, Nr. 3 (Odense, 1960/61).
Lund, K., and Holm-Pedersen, F.: Svane Sang (Odense, 1956).
Lubbock, B.: The Last of the Windjammers, Vols I and II (Glasgow, 1960).
Lubbock, B.: The Log of the Cutty Sark (Glasgow, 1960).
Lubbock, B.: The Nitrate Clippers (Glasgow, 1953).

MacMullen, J.: Star of India, The Log of an Iron Ship (Berkely, Calif., 1961).
Martinez-Hidalgo, J. M.: Columbus' Ships (Barre, Mass., 1966).
Mutiny on the Bounty (MGM Film Inc., London, 1962).

Naish, G. P. B.: Nelson and HMS Victory (London, 1965), Vasa, her place in history (National Maritime Museum Greenwich).

Ohrelius, B.: Vasa, The King's Ship

Polland, L. D.: The Frigate Constellation, An Outline of the present Restoration (Baltimore, 1966).

Rogge, B., and Busch, O.: Weisse Segel — Weite Meere (Berlin, 1942).
Rohrbach, P., Piening, H., and Schmidt, F.: Die Geschichte einer Reederei (Hamburg, 1960).

Sea Breezes (Liverpool, various issues).
Stackelberg, Frh. v.: Rahsegler im Rennen (Flensburg, 1965).
Steen Steensen, R.: Fregatten Jylland (Copen-hagen, 1961).

Tod, G. M. S.: The Last Sail Down East (Barre, Mass., 1965).
Underhill, H. A.: Deep Water Sail (Glasgow, 1955).

Underhill, H. A.: Sail Training and Cadet Ships (Glasgow, 1956).
Underhill, H. A.: Masting and Rigging the Clipper Ship and Ocean Carrier (Glasgow, 1958).
Underhill, H. A.: Sailing Ship Rigs & Rigging (Glasgow, 1955).

Villiers, A., and others: Men, Ships and the Sea (Washington, 1962).
Villiers, A.: Sailing Eagle (New York, 1955).
Villiers, A.: The Cutty Sark, Last of a Glorious Era (London, 1957).

Weyers Flotten-Taschenbuch (Munich, several years' editions).
Windjammer, modern adventure in Cine-miracle (New York, 1958).
Winter, H.: Die Kolumbus-Schiffe (Magdeburg, 1944).
Worcester, H.M.S. (Thames Nautical Training College, Greenhithe, 1965).

Zetsche, S., Barthel, F., and Hauschildt, A. W.: 'Segelschulschiff Dewarutji' (Hanse, Zentralorgan für Schiffahrt - Schiffbau - Häfen, Hamburg, Nr. 51/52, 1953).

Acknowledgements for photographs

Anthony's Pier 4 Restaurant, Boston (1), E. M. DA Armanda, Servicio De Fotografia, Lisbon (2), I. Aaserud Billedsentralen, Oslo (1)

Blohm & Voss AG, Hamburg (1), John Blue (1), Brigantine Incorporated, Kingston (1), G. Barkowsky, Berlin (1), Beken of Cowes (3), William Bartz (1), Buque-Museo Fragata A. R. A. (1), Robert Boehme, Seattle (1)

Comissao Consultiva National Das Pescarias Do Noroeste Do Atlantico, Lisbon (3), Maurice Crosby Photography Ltd., Halifax (1)

A. Duncan, Gravesend, Kent (1), Deutscher Schulschiff-Verein, Bremen (1), Paul Dziuban, Toronto (1)

Escuela De Maniobra, El Ferrol de Caudillo (1), Buque Escuela Esmeralda (1)

Fotoboat Company, Santa Barbara, Calif. (1), Fototeca Uff. Propaganda, Stato Maggiore Marina, Rome (1), Fram-Museum, Oslo-Bygdøy (1)

Lars Grönstrand, Abo (3), Capt. J. S. Gibb (1), Gremio Dos Armadores De Navios Da Pesca Do Bacalhau, Lisbon (1), Segelschulschiff *Gorch Fock* (1)

Howell's Photo Studio, Vineyard Haven, Mass. (1), Hawrylow, Melbourne (1), Kieler Howaldtwerke (1)

Institute for Seatraining, Tokyo (5)

Gordon Jones, Seattle (1)

Koninklijke Marine, Den Haag (1), Capt. A. Kimberly (2), A. F. Kersting, London (1), Karl Kortum, San Francisco (1), Henry Kabot, Gdynia (5), Kenter (1)

A. C. Littlejohns Bideford, Devon (1), A. Lusi Ltd., London (1), H. M. Lawrence, Vineburgh, Washington D. C. (1), Training ship *Libertad* (1), F. A. Mac Lachlan, Kingston (1), Kaj Lund, Kopenhagen (3), Lynn Photo-Service Ship Bottom (1), Foto Lusarte, Lisbon (1), Lloyd's Register of Shipping, London (1), Lamont Geological Observatory, New York (1)

Metro Goldwyn Mayer Inc., New York (1), Maritime Museum, Vancouver B. C. (1), MCS Film KG, München (1), Ministerio Da Marinha, Rio de Janeiro (1), Ministero Difesa Marina, Centro Fotografico dell Ufficio Documentazione, Rome (1), L. S. Martel, Mystic Seaport, Conn.

(5), Jerry Mac Mullen, San Diego, Calif. (1), Ministerio de Defensa Nacional, Santiago, Chile (1), Maine Coast Cruises, Castine (1), Ministère Des Armées, Paris (3)

Niarchos (London) Ltd. (1), Navigationsuddannelsesradet Statens Skoleskib „Danmark" (1), Kapt. J. P. Nørgaard (1), National Maritime Museum, Greenwich (1), New Zealand Information Service, Wellington (1), National Maritime Historical Society, Washington (1)

Official Plimoth Plantation Photo (1), L. B. Owen (1), Østlandets Skoleskib (1), Outward Bound Moray Sea School (1), G. A. Osbon (1), Ocean Wide Film and TV Productions, Berlin (1)

Pressebureau APN, Copenhagen (1), Andrew Pine, Savannah, Georgia (1), Parceria Geral de Pescarias, Lisbon (1), Pascal u. Filhos, Aveiro (1), Pennsylvania Historical And Museum Commission, Harrisburg, Penn. (1), Ports and Lights Administration, Alexandria (1)

W. A. Robinson, Papete (1), Eilen Ramsay (1)

Stülcken-Werft, Hamburg (2), Sail Training Association (1), Skyfotos, Lympne Airport, Kent (3), Stato Maggiore della Marina, Ufficio Propaganda (1), Capt. J. Sharp (1), Sørlandets Seilende Skoleskibs Institution (1), Les Scott, Virgin Islands Tourist Bureau (1), Statens Sjøhistoriska Museum, Stockholm (1), Star Spangled Banner Flag House Association of Baltimore (1), South Street Seaport Museum (1), San Francisco Maritime Museum (3), Bergens Skoleskib (1), The author (60), Royal Swedish Navy (1), F. u. M. Schaefer Brewing Co., New York (1)

Tabor Academy, Marion, Mass. (1)

U. S. Navy Photo (1), U. S. Coast Guard Official Photo (1), University for Piscatory Sciences, Tokyo (2)

Alan Villiers (1)

Barclay H. Warburton, Boston (1), Windjammer Cruises Inc., Miami Beach, Florida (3)